This rich and provocative study assesses Herbert Spencer's pivotal contribution to the emergence of liberal utilitarianism, as well as the conceptual and logical integrity of his version of it. Spencer, as much as J. S. Mill, provided liberal utilitarianism with its formative contours. Like Mill, Spencer tried to reconcile a principle of liberty and strong moral rights with a utilitarian, maximizing theory of good. He endeavored, like Mill, to make utilitarianism more ethically attractive by fortifying it with powerful deontological constraints on the pursuit of utility. And yet, insofar as rights were indefeasible for Spencer, his liberal utilitarian amalgam was more unstable than Mill's. In aggressively trying to occupy what Samuel Scheffler has referred to as "a non-existent middle ground" between utility and rights, Spencer's liberal utilitarianism powerfully reveals the philosophical stakes at issue in trying to systematize liberalism by liberalizing utilitarianism.

This is a major contribution to understanding nineteenth-century political thought and to utilitarian studies, and will be of interest to graduates and scholars in the fields of political theory, moral and political philosophy and the history of political thought.

IDEAS IN CONTEXT 49

EQUAL FREEDOM AND UTILITY

IDEAS IN CONTEXT

The books in this series will discuss the emergence of intellectual traditions and of related new disciplines. The procedures, aims and vocabularies that were generated will be set in the context of the alternatives available within the contemporary frameworks of ideas and institutions. Through detailed studies of the evolution of such traditions, and their modification by different audiences, it is hoped that a new picture will form of the development of ideas in their concrete contexts. By this means, artificial distinctions between the history of philosophy, of the various sciences, of society and politics, and of literature may be seen to dissolve.

The series is published with the support of the Exxon Foundation.

A list of books in the series will be found at the end of the volume.

EQUAL FREEDOM AND UTILITY

Herbert Spencer's Liberal Utilitarianism

D. WEINSTEIN

Wake Forest University

PUBLISHED BY THE PRESS SYNDICATE OF THE UNIVERSITY OF CAMBRIDGE
The Pitt Building, Trumpington Street, Cambridge CB2 1RP, United Kingdom

CAMBRIDGE UNIVERSITY PRESS
The Edinburgh Building, Cambridge CB2 2RU, United Kingdom
40 West 20th Street, New York, NY 10011–4211, USA
10 Stamford Road, Oakleigh, Melbourne 3166, Australia

First published 1998

Printed in the United Kingdom at the University Press, Cambridge

Typeset in Baskerville 10/12.5 pt. [CE]

A catalogue record for this book is available from the British Library

Library of Congress cataloguing in publication data

Weinstein, D. (David). 1949–
Equal freedom and utility : Herbert Spencer's liberal utilitarianism – D. Weinstein.
p. cm. – (Ideas in context : 49)
Includes bibliographical references and index.
ISBN 0 521 62264 6 (hb)
1. Social choice. 2. Utilitarianism. 3. Liberalism.
4. Spencer, Herbert, 1820–1903.
I. Title. II. Series.
HB846.8.W45 1998
192–dc21 97–27895 CIP

ISBN 0 521 62264 6 hardback

For my parents
To the Sierra night sky

Contents

Acknowledgements

My study of Spencer's liberal utilitarianism began too many years ago when Martin Seliger of The Hebrew University of Jerusalem suggested that I "have a look at Spencer." I have now had a long and rather hard "look," incurring many debts along the way.

I owe a great deal to Richard E. Flathman, my mentor at The Johns Hopkins University. Dick Flathman gave me the conceptual tools without which this book would have remained too unphilosophical and, therefore, certainly pedestrian. Dick taught me the virtues of thinking rigorously and cautiously. I hope that I have succeeded in doing both in some small measure here. Dick also understood the practical importance of his students finishing their Ph.D.s before dotage set in so that there would still be time left for a life and an academic career. For this, I am grateful beyond measure.

I am equally indebted to J. G. A. Pocock who taught me that there was much more to the history of political thought than just thinking about past political thought. From John Pocock, I learned that thinking about the past should proceed archaeologically even though the best archaeology is invariably a rethinking.

Three others, in particular, have taken precious time to comment upon larger and smaller pieces of this manuscript over the years. They are J. B. Schneewind, John Gray and the late Judith Shklar. I am beholden to all three. I am just as indebted to the exceptionally insightful, anonymous reviewers of earlier drafts of this book.

Many other colleagues and friends have influenced my thinking about Spencer in particular, and about the history of political thought in general, in subtler though no less determining ways. Avital Simhony, as unsparing a critic as she is a close friend, has pushed my thinking forward conceptually and chronologically. Now on to the new liberalism! For helping me thread my way through the threatening shoals of liberal utilitarianism, I must also thank

Michael Freeden, Fred Rosen, Peter Nicholson and Jonathan Riley. Avihu Zakai, Yaron Ezrahi, Jerry Gaus and Dick Polenberg deserve many thanks as well.

To Ginni Walsh especially, I owe what can never be repaid. When I faltered and doubted, she always became more convinced.

A Scheinbrun Fellowship at The Hebrew University of Jerusalem gave me two years (1987-8) of limited teaching, much reading and even some writing. "Equal Freedom, Rights and Utility in Spencer's Moral Philosophy," *The History of Political Thought*, 11 (1990), 119–42, was a fruit of those sharp-edged Jerusalem years. More recently (1994), Wake Forest University awarded me a Z. Smith Reynolds Research Leave which proved invaluable in bringing this project to a close.

My colleagues in the Department of Politics at Wake Forest deserve to be commended for their valor in putting up with my too-predictable humor, and for standing by me, over the years. Kathy Smith and Hank Kennedy have been rocks of salvation.

In Gale Sigal, I met a fellow traveler in spirit, love and the life of mind. More than anyone, she exemplifies what it means to be an intellectual, and a Bronx-raised intellectual at that.

To my parents I owe most of all. From the disciplined simplicity of prairie modernism to the virtue of toleration, they showed me just about all I ever really needed to know in order to live as I should.

Note on the text

I have placed some references in parentheses, rather than in the footnotes, if the text has previously been footnoted in full or if the context of my discussion clearly indicates the book or article being cited or referred to. Whenever possible, I have used original editions or reprints of older books. Otherwise, I have used modern standard editions.

Introduction

When John Rawls' magisterial *A Theory of Justice* rang the death knell of utilitarianism anew by declaring that it utterly failed to take "seriously the distinction between persons," utilitarianism's bad reputation in the eyes of many was reconfirmed. But Rawls leveled his liberal neo-Kantian weaponry at classical, Sidgwickian utilitarianism, leaving untouched improved varieties fortified with liberal principles. Indeed, much utilitarian theorizing in recent years has attempted to rescue utilitarianism by infusing it with robust liberal constraints on what can be done to individuals in the name of maximizing utility. What has been rescued has come to be known as "liberal utilitarianism."

Liberal utilitarianism is a variety of indirect utilitarianism that accents the development of individuality as importantly constitutive of happiness. Liberal utilitarianism is also vigorously juridical, giving pride of place to strong basic rights. This latter feature endows liberal utilitarianism with its solid indirect utilitarian credentials. Unlike direct utilitarians, who hold that the principle of utility serves both as a normative standard for assessing classes of actions and institutions and as a direct source of moral obligation, liberal utilitarians do not burden the principle of utility with this double liability. As indirect utilitarians, they permit the principle of utility to serve as a standard for assessing classes of actions and institutions while denying it service as a source of direct obligation. For them, strong moral rights serve as sources of direct obligation, making their version of indirect utilitarianism *liberal* utilitarianism. Liberal utilitarians hold that general utility is best maximized over the long run when individuals assiduously fulfill their fundamental juridical obligations and thereby indirectly promote the flourishing of individuality. Maximizing happiness consists in fostering individuality which, in turn, requires that we channel our actions along broad avenues permitted by stringent moral rights.

The distinction between direct and indirect utilitarianism (including liberal versions of the latter) is sometimes depicted as resting on the distinction between a criterion and a decision procedure. According to James Griffin, "The distinction is one of the most important developments in utility theory of recent decades."[1] As a criterion of right action, the principle of utility is capable of distinguishing between right and wrong actions. But as an action-guiding, decision procedure, it is woefully clumsy and even perilous. Unfortunately, we are neither impartial enough nor intelligent enough direct maximizers of general utility. Were we always to appeal directly to the principle of utility for action guidance, we would often fail miserably and sometimes with great cruelty. Thus, we need handier, unvarnished decision procedures; procedures that do not themselves prescribe overwhelmingly complex, maximizing calculations. As Griffin says of such a strategy:

> The principles that we use in deciding how to act, on the other hand, can take account of human limitations; they might turn out to be much like the principles of common-sense ethics, or a tidied-up version of them, allowing a large measure of partiality and easing demands on our powers of calculation. All that utilitarians need hold out for is that our actions are right if, and only if, they most promote utility overall. ("Distinction," pp. 179–80)

Liberal utilitarianism, as a version of indirect utilitarianism, recommends strong moral rights as the basic "principles we use in deciding how to act." For liberal utilitarianism, rights function as key decision procedures.

Injecting utilitarianism with robust decision procedures such as moral rights creates several fundamental dilemmas for utilitarians, not the least of which concerns utilitarianism's identity. By making their decision procedures so robust, liberal utilitarians risk subsuming the principle of utility as a meaningful criterion of right action. Where decision procedures so overwhelm the principle of utility for all practical purposes, it remains debatable whether liberal utilitarianism has simply metamorphosed into just plain liberalism. The hegemony of decision procedures may be nothing less than a

[1] James Griffin, "The Distinction Between Criterion and Decision Procedure: A Reply to Madison Powers," *Utilitas*, 6 (1994), 179.

veiled triumph of the right over the good. To borrow from Griffin again, "If utility calculation is squeezed out of a quite large part of moral life, if it is relegated to the extremes and to manageable small-scale matters, if, that is, those are the only situations in which utilities can be calculated to a sufficient degree of reliability, then does enough remain to be called 'utilitarianism'?" ("Distinction," p. 181)[2]

Others have impugned liberal utilitarianism on related grounds for trying to impose liberal constraints on the pursuit of utility. In particular, several philosophers have deemed indefeasible moral rights and the principle of utility irreconcilable. For instance, David Lyons has vigorously argued that strong rights and utility are incommensurable because stringent rights corrupt utilitarianism by introducing a second, alien criterion of good with its own separate "moral force."[3] Alan Ryan and John Charvet have similarly criticized Mill's liberal utilitarianism. Despite his enthusiasm for Mill, Ryan nonetheless shares Lyons' reservations about Mill's utilitarianism, reproaching Mill for suppressing the logical "conflict" between the requirements of justice and the requirements of utility.[4] Charvet likewise complains that, despite Mill's Herculean efforts, justice and utility cannot be integrated without one of them being devalued.[5] And John Gray, formerly one of liberal utilitarianism's champions, has switched sides, repudiating liberal utilitarianism as unworkable.[6]

Notwithstanding the logical cogency of liberalizing utilitarianism by investing it with strong rights, liberal utilitarianism commands a rich, variegated genealogy. Even Jeremy Bentham is arguably a liberal utilitarian if we follow P. J. Kelly. According to Kelly, in *Utilitarianism and Distributive Justice*, Bentham's utilitarianism was multi-layered, combining direct and indirect utilitarian strategies. Kelly says that the "overall object" of his study "is to argue that Bentham did not intend to supply a direct utilitarian theory of moral obligation, but rather that he employed a utilitarian theory of justice

[2] Griffin continues, "If the limitations of human knowledge pose a serious problem for utilitarianism (as I myself think they do), it is not to be solved by invoking a form of the distinction between criterion and decision procedure that allows the criterion to rise serenely clear of the life of accommodations and compromises that limited people like us must lead" ("Distinction," pp. 181–2).

[3] David Lyons, "Utility and Rights" in John W. Chapman and J. Roland Pennock (eds.), *Ethics, Economics and the Law* (New York University Press, 1982), Nomos 24.

[4] Alan Ryan, *The Philosophy of John Stuart Mill* (London: Macmillan Press, 1987), p. 228.

[5] John Charvet, *A Critique of Freedom and Equality* (Cambridge University Press, 1981), p. 95.

[6] John Gray, "Mill's and Other Liberalisms" in John Gray (ed.), *Liberalisms: Essays in Political Philosophy* (London: Routledge, 1989), pp. 218–24.

which provided the framework within which individuals could pursue their own conceptions of well-being."[7] Nor, in Kelly's view and contrary to H. L. A. Hart, did Bentham advocate a straightforward indirect theory of obligation in which the principle of utility merely functions as a criterion for determining juridical rules which are the real sources of moral obligation. Bentham's "system of obligations provides a framework within which individual agents can act on direct utilitarian reasons, without their actions undermining the conditions of social interaction on which the most important sources of utility depend." Hence, Bentham "combines aspects of a direct and indirect utilitarian theory" that is sensitive to the basic conditions of utility-generating stability while also providing individuals with ample scope to pursue utility directly (p. 69). Thus Gertrude Himmelfarb's shopworn complaint, that Benthamite utilitarianism reveals that "the principle of the greatest happiness of the greatest number was as inimical to the idea of liberty as to the idea of rights," may be unwarranted.[8]

Liberal utilitarianism, then, may have a deeper ancestry than is usually believed. In any case, J. S. Mill was indisputably nothing less than a liberal utilitarian. How else can we account for the way his moral theory continues to resonate so powerfully in current debates about liberalism versus utilitarianism and in recent efforts to forge some kind of tenuous amalgam from them? How else can we explain James Fitzjames Stephen's criticisms of Mill that so closely mirror more recent criticisms of liberal utilitarianism by Lyons, Ryan, Charvet and Gray? As Stephen once observed of Millian utilitarianism:

> Why should [anyone] prefer obedience to a rule to a specific calculation in a specific case, when, after all, the only reason for obeying the rule is the advantage to be got by it, which by the hypothesis is not an advantage, but a loss in the particular case? A given road may be the direct way from one place to another, but that fact is no reason for following the road when you are offered a short cut. It may be a good general rule not to seek for more than 5 per cent in investments, but if it so happens that you can invest at 10 per cent with perfect safety, would not a man who refused to do so be a fool?[9]

[7] P. J. Kelly, *Utilitarianism and Distributive Justice* (Oxford University Press, 1990), p. 43.

[8] For Himmelfarb's criticism, see her "The Haunted House of Jeremy Bentham" in R. Herr and H. T. Parker (eds.), *Ideas in History* (Durham, N.C.: Duke University Press, 1965), p. 235.

[9] James Fitzjames Stephen, "Note on Utilitarianism," *Liberty, Equality and Fraternity* [1873] (University of Chicago Press, 1991), p. 277.

Modern proponents of liberal utilitarianism have taken it to higher levels of sophistication hoping to meet criticisms like Stephen's. In *Liberal Utilitarianism*, Jonathan Riley attempts to combine the virtues of both liberalism and utilitarianism while avoiding their respective flaws. In the eyes of many, according to Riley, liberalism is thought of as having extensive ethical appeal at the cost of sacrificing coherence insofar as the core values celebrated by liberals are tragically incommensurable. Ironically, liberalism's lack of coherence stems from its very appeal. Utilitarianism, on the other hand, is frequently castigated precisely because of its notorious coherence that allegedly subverts individual integrity in the name of systematically maximizing utility. Riley, by contrast, strives to liberalize utilitarianism and to systematize liberalism by defending a form of utilitarianism that possesses *both* liberal ethical appeal and formal coherence.

Riley's defense of liberal utilitarianism combines axiomatic social choice theory and a "new interpretation of Mill's liberal version of utilitarianism."[10] Riley argues that by sufficiently restricting the domain of our conception of utility, we can fortify utilitarianism's liberal credentials without undermining its systematic coherence. Moreover, in Mill, according to Riley, we have a promising basis of how to proceed. For Riley, Mill's conception of good is "utility in the largest sense," of which security (justice) and individuality are the foremost components or kinds of utility. Mill ranks these kinds of utility lexically, so that our interest in security outranks our interest in individuality. That is, "utility in the largest sense" results when all individuals cultivate their individualities subject to respecting one another's rights to security with the right to liberty, as embodied in Mill's liberty principle, being pivotal. The lexical priority of security over individuality restricts the domain of preferences, thereby insuring liberal ethical appeal. And overall coherence is preserved because utility defined this way, as the harmonious realization of security and individuality, remains the ultimate standard of value by which right action is systematized.

Riley's liberal utilitarian rendering of Mill shares much with John Gray's largely favorable assessment of Mill in *Mill on Liberty: A Defence*, an assessment that Gray has since disavowed. There are,

[10] Jonathan Riley, *Liberal Utilitarianism: Social Choice Theory and J. S. Mill's Philosophy* (Cambridge University Press, 1988), p. 329.

nevertheless, subtle differences between Riley's and Gray's Mill and, by implication, subtle differences in their respective approaches to the larger enterprise of liberal utilitarianism. For Riley, Mill was a "disposition" utilitarian because of the importance that Mill placed on moral self-development as a feature of individuality. As an evolving disposition, moral self-development fosters happiness by fostering habitual respect for rights, making moral individuality the wellspring of security. Though lexically more important, security depends upon correct moral dispositions. Gray, by contrast, lays greater stress on moral rights themselves, on the *external* conditions of utility maximization. Consequently, his Mill is less of an *internal* dispositional utilitarian than Riley's.

A measure of irony characterizes Riley's interpretation and defense of Millian liberal utilitarianism compared to Gray's. Whereas Riley accentuates the dispositional features of moral individuality of Mill's liberal utilitarianism, he nonetheless holds that security is a lexically more important kind of utility. Gray, on the other hand, lays less stress on dispositional attributes and more on moral rights and yet regards individuality as ultimately more significant.[11]

Another compelling defense of liberal utilitarianism is Wayne Sumner's *The Moral Foundations of Rights*. Like Riley and Gray, Sumner maintains that an indirect utilitarian strategy that places powerful juridical constraints on the pursuit of general utility is the best strategy for maximizing general utility. But unlike them, he does not invoke Mill so extensively in championing the cause of liberal utilitarianism. And unlike them, he concedes that liberal utilitarianism can accommodate not just stringent, though ultimately defeasible, rights but indefeasible rights as well.[12]

Liberal utilitarianism, then, possesses a venerable genealogy. But Mill, and arguably Bentham, did not usher in liberal utilitarianism alone. Herbert Spencer, as much as Mill, gave liberal utilitarianism its formative personality.

Equal Freedom and Utility: Herbert Spencer's Liberal Utilitarianism assesses Spencer's pivotal contribution to the emergence of what *we*

[11] See especially chapter 4 in John Gray, *Mill on Liberty: A Defence* (London: Routledge and Kegan Paul, 1983).

[12] For Sumner's defense of stringent consequentialist rights, see especially chapter 6, "Consequentialist Rights," in Wayne Sumner, *The Moral Foundations of Rights* (Oxford University Press, 1987).

now call liberal utilitarianism as well as the success of his version of it.[13] My study analyzes Spencer's unprecedented and problematic endeavor to take moral rights seriously as stringent decision procedures while simultaneously insisting that their consequentialist instrumentality not disappear from view. For Spencer, moral rights are not metaphysical absolutes even if a single stringent set of them proves contingently superior in maximizing happiness. Though moral rights mimic natural rights in their stringency, though they are shadows of natural rights, their ultimate justification nevertheless lies in the practice of utility.

Like Mill, Spencer endeavored to make utilitarianism more ethically attractive by constraining the pursuit of utility with potent moral rights. And yet, insofar as moral rights were *indefeasible* for Spencer, particularly in his earlier works such as *Social Statics*, his liberal utilitarian amalgam was more daring and unstable than Mill's. Though stringent, Millian rights are ultimately *defeasible* and consequently Mill's version of liberal utilitarianism is less rigorously liberal and therefore less logically precarious.

Since Spencer's liberal utilitarianism resembles Mill's so closely, we ought to regard Spencer's version of it as seriously as we regard Mill's. If much of *our* current philosophical interest in Mill stems from his contribution to the issue of the logical compatibility between strong moral rights and utility, then we should find Spencer's contribution to this issue even more intriguing. If Mill's liberal utilitarianism is heroic, then Spencer's is all the more so. After a preliminary chapter on Spencer's evolutionary theory and a second chapter devoted to examining his principle of equal freedom, in the next three chapters I explore the relationship between moral rights and the principle of utility. The chapters on equal freedom and moral rights constitute the core of my study of Spencer.

Spencer, then, was a liberal utilitarian. Such a characterization of him implies, of course, that he embraced a hedonic theory of good. G. E. Moore's accusations notwithstanding, Spencer never defined good in a callous and chilling way. He certainly never defined good as survival of the fittest and therefore did not commit the naturalistic

[13] Spencer never used the expression "liberal utilitarianism" when referring to his own moral and political theory. Mill didn't either, to the best of my knowledge. The fact that neither Mill nor Spencer explicitly identified themselves as liberal utilitarians naturally opens liberal utilitarian interpretations of them to the charge of being rational reconstructions.

fallacy in the manner attributed to him by Moore.[14] For Spencer, good was happiness if it was anything. And, generally speaking, maximizing good entailed operationalizing good universalistically. However, Spencer sometimes inconsistently advocated operationalizing good egoistically. This inconsistency only muddied the contours of his liberal utilitarian visage, making him easier prey to mistaken identity and self-serving appropriation such as Moore's.

Spencer's moral reasoning regarding good, then, was neither as logically inadequate as Moore's caricature suggests nor entirely successful either, given that Spencer sometimes wavered in his commitment to universalistic hedonism. For Spencer, maximizing happiness generally meant maximizing happiness universally and distributively for *all* members of society, even though egoistic lapses occasionally vitiated his theory of good.

The liberal credentials of Spencer's maximizing theory stem from another feature of Spencer's moral reasoning, namely the deductive manner in which moral rights ostensibly followed from the principle of equal freedom. This principle stipulates that: "Every man is free to do that which he will provided he infringes not the equal freedom of any other man."[15] According to Spencer, as we shall see, moral rights were logical derivations of equal freedom. Insofar as the principle of equal freedom was indispensable to maximizing happiness, and insofar as moral rights were "corollaries" of equal freedom, unswerving respect for them was equally indispensable to maximizing happiness. Hence, Spencer proudly characterized his brand of liberal utilitarianism as "rational" utilitarianism. In contrast to merely "empirical" varieties of utilitarianism such as Bentham's, "rational" utilitarianism was supposedly rigorously logical. Its logical rigor inoculated it from being continually modified in the name of brute expediency, unlike "empirical" utilitarianism. Where "empirical" utilitarians were never shy about forever refitting the right for the sake of the good, "rational" utilitarians sanctified the right for the sake of the good. Only "rational" utilitarianism took stringent moral rights as the sole theory of right worthy of reverence before the altar of good. Only "rational" utilitarianism was ethically appealing by building on our deepest and most cherished liberal convictions. Only "rational" utilitarianism, as far

[14] G. E. Moore, *Principia Ethica* (Cambridge University Press, 1984), chapter 2.

[15] Herbert Spencer, *The Principles of Ethics* [1879–93], 2 vols. (Indianapolis: Liberty Classics, 1978), vol. II, p. 62.

as Spencer was concerned, provided firm methodological foundations on which liberal utilitarianism could be safely built.

But Spencer's "rational" utilitarianism rests on a specious methodology. Contrary to what Spencer holds, moral rights cannot possibly be strict, logical derivations from equal freedom. Hence his hopes of replacing merely "empirical" Benthamite utilitarianism with a more methodologically rigorous "rational" variety founder. In the end, Spencer's liberal utilitarianism proves to be just as irrefutably "empirical," methodologically speaking, as any other version of utilitarianism. So, Spencer's claim that his brand of utilitarianism was not just an improvement over Bentham's, but also methodologically different from Bentham's, is overexaggerated. And if Kelly is correct that Bentham was a liberal utilitarian, then the differences between Bentham and Spencer may be smaller still. Chapter 6 examines Spencer's contention that he was a "rational" utilitarian as well as Moore's caricature of Spencer's moral theory as exemplifying crude ethical naturalism.

Some of the practical applications of Spencer's liberal utilitarianism, such as his support for land nationalization, further reveal the fundamentally empirical nature of his utilitarian reasoning. Land nationalization and related issues are addressed in chapter 7.

Spencer's liberal utilitarianism is hydra-headed not least because it is overlaid with so many complicating theoretical concerns stemming from his biology, psychology and sociology. And there is so much Spencer; "yards of Spencer" as J. B. Schneewind once put it.[16] Making sense of Spencer is an exegetical labyrinth even for the initiated. Hence, there are ample reasons for proceeding cautiously when interpreting Spencer's liberal utilitarianism. And consequently there are added reasons not to be imprudently sanguine about the success of his version of it.

My study of Spencer claims that he was a liberal utilitarian. He began as one and he ended as one. In other words, Spencer's moral and political thought exhibits greater systematic integrity than the received view of his thought acknowledges.[17] My study also examines the myriad problems with his version of liberal utilitarianism, which were often not insignificant.

[16] Schneewind's remark was made in a conversation with me about Spencer.

[17] However, see T. S. Gray, *The Political Philosophy of Herbert Spencer: Individualism and Organicism* (Aldershot: Avebury, 1996), for a recent attempt to reconcile the tension between Spencer's individualism and his organicism.

Precisely because of these flaws, Spencer's contribution to the larger problematic enterprise of liberal utilitarianism accentuates its pitfalls and intellectual dividends in a revealing way. The challenges of trying to ground the principle of equal freedom and moral rights in the principle of utility are not just considerable but also timely and significant for us. As a consequence, Spencer's unusual version of liberal utilitarianism is engaging and deserving of our critical attention. Neo-Kantians, in particular, dare not ignore him, lest they foolishly think that the final blows to the venerable ghost of Sidgwick and nineteenth-century utilitarianism were dealt in the battle cry of *A Theory of Justice*.

If we need to read our Sidgwick as spadework for reading Rawls, then we need to read our Spencer too.

CHAPTER I

Social evolution

There is something intuitively appealing, perhaps even something inspiring, about the principle of equal freedom. For Herbert Spencer, equal freedom was pivotal because it was the fount of individual flourishing and well-being and, therefore, of much that is ennobling in human beings. The principle of equal freedom comprised the core decision procedure of his utilitarianism and was, therefore, the source of its liberal authenticity.

However, equal freedom (and Spencer's liberal utilitarianism as well) cannot be adequately understood when separated from the deeper context of Spencer's theory of social evolution. Therefore, an examination of his social evolutionary theory must precede any discussion of his moral and political theory.

I shall begin by briefly discussing Spencer's metaphysical first principles. We shall situate his moral and political theory within the larger context of his broader metaphysical commitments. The second section addresses Spencer's treatment of human prehistory. The next section introduces some dominant motifs from Spencer's theory of social evolution, such as the view that war and population growth have been engines of social and moral progress, his claim that social evolution exhibits increasing integration and heterogeneity and his conviction that liberal "industrial" societies were the evolutionary fruit of successful "militant" societies. The final section of this chapter addresses two crucial features of Spencer's theory of social evolution that are especially germane to his moral and political theory, namely his theories of character formation and of the inheritance of acquired characteristics.

FIRST PRINCIPLES

For Spencer, social evolution was a facet, albeit a critically important one, of a grander evolutionary drama. This larger drama, laid out in considerable detail in *First Principles*, encompassed all of inorganic as well as organic evolution. Published in 1862, *First Principles* was intended as a metaphysical prolegomena to all of Spencer's subsequent writings, particularly the "Synthetic Philosophy." The "Synthetic Philosophy" consisted of *The Principles of Psychology* (1855, 2nd edn. 1870–2), *The Principles of Biology* (1864–7), *The Principles of Sociology* (1876–96) and *The Principles of Ethics* (1879–3). According to H. S. Shelton, an early twentieth-century critic of Spencer, the "Synthetic Philosophy" was written to "illustrate the applicability" of the fundamental ideas that Spencer first set out in *First Principles.*[1]

First Principles argues that the universe is evolving in complexity. As it evolves, the universe subdivides relentlessly into increasingly intricate aggregates. Moreover, these aggregates gradually become increasingly differentiated. Their parts become increasingly dissimilar as the aggregates themselves become increasingly dissimilar. Hence, the universe is becoming ever more heterogeneous. As Spencer defines the "law" of cosmic evolution: "Evolution is an integration of matter and concomitant dissipation of motion, during which the matter passes from an indefinite, incoherent homogeneity to a definite, coherent heterogeneity, and during which the retained motion undergoes a parallel transformation."[2]

Spencer fortified this "law" of evolution with his principle of the Persistence of Force and with his Laws of the Instability of the Homogeneous and of the Multiplicity of Effects. Because Force or Energy, though unremitting, never expands uniformly, all primitively homogeneous phenomena become heterogeneous under the imprint of incidental forces. Homogeneity, in short, is inherently unstable. And thanks to the Law of the Multiplicity of Effects, incidental forces engender new forces that accelerate the rate by which homogeneity evolves into heterogeneity.[3] Nonetheless, the cosmic

[1] H. S. Shelton, "Spencer's Formula of Evolution," *The Philosophical Review*, 19 (1910), 243.
[2] Herbert Spencer, *First Principles* [1862] (London: Williams and Norgate, 1915), p. 321.
[3] For an especially concise statement of the Law of the Multiplicity of Effects, see Spencer's 1857 "Progress: Its Law and Cause," *Essays: Scientific, Political and Speculative* [1868–74], 3 vols. (London: Williams and Norgate, 1901), vol. 1, p. 37. Also see Herbert Spencer, *An Autobiography*, 2 vols. (London: Watts, 1904), vol. 1, pp. 176 and 384 and David Duncan (ed.), *The Life and Letters of Herbert Spencer* (London: Methuen and Co., 1908), pp. 541 and 546 for

march of heterogeneity does not continue indefinitely but eventually reaches equilibrium and is followed by dissolution.

For Spencer, then, the cosmos was ineluctably evolving. Broadly speaking, all inorganic and organic phenomena were inexorably becoming more integrated, specialized and heterogeneous. And this was no less true of social evolution, for social evolution was just a mode of the larger cosmic drama:

> Now, we propose in the first place to show, that this law of organic progress is the law of all progress. Whether it be in the development of the Earth, in the development of Life upon its surface, in the development of Society, of Government, of Manufactures, of Commerce, of Language, Literature, Science, Art, this same evolution of the simple into the complex, through successive differentiations, holds throughout. From the earliest traceable cosmical changes down to the latest results of civilization, we shall find that transformation of the homogeneous into the heterogeneous, is that in which progress essentially consists. (*Essays*, vol. I, p. 10)

Social evolution, in other words, has been characterized by the emergence of increasingly complex, heterogeneous societies whose members were increasingly interdependent and increasingly individuated. Social progress has been nothing less than intensifying specialization, thickening interdependence, deepening individualization and expanding diversity.[4]

PRESOCIAL POLITICS

In the beginning, there was the "presocial state." Variously described by Spencer as an "original predatory life," an "antecedent state" and an "original state," our "primitive circumstances" were plainly unstable. Though he never discusses early human history systematically, we can nevertheless reconstruct how Spencer viewed its broad contours.

Coleridge, Schelling and Von Baer's influence on Spencer's *First Principles*. Spencer owed to Schelling the idea that all species were characterized by increasing individuation. He owed the claim that all development was from the homogeneous to the heterogeneous to Von Baer.

[4] For a comprehensive discussion of Spencer's theory of social evolution as part of his cosmology, see M. W. Taylor's largely excellent *Men Versus the State: Herbert Spencer and Late Victorian Individualism* (Oxford University Press, 1992). In Taylor's view, Spencer "aimed at nothing less than a mechanical interpretation of the universe in which every event could be explained in terms of the relations of cause and effect between incident forces" (p. 77). Hence, for Taylor, "Spencer's doctrine of evolution was neither Darwinian nor Lamarckian, although both Lamarckian and Darwinian factors can be seen to have been incorporated in the theory of evolution which he propounded" (p. 76).

Sometimes Spencer claims that humans once lived blissfully isolated lives. For instance, in his early *Social Statics* (1851), he says that human violence emerged when humans first began living socially, implying that they previously lived asocially and peacefully.[5] In *The Principles of Ethics*, published over forty years later, Spencer contrasts "social life" with the "presocial state" again implying that humans once lived asocially (vol. I, p. 290).

Sometimes Spencer depicts our earliest beginnings as substantially social and harmonious. In *The Man Versus the State* (1884), he says that "in these exceptional [beginning] circumstances, unaggressive and for special reasons unaggressed on, there is so little deviation from the virtues of truthfulness, honesty, justice and generosity, that nothing beyond an occasional expression of public opinion by informally-assembled elders is needed."[6]

But at other times Spencer describes early human history as being extremely incommodious. He sometimes suggests that humans originally lived anti-socially and violently. For instance, in *Social Statics*, he says that we initially lived "predatory" lives requiring that each "should sacrifice the welfare of other beings to his own" (p. 58). Life was "savage," steeped in "perpetual antagonism" and overflowing with "aggression, dispute, anger, hatred and revenge" (pp. 58, 176–7).

Spencer's conception of our "presocial," primitive beginnings is inconsistent. Moreover, incoherent implications follow from at least one of his earlier versions of this conception, where he describes the quitting of "presocial" politics as a social contract.[7] That is, inasmuch as our origins were deeply asocial and "unsituated," they would have been languageless and thus devoid of the cognitive skills

[5] Herbert Spencer, *Social Statics* [1851] (New York: Robert Schalkenbach Foundation, 1970), p. 57.

[6] Herbert Spencer, *The Man Versus the State* [1884] (Indianapolis: Liberty Classics, 1981), p. 71. Also see *The Principles of Ethics*, vol. II, p. 222, where Spencer says that humans originally lived tribally, peacefully and without any sort of central authority.

[7] Even in the later *The Principles of Ethics*, vol. II, p. 36, remnants of social contract linger in his thinking: "We come now to the truth – faintly indicated among lower beings – that the advantages of cooperation can be had only by conformity to certain requirements which association imposes. The mutual hindrances liable to arise during the pursuit of their needs by individuals living in proximity, must be kept within such limits as to leave a surplus of advantage obtained by associated life." In other words, originally living separately and antagonistically, individuals gradually opt for primitive association. Small groups form as members dimly begin appreciating the "advantages of cooperation." They slowly realize that some manner of mutual forbearance is required if they are to pursue their respective "ends" with success.

required for making social contracts. However, contractual strategies would be possible if "presocial" politics were sufficiently social, as Spencer's second and third versions of presociality seem to be. Contractual deliverance from the second version of presociality would constitute a move *within* sociality or *within* situatedness from thinner to thicker kinds of sociality. Similarly, contractual resolution to the third version would also occur *within* sociality though this time from social savagery to social cooperation. In his later writings, where he discards social contract theory in favor of an evolutionary account of politics, Spencer seems vaguely aware of these conceptual shortcomings. Faulting Hobbes' social contract theory in the manner of Rousseau, Spencer observes:

> If the admired philosopher Hobbes, instead of deducing his theory of the state from a pure fiction, had prepared himself by ascertaining the facts as they are actually presented in groups of primitive men, or men in the first stages of social life, he never would have propounded it. Had he known something more of savages as they really exist, he would not have ascribed to them those *ideas* of social order and its benefits, which are the products of *developed* social life; and he would have learned that subordination to a ruling power is at the outset not in the least prompted by the motive he assigns. (my italics)[8]

Spencer's theory of "presocial" politics was never carefully formulated and is therefore unsatisfying. Earlier versions varied considerably, as did later versions. One version was implausible, if not simply incoherent. Even after becoming a devoted advocate of evolutionary theory, Spencer never elaborated upon his theory of "presocial" politics as one might expect. Consequently, Spencer's liberal utilitarianism rested on unsettled historical foundations. By contrast, his theory of "social" politics, both in its earlier and later versions, was much more sophisticated, if not always convincing.

POLITICS AND SOCIAL EVOLUTION

After *Social Statics*, Spencer became a dedicated advocate of theorizing history through the lens of social evolution. In his 1899 intellectual autobiography, "The Filiation of Ideas," he insists that he, and not Darwin, first introduced the concept of evolution in his

[8] *The Principles of Ethics*, vol. II, pp. 221–2.

1857 "Progress: Its Law and Cause,"[9] Besides typifying Spencer's exaggerated sense of originality, this boldfaced claim nevertheless signals the centrality which evolutionary theorizing came to play for him. Such theorizing soon invested his entire understanding of society and politics.

In his post-*Social Statics* writings, Spencer held that, roughly speaking, political history evolved through four basic phases. These are (1) primitive societies characterized by informal political cooperation, (2) "militant" societies dominated by regimented, centralized political authority, (3) "industrial" societies distinguished by the relaxation of centralized political authority and the emergence of liberal values and, finally, (4) liberal utopias where government withers away.

For Spencer, primitive societies were distinguished by a "certain concreteness," by possessing a "general likeness of arrangements throughout the area occupied," by having a modicum of "constancy" that comes with "settled life."[10] And significantly, they were distinguished by fledgling, lasting patterns of "cooperation" for the sake of achieving "combined action against enemies" and for the sake of better "facilitating sustenation by mutual aid" and of better satisfying "companionship" needs (*The Principles of Ethics*, vol. II, pp. 203–4). Such cooperation, though, was politically informal.

The transition to the third phase of social evolution, that is, from limited informal cooperation to formal politicized cooperation and cohesiveness, continues gradually. War, in particular, facilitates this transition: "The first fact is that where there neither is, nor has been, any war there is no government" because "government is initiated and developed by the defensive and offensive actions of a society against other societies" (vol. II, pp. 222, 224). These actions are, in turn, rooted in one overriding cause, namely physical encounters between primitive societies. Primitive societies, in other words, expand, become more numerous, and begin to press upon one another. They "come to be everywhere in one another's way" (vol. II, p. 37). Conflict ensues. Success in war requires group

[9] Herbert Spencer, "*The Filiation of Ideas*" in Duncan (ed.), *The Life and Letters of Herbert Spencer*, p. 55. Spencer also claims that he was the first to use the expression "survival of the fittest" which he says he introduced in place of Darwin's teleologically laden "natural selection." See Herbert Spencer, "The Survival of the Fittest," *Nature* (February 1, 1872), 263.

[10] Herbert Spencer, *The Principles of Sociology* [1876–96], 3 vols. (New York: D. Appleton and Co., 1883), vol. I, p. 466.

solidarity and tighter cooperation, which fosters nascent political authority: "When many tribes unite against a common enemy, long continuance of their combined action makes them coherent under some common control. And so it is subsequently with still larger aggregates" (*The Principles of Sociology*, vol. II, p. 286).[11]

Wars, at first occasional, cause prominent tribal warriors to assume temporary influence for the duration of conflict. As war becomes chronic, their influence becomes customary and firmly entrenched. Chronic warfare, furthermore, selects out social aggregates exhibiting weaker solidarity and weaker central authority. Victory in war consolidates their more successful rivals, causes them to expand and enhances the power of their leaders. This power eventually becomes absolute and sweeping: "When, by this process, nations are formed and chiefs grow into kings, governmental power, becoming absolute, becomes also coextensive with social life" (*The Principles of Ethics*, vol. II, p. 223).[12]

Victory, consolidation and territorial growth accompanies those political units in which militancy and subordination are greatest. In the inter-societal "struggle for existence," success favors the most thoroughly militant in which the "fighting part includes all who can bear arms and be trusted with arms, while the remaining part serves simply as a permanent commissariat" (*The Principles of Sociology*, vol. II, p. 570).

Warfare spreads and intensifies thanks to the emergence of two new factors which are themselves, in turn, products of social cohesion engendered by warfare. First, as deceased tribal chiefs become mythological personalities, their "unsettled feuds" become a "duty" demanding continuation. Even in the absence of such feuds, divine pleasure frequently requires periodic aggression: "Hence such a fact as that told of the Fijian chief, who was in a state of mental agony because he had displeased his god by not killing enough of the enemy" (*The Principles of Ethics*, vol. I, p. 344).[13] Second, warfare, especially after the rise of feudalism in Europe, is fueled by new anti-social vices which arise as societies congeal. These vices include

[11] See also vol. II, p. 286 for Spencer's remark that "Cooperation in war is the chief cause of social integration."

[12] See also "Social Effects of War – Benefits" in Alfred W. Tillett's collection of excerpts from Spencer entitled *Militancy Versus Civilization* (London: P. S. King and Co., 1915).

[13] Notice that Spencer uses contemporary anthropology to support his account of early social evolution. This "conjectural" method of using modern "rude" cultures to speculate about early social evolution was typical of Spencer especially in *The Principles of Sociology*.

avarice, deceit, thievery, and "other excesses of an unbridled soldiery" (vol. 1, p. 388).

War, then, has caused the "extirpating" of feebler social aggregates by more vigorous and advanced ones. "By force alone" have smaller social aggregates expanded and made themselves into nations. Moreover, and crucially, the habits and practices of conquest and subordination have taught humans the habits and "discipline of submission" which have gradually fitted them for "submission to that code of moral law" by which their conduct has become more ethical.[14]

For Spencer, population growth was an equally important source of social progress. Insofar as conflict results from people coming to be "everywhere in one another's way," population had to have become sufficiently dense so as to engender social friction. In short, population growth led to war which, in turn, caused social progress.

Although Spencer never acknowledged Malthus' influence, this influence is palpable especially in Spencer's earlier works when Malthus still cast a large shadow across the English intellectual landscape.[15] Spencer's early 1852 essay, "A Theory of Population Deduced From the General Law of Animal Fertility," succinctly analyzes the role of population pressure in social evolution and plainly betrays Malthus' legacy. As Spencer writes at the conclusion:

> The gradual diminution and ultimate disappearance of the original excess of fertility could take place only through the process of civilization; and, at the same time, the excess of fertility has itself rendered the process of civilization inevitable. From the beginning, pressure of population has been the proximate cause of progress. It produced the original diffusion of the race. It compelled men to abandon predatory habits and take to agriculture. It led to the clearing of the earth's surface. It forced men into the social state; made social organization inevitable; and has developed the social sentiments. It has stimulated progressive improvements in production, and increased skill and intelligence. It is daily pressing us into closer contact and more mutually-dependent relationships. And after

[14] Herbert Spencer, *The Study of Sociology* [1873] (Ann Arbor: University of Michigan Press, 1969), pp. 174–8.

[15] As R. M. Young has observed, "Malthus' biographer says that it rained refutations of Malthus for thirty years. The resulting controversy sprouted everywhere. Malthus' ideas were as commonplace in the first half of the nineteenth century as Freud's were in the twentieth." See his *Darwin's Metaphor* (Cambridge University Press, 1985), p. 26. Of course, Darwin and Wallace owed much to Malthus in separately discovering the principle of natural selection. How much they owed to him, especially in the case of Darwin, is controversial. See, in particular, Derek Freeman, "The Evolutionary Theories of Charles Darwin and Herbert Spencer," *Current Anthropology*, 15 (1974).

having caused, as it ultimately must, the due peopling of the globe, and the bringing of all its habitable parts into the highest state of culture – after having brought all processes for the satisfaction of human wants to the greatest perfection–after having, at the same time, developed the intellect into complete competency for its work, and the feelings into complete fitness for social life – after having done all this, we see that the pressure of population, as it gradually finishes its work, must gradually bring itself to an end.[16]

This passage makes broad claims about the impact of population pressure. Population pressure scattered humans and compelled them to take up agriculture as well as more sophisticated modes of production. It forced humans to live socially making them interdependent and causing them to develop "social sentiments." The latter consequence is significant for by "social sentiments," Spencer means nascent morality.[17]

Spencer, then, and particularly in his earlier writings, believed that population pressure indirectly caused social progress. War, that great engine of social evolution, presupposes social friction which, in turn, results from population growth and pressure on overextended subsistence resources.

Though he held that war and population pressure were initially important stimuli of social evolution, Spencer denied that they were permanent fixtures of human history. Both were losing their significance and atrophying like useless biological appendages. His later writings, such as *The Principles of Sociology*, stress this claim repeatedly:

Recognizing our indebtedness to war for forming great communities and developing their structures, we may yet infer that the acquired powers, available for other activities, will lose their original activities. While conceding that without these perpetual bloody strifes, civilized societies

[16] Herbert Spencer, "A Theory of Population Deduced From the General Law of Animal Fertility" [1852] in J. D. Y. Peel (ed.), *Herbert Spencer on Social Evolution* (University of Chicago Press, 1972), p. 37. Spencer later claimed that this essay proved that he nearly stumbled on to the theory of natural selection seven years before Darwin's 1859 *The Origin of Species*. For valuable discussions of Spencer's essay, see J. D. Y. Peel, *Herbert Spencer: The Evolution of a Sociologist* (New York: Basic Books, 1971), pp. 137–9 and John C. Greene, "Biology and Herbert Spencer" in John C. Greene, *Science, Ideology and World View* (Berkeley: University of California Press, 1981), pp. 76–7.

[17] Spencer also remarks that, as it abates, thanks to declining human fertility, population pressure will have engendered a "state of things which will require from each individual no more than a normal and pleasurable activity . . . Consequently, in the end, the obtainment of subsistence will require just that kind and that amount of action needful to perfect health and happiness." Spencer, "A Theory of Population," pp. 36–7.

could not have arisen, and that an adapted form of human nature, fierce as well as intelligent, was a needful concomitant; we may at the same time hold that such societies having been produced, the brutality of nature in their units which was necessitated by the process, ceasing to be necessary with the cessation of the process, will disappear. (vol. II, p. 242)[18]

As warfare becomes less chronic, a new historical epoch characterized by industrialization arises. Prolonged success in war makes "industrial" civilization possible. By defeating and absorbing enemies, militarily successful societies not only expand but stabilize. Such societies, as they stabilize, begin "compounding" and "recompounding," intensifying social integration and causing the division of labor and commerce to appear. "Compound" societies evolve, in turn, into "doubly compound" and "trebly compound" societies. Until the advent of capitalism, social "compounding" and "recompounding" produce political hierarchy and economic inequality. Liberal capitalism, however, constitutes a turning point in social evolution. Socio-economic integration and differentiation deepen while political absolutism, hierarchy and economic inequality wane. "Militant" social evolution succumbs to "industrialism."

"Militancy," then, is an invaluable though happily impermanent phase of social evolution. Inflexibly hierarchical and economically autarkical, "militant" societies eventually are too repressive, inefficient and listless to compete with "industrial" societies.

By healthy contrast, "industrial" societies are dynamic and merely "negatively regulative" insofar as state responsibilities shrink by becoming highly "specialized" and restricted to protecting citizens against force and fraud at home and aggression from abroad. "Industrial" societies, consequently, are grounded in contractual, voluntary cooperation. Their members display a "strong sense of individual freedom, and a determination to maintain it" as well as an "unusual respect for the claims of others" and "others' individualities" (*The Principles of Sociology*, vol. II, pp. 628–9).[19] Their members

[18] See as well Spencer, *The Principles of Sociology*, vol. II, pp. 664–5: "From war has been gained all that it had to give. This peopling of the Earth by the more powerful and intelligent races, is a benefit in great measure achieved; and what remains to be done, calls for no other agency than the quiet pressure of a spreading industrial civilization on a barbarism which slowly dwindles."

[19] See as well Spencer, *The Principles of Sociology*, vol. II, p. 608, where Spencer says that with industrialism, "the individuality of each man shall have the fullest play compatible with the like play of other men's individualities."

develop these attitudes because "every act of exchange" fosters them (vol. II, p. 309). Furthermore:

> This relation, in which the mutual rendering of services is unforced and neither individual subordinated, becomes the predominant relation throughout society in proportion as the industrial activities predominate. Daily determining the thoughts and sentiments, daily disciplining all in asserting their own claims while forcing them to recognize the correlative claims of others, it produces social units whose mental structures and habits mould social arrangements into corresponding forms. There results this type characterized throughout by that same individual freedom which every commercial transaction implies. The co-operation by which the multi-form activities of the society are carried on, becomes a voluntary co-operation. (vol. I, pp. 589–90)[20]

"Industrial" societies, because of their dynamism and commitment to promoting freedom, prosper at the expense of their "militant" rivals. And those "industrial" societies that are most committed to freedom and respecting basic rights flourish most of all. As Spencer contends:

> For it is clear that, other things equal, a society in which life, liberty, and property, are secure, and all interests justly regarded, must prosper more than one in which they are not; and, consequently, among competing industrial societies, there must be a gradual replacing of those in which personal rights are imperfectly maintained, by those in which they are perfectly maintained. So that by survival of the fittest must be produced a social type in which individual claims, considered as sacred, are trenched on by the State no further than is requisite to pay the cost of maintaining them, or rather, of arbitrating among them. (*The Principles of Sociology*, vol. II, p. 608)[21]

The conceptual distinction between "militancy" and "industrialism" was fairly commonplace in nineteenth-century England, especially by the time Spencer embraced it in his later works. According to J. D. Y. Peel, it figured in the thinking of Cobden and Bright and in the propaganda of the Anti-Corn Law League (*Herbert*

[20] For Spencer's most systematic analyses of "militant" and "industrial" societies, see his chapters "The Militant Type of Society" and "The Industrial Type of Society" in *The Principles of Sociology*, vol. II.

[21] See also Spencer, *The Principles of Sociology*, vol. II, p. 610, where Spencer similarly observes, "For when, the struggle for existence between societies by war having ceased, there remains only the industrial struggle for existence, the final survival and spread must be on the part of those societies which produce the largest number of the best individuals – individuals best adapted for life in the industrial state."

Spencer: The Evolution of a Sociologist, pp. 76 and 193). It was also employed later by such intellectual contemporaries of Spencer as Henry Maine and Walter Bagehot. For Maine, the development of civilization was nothing less than the transformation of "status" societies into "contract" societies. Whereas, in the former, law is little more than the codified commands of rulers, in the latter, law becomes depersonalized by becoming supreme and by focusing on protecting individual rights.[22] Spencer, by the way, frequently employed the notions of "status" and "contract" when contrasting militancy and industrialism. However, though he knew Maine personally, there is no direct evidence that he borrowed these categories from him.

For Bagehot, who worked for *The Economist* during the mid-1800s like Spencer (but after Spencer resigned), certain societies succeeded for many of the same reasons offered by Spencer. Those societies enjoying greater solidarity, religious identity and military skill have tended to supplant those in which these qualities have been weaker. Such success, in turn, has engendered stability and, ultimately, industrial development. And successful industrial development was fast leading to the triumph of what Bagehot labeled the "age of discussion."[23]

The distinction between "militancy" and "industrialism" continues to enchant social and political theorists. Michael Oakeshott, in particular, deploys similar conceptual language. For Oakeshott, "enterprise associations," like Spencer's "militant" societies, are command societies that are hierarchical, control material resources, supervise beliefs, assign employment and allocate rewards. By contrast, "civil associations," like Spencer's "industrial" societies, enforce non-substantive rules of conduct without narrowly specifying what citizens must do. As one of Oakeshott's sympathetic interpreters puts this distinction, "enterprise government runs men's lives, civil government rules them."[24]

The fifth and closing epoch of Spencerian social evolution is

[22] See, in particular, the chapter entitled "Primitive Society and Ancient Law" in Henry Maine, *Ancient Law* [1861] (New York: H. Holt, 1906).

[23] For Bagehot's version of this socio-historical dichotomy, see his *Physics and Politics* (New York: A. A. Knopf, 1948).

[24] John Liddington, "Oakeshott: Freedom in a Modern State" in John Gray and Z. A. Pelczynski (eds.), *Conceptions of Liberty in Political Philosophy* (New York: St. Martin's Press, 1984), p. 307.

nothing less than liberal capitalist utopia. As the culmination of human history, liberal utopia constitutes the realization of everyone's freedom. It entails mutual respect between citizens and, thus, generates social well-being. It also entails peace between liberal states and the marginalization of non-liberal ones. The triumph of liberalism is nothing less than the victory of liberalism over its antiquated rivals everywhere. Liberal utopia, then, is as much the victorious conclusion of "industrialism" as it is the emergence of a *separate* and final epoch of human history.

Spencer did not always indulge in such Enlightenment fantasies. As he grew older, he conceded that "industrialism" could relapse into "militancy." The spread of socialism in Europe at the end of the nineteenth century sobered his optimism about the future of liberalism. As far as Spencer was concerned, socialism re-militarized liberal societies and made them imperialistic. But Spencer's doubts were never systematically integrated into his social evolutionary theory. They were never elaborately conceptualized and remained simply an undercurrent anxiety. Spencer was too much a committed liberal, too much of a child of modernity, to abandon so easily his faith in the utility-generating powers of freedom once it had sufficiently taken root in society.

USE-INHERITANCE AND MORAL PROGRESS

Before we analyze Spencer's theory of freedom, we must first address the interrelationship between use-inheritance, or the inheritance of acquired characteristics, and moral progress in his theory of social evolution. Throughout his writings, Spencer held that our moral "character" was "indefinitely modifiable," though modifications occurred imperceptibly. Accordingly, Spencer chastised those whose unscientific myopia convinced them otherwise:

> While it was held that the stars are fixed and that the hills are everlasting, there was a certain congruity in the notion that man continued unchanged from age to age; but now when we know that all stars are in motion, and that there are no such things as lasting hills – now when we find all things throughout the universe to be in a ceaseless flux, it is time for this crude conception of human nature to disappear out of our social conceptions; or rather – it is time for its disappearance to be followed by that of the many narrow notions respecting the past and the future of society, which have grown out of it, and which linger notwithstanding the loss of their root. For,

avowedly by some and tacitly by others, it continues to be thought that the human heart is as "desperately wicked" as it ever was, and that the state of society hereafter will be very much like the state of society now. (*The Study of Sociology*, p. 108)[25]

The inherent malleability of character is a condition for the emergence of liberal institutions and liberal morality as far as Spencer was concerned. This malleability allows individuals to take advantage of changing social circumstances in order to learn new patterns of mutual respect. Nascent "industrialism" encourages individuals to begin asserting their claims to pursue happiness while simultaneously "respecting the [like] claims of others." And this transformation of our moral character, this waxing ethos of mutual forbearance, amounts to nothing less than the steady fulfillment of "everyone's individuality" and happiness (*Social Statics*, p. 389).[26]

So, the development of liberal forbearance is concomitant with the evolution of "industrial" society because this forbearance awakens under growing security, internal stability and expanding productive relations which are, in turn, ultimately traceable to the establishment of national integrity through successful military competition and expansion. In other words, character exploits changed circumstances and begins flourishing. "Civilization," according to *Social Statics*, "seems rather the development of man's latent capabilities under the action of favorable circumstance" (p. 372). And according to "The Filiation of Ideas":

> There is [in *Social Statics*] a perpetual assumption of the moral modifiability of Man, and the progressive adaptation of his character to the social state. It is alleged that his moral evolution depends on the development of sympathy, which is held to be the root of both justice and beneficence. This change of mental nature is ascribed to the exercise of the sympathetic emotions consequent upon a peaceful social life, and, therefore, tacitly implies the inheritance of functionally-produced changes of structure. (*The Life and letters of Herbert Spencer*, p. 540)

The above passage not only illustrates Spencer's belief in humankind's moral modification under the favorable opportunities of peace, stability and industry. It also highlights Spencer's early

[25] By those who view the "human heart" as "desperately wicked," Spencer probably means Hobbes.

[26] Also see Spencer to Horace Seal, July 11, 1893 in Duncan (ed.), *The Life and Letters of Herbert Spencer*, p. 354, where Spencer says that growing individualism, based on "elaborate . . . mutual dependence," characterizes moral progress.

Lamarckianism, which became central to his later moral theory, as we shall shortly see. By the 1870s, Spencer had become a dedicated advocate of the inheritance of acquired characteristics as the principal mechanism of human mental and moral development. But it wasn't until 1886, in "The Factors of Organic Evolution," that he published his most succinct defense of his Lamarckian convictions. The essay's preface is especially revealing:

> Though mental phenomena of many kinds, and especially of the simpler kinds, are explicable only as resulting from the natural selection of favourable variations; yet there are, I believe, still more numerous mental phenomena, including all those of any considerable complexity, which cannot be explained otherwise than as results of the inheritance of functionally-produced modifications . . .
>
> Of course there are involved the conceptions we form of the genesis and nature of our higher emotions; and by implication, the conceptions we form of our moral intuitions. If functionally-produced modifications are inheritable, then the mental associations habitually produced in individuals by experiences of the relations between actions and their consequences, pleasurable or painful, may, in the successions of individuals, generate innate tendencies to like or dislike such actions. But if not, the genesis of such tendencies is, as we shall see, not satisfactorily explicable.
>
> That our sociological beliefs must also be profoundly affected by the conclusions we draw on this point, is obvious. If a nation is modified en masse by transmission of the effects produced on the natures of its members by those modes of daily activity which its institutions and circumstances involve; then we must infer that such institutions and circumstances mould its members far more rapidly and comprehensively than they can do if the sole cause of adaptation to them is the more frequent survival of individuals who happen to have varied in favourable ways.[27]

For Spencer, then, human evolution is affected by natural selection, though natural selection declines in significance as human evolution becomes mostly mental and moral. Use-inheritance is the more powerful engine of evolutionary change in general and it is un-

[27] Herbert Spencer, "The Factors of Organic Evolution," *Essays*, vol. 1, pp. 463–5. See, as well, p. 424 where Spencer says that the "inheritance of functionally-produced changes has been not simply a co-operating factor in organic evolution, but has been a co-operating factor without which organic evolution, in its *higher forms* at any rate, could never have taken place" (my italics). "The Factors of Organic Evolution" first appeared in *The Nineteenth Century* in April and May 1886 and was republished in 1887 as a pamphlet. Also see Herbert Spencer, "The Inheritance of Acquired Characteristics," *Nature* (March 6, 1890). Spencer embraced Lamarckianism after reading Lyell's *Principles of Geology* (1830), in 1840. Arguing against use-inheritance, Lyell succeeded in convincing Spencer of its validity.

questionably the best mechanism for explaining how our mental and moral faculties have evolved. Thus, as far as Spencer was concerned, Darwin was a great naturalist, though his evolutionary sociology and moral theory remained radically incomplete. By relying so heavily on natural selection as an account of all evolutionary development, Darwin handicapped his theory's ability to handle human progress.

The extent of the differences between Spencer's and Darwin's theories of evolution has been a matter of some dispute. Many historians of science insist that whereas Spencer was a confirmed Lamarckian, Darwin rejected Lamarckianism. For instance, Freeman argues that the "theories of Darwin and Spencer were unrelated in their origins, markedly disparate in their logical structures, and differed decisively in the degree to which they depended on the supposed mechanism of Lamarckian inheritance and recognized 'progress' as inevitable" ("The Evolutionary Theories of Charles Darwin and Herbert Spencer," p. 213). Greene, on the other hand, claims that although *The Origin of Species* "owed nothing to Spencer," *The Descent of Man* is "Spencerian in two ways" by stressing competitive struggle and "inherited effects of mental and moral training" as explanations of social progress.[28] Whatever the *extent* of the differences, Spencer never dismissed natural selection out of hand nor did Darwin totally reject inheritance of acquired characteristics. Indeed, by the final 1872 revision of *The Origin of Species*, Darwin warmed to the significance of use-inheritance, though natural selection always remained the predominant mechanism of evolution for him.[29] Darwin's unsettled views about the inheritance of acquired characteristics were reflected in his ambivalent assessment of Spencer. By and large, Darwin thought Spencer a remarkable sociologist but an inadequate scientist.[30] Had Darwin lived

[28] John C. Greene, "Comments on Freeman," *Current Anthropology*, 15 (1974), 224.

[29] Darwin and Spencer differed in another important respect. Whereas Spencer aspired to explain the evolution of the entire cosmos, Darwin was less ambitious, focusing primarily upon the physical transformation of earthly species.

[30] For Darwin's favorable estimation of Spencer, see Darwin to Herbert Spencer, 25 November, 1858 in F. Darwin (ed.), *The Life and Letters of Charles Darwin* [1887], 3 vols. (New York: Basic Books, 1959), vol. I, p. 497. Darwin begins by thanking Spencer for a complimentary copy of his *Essays: Scientific, Political and Speculative.* He then refers to the forthcoming publication of *The Origin of Species*, adding: "I treat the subject simply as a naturalist, and not from a general point of view, otherwise, in my opinion, your argument could not have been improved on, and might have been quoted by me with great advantage." But see also Darwin's somewhat less enthusiastic remarks, eight years later, in Darwin to J. D. Hooker, December 10, 1866, *The Life and Letters of Charles Darwin*, vol. II, p. 239. Referring to Spencer's *Principles of Biology* [1864–7], Darwin says that it is

another ten years to witness Weismann's devastating criticisms of Lamarckianism and the beginning of advances in cytology, his views of Spencer surely would have become more negative. As Lamarckianism fell into greater and greater discredit, Spencer became a shriller proponent of it. In 1893, he published "The Inadequacy of 'Natural Selection'" in *The Contemporary Review*, arguing, in effect, that without the inheritance of acquired characteristics, evolution never would have occurred.[31] Thereafter followed several exchanges with August Weismann also published in *The Contemporary Review* from 1893 to 1895, and a final defense of Lamarckianism, "Some Light on Use-Inheritance," published 1902 a year before Spencer died.[32]

In his exchange with Spencer, Weismann complained that use-inheritance was not credible because it could not account for important biological changes. For instance, use-inheritance could not explain the disappearance of wings in worker ants because "workers are sterile and can transmit nothing at all."[33] Being sterile, earlier generations of workers could not possibly have passed along to subsequent generations their atrophying, little-used wings. Therefore, the disappearance of wings in workers must have been caused, not by inheritable disuse, but by some other biological mechanism. Second, even if workers had progeny, their wings are "passive organs whose perfection in no way depends on their being employed; they are complete before they are used, and are rather injured by wear than strengthened by use."[34] Wing use or disuse, in short, neither causes wings to develop nor to degenerate, making use or disuse irrelevant to biological evolution. The same is true, Weismann cautions, of the shells of shellfish and the hard outer surfaces of

"wonderfully clever" and "mostly true." He adds, however, that had Spencer "trained himself to observe more . . . he would have been a wonderful man." For a wholly negative evaluation, see Charles Darwin, *The Autobiography of Charles Darwin* [1892] (London: Collins, 1958), pp. 108–9, where Darwin observes: "His [Spencer's] deductive manner of treating every subject is wholly opposed to my frame of mind. His conclusions never convince me." Furthermore, his fundamental generalizations "do not seem to me to be of any strictly scientific use. They partake more of the nature of definitions than laws of nature."

31 Herbert Spencer, "The Inadequacy of 'Natural Selection,'" *The Contemporary Review*, 63 (1893).

32 For his 1902 essay, see Herbert Spencer, "Some Light on Use-Inheritance," *Facts and Comments* (London: Williams and Norgate, 1902). Spencer republished several of his later essays defending Lamarckianism in his 1898 revised *Principles of Biology*.

33 August Weismann, "The All-Sufficiency of Natural Selection: A Reply to Herbert Spencer," *The Contemporary Review*, 64 (1893), 316.

34 Ibid., p. 317.

insects. He concludes: "Innumerable *positive* variations likewise do not admit of explanation by the Lamarckian principle, because the parts involved have only a passive function, and therefore are not strengthened by functioning . . . A muscle can become larger through use, but a claw, a fringe of bristles, an indentation, or a spine of an arthropod cannot by use become thicker, longer, or stronger."[35]

According to Weismann, only "panmixia" can plausibly explain the degeneration of passive organs such as insect wings. The theory of panmixia holds that as organs or parts of organs become superfluous for survival (such as ant wings), they decline from the height of their adaptive refinement. As the pressures from selection wane, such organs or their parts atrophy through variation, often persisting as rudimentary, inessential appendages. Hence, survival disutility, not inheritable disuse, explains their decline and disappearance: "The first impetus, then, to the 'upward' or 'downward' development of an organ is due not to its greater or lesser activity, but to its degree of utility."[36] In sum, according to Weismann, natural selection is the "only possible explanation that we can conceive" of with respect to all forms of biological metamorphoses.[37] All alternative accounts, including use-inheritance, leave too much unexplained.

In contrast to Weismann, Spencer complained that insofar as natural selection generated infinitesimal variations in each new generation, it couldn't plausibly account for the relative speed of most biological evolution. Tiny fortuitous variations, Spencer surmised, could not possibly enhance an organism's chances of survival appreciably and, hence, could not possibly advance the adaptive powers of its descendants very much.[38] Moreover, natural selection was incapable of explaining the increasing tactile discriminativeness of the tip of the human finger or human tongue. Spencer observes: "Having shown that discriminativeness increases with practice, I pointed out that, if there is inheritance of acquired characters, these

[35] August Weismann, "Heredity Once More," *The Contemporary Review*, 68 (1895), 451.

[36] Ibid., 432. Also see p. 448 where Weismann says of the evolution of the human ankle joint: "As the result of some beautiful comparative studies, Tornier has recently tried to prove that the function always produces the joint, not the joint the function; but, strongly as appearances support this view, it is, nevertheless, only apparently true; in reality the transformation of form precedes the variation of function in point of time . . . The joint cannot possibly be formed as a result of function, seeing that it can only be made use of when it is complete and hardened, and is no longer variable."

[37] Ibid., 455.

[38] Spencer, "The Inadequacy of 'Natural Selection,' " pp. 165–6.

differences are completely accounted for – are, indeed, necessary corollaries; and I then asked whether it was possible to account for them otherwise." Not surprisingly, Spencer insists that these differences can't be explained in any other way. Thus, on Weismann's own principle that an explanation is justified if phenomena are inexplicable without it, Spencer concludes that "the inheritance of acquired characters must be admitted."[39] In sum, natural selection, and not use-inheritance as Weismann insists, leaves too much unexplained.

The earlier passage from "Factors of Organic Evolution" is also striking because it suggests that use-inheritance, associationist psychology, moral intuitionism and utility are deeply intertwined. Actions that have tended to produce pleasure or pain have tended to generate fixed mental associations in individuals between the types of action and pleasure or pain. These psychological associations have been, furthermore, accompanied by pangs of approval or disapproval insofar as we naturally feel approval for actions which produce pleasure and disapproval for those which produce pain. And thanks to the biological mechanism of use-inheritance, these pangs of approval and disapproval have, in turn, become inherited as moral intuitions of approval and disapproval gradually strengthening and becoming more instinctive over time. Hence, human behavior was becoming, slowly and unavoidably, more spontaneously moral. In the words of E. L. Youmans, founder of *Popular Science Monthly* and one of Spencer's American disciples: "Mental and moral faculties were viewed [by Spencer] as products of inherited experiences that have become organized in the nervous constitutions of higher beings . . . The principle of the evolution of ideas in the hereditary intelligence of the race, and of the evolution of moral sentiments in its hereditary conscience, reconciles the

[39] Herbert Spencer, "Heredity Once More," *The Contemporary Review*, 68 (1895), 608. Also see Spencer's rhetorical question: "But now if the sufficiency of an assigned cause cannot in any case be demonstrated, and if it is 'really very difficult to imagine' [as Weismann admits] in what way it [natural selection] has produced its alleged effects, what becomes of the 'all sufficiency' of the cause?" "A Rejoinder to Professor Weismann," *The Contemporary Review*, 64 (1893), 893. But see, as well, Spencer's concession that use-inheritance is not the exclusive vehicle of evolutionary development: "Though 'The Origin of the Species' proved to me that the transmission of acquired characters cannot be the sole factor in organic evolution, as I had assumed in 'Social Statics' and in 'The Principles of Psychology,' published in pre-Darwinian days, yet I have never wavered in the belief that it is *a* factor, and an all-important factor." "Weismann Once More," *The Contemporary Review*, 66 (1894), 610.

conflicting schools of intuitionalism and utilitarianism in mental and moral philosophy."[40]

Spencer's marriage of many of these concepts was not unprecedented. For instance, Mill also married associationist psychology and utility to explain our intuitions and a priori convictions. However, Mill restricted his account to associational patterns learned in individual lives only, whereas Spencer included patterns inherited across lives.[41]

Among recent interpreters of Spencer, M. W. Taylor has perceptively grasped the centrality of use-inheritance for Spencer's moral psychology and for his theory of moral progress. Taylor argues that, for Spencer, moral intuitions are inheritable precisely because each mental sensation corresponds to a physiological event in our nervous systems. Like all complex sensations, moral approval or disapproval have their physiological dimensions. Because these physiological dimensions are inheritable, their emotive counterparts are likewise inheritable (*Men Versus the State*, pp. 112–13).[42]

According to Spencer, then, human nature gradually adjusts itself to the requirements of sociality as associations between specific moral ideas and specific behaviors are transmitted and strengthened from generation to generation. This adjustment occurs, moreover, because it makes sociality more commodious. Hence, this adjustment is ultimately grounded in utility.

Moral judgement, moreover, develops by becoming more nuanced and influential because it also serves as a formidable weapon in the inter-societal struggle for existence. That is, societies in which moral sentiments are comparably stronger and more widespread tend to be more successful *vis-à-vis* other societies. Societies in which mutual respect and forbearance are comparatively more

[40] E. L. Youmans, "Spencer's Evolution Philosophy," *The North American Review*, 129 (1879), 394.

[41] See J. S. Mill, *An Examination of Sir William Hamilton's Philosophy* [1865] in John M. Robson (ed.), *The Collected Works of John Stuart Mill*, 33 vols. (University of Toronto Press, 1979), vol. IX, pp. 143–5 and Spencer's "Mill versus Hamilton – The Test of Truth," *Essays*, vol. II,. For a succinct account of Spencer's psychology, see C. U. M. Smith, "Evolution and the Problem of Mind: Part I Herbert Spencer," *Journal of the History of Biology* 15 (1982).

[42] Note Taylor's observation that, thanks to Spencer, "The trains of ideas of classical associationism were now deemed to run on physiological tracks worn by the associations of many previous generations, and hence they were substantially predetermined for any given individual. Such biological tracks, i.e. the stands of nervous fibre, changed only slowly, over the course of many generations, while particular configurations of nervous structure were transmitted from parent to children according to the Lamarckian inheritance of acquired characteristics."

advanced tend to be more harmonious and happier and therefore more vigorous and productive. In Spencer's words:

> By virtue of this process there have been produced to some extent among lower creatures, and there are being further produced in man, the sentiments appropriate to social life . . . Conversely, conduct restrained within the required limits, calling out no antagonistic passions, favors harmonious cooperation, profits the group, and, by implication, profits the average of its individuals. Consequently, there results, other things equal, a tendency for groups formed of members having this adaptation of nature, to survive and spread. (*The Principles of Ethics*, vol. II, p. 43)[43]

Use-inheritance and associationism, then, play salient roles in Spencer's theory of social and moral evolution. In conjunction with natural selection, they determine human progress. However, whereas natural selection, use-inheritance and associationism jointly account for progress during formative "militant" epochs of social evolution, use-inheritance and associationism best account for progress after the emergence of "industrialism."

For Spencer, social and moral evolution were roughly complementary if not synonymous phenomena. As "militant" societies emerged from the desultory meagerness of presociality, they began exhibiting increasingly sophisticated patterns of internal cooperation which tended to favor those societies which displayed superior efficiency and unitary sense of purpose. And since cooperative efficiency *proscribes* certain kinds of behavior, cooperation began becoming effectively moral in nature. The emergence of "militancy" was simultaneously the emergence of rule-governed, moral behavior.

The transformation of "militancy" into "industrialism" was similarly, for Spencer, a matter of social and moral progress. With the spread of "industrial" societies, cooperation has become more complex, self-reflective and freer for everyone equally. It has become more moral precisely because it has become freer for everyone equally.

In other words, morality and cooperation have flourished as industrialism has flourished. And industrial prowess has, in turn, thrived as morality and cooperation have matured. As a result, "industrial" societies have become increasingly productive, moral

[43] See also Spencer, *The Principles of Ethics*, vol. I, pp. 334–5, where Spencer argues that, at a certain advanced stage of social evolution, altruism likewise tends to favor those societies where it is more developed.

and commodious, supplanting and overpowering societies which have lingered behind in the cold and crippling shadows of "militancy."

The principle of equal freedom was the normative crucible of this triumphal ascent of liberal industrialism for Spencer. The triumph of liberal industrialism was nothing less than the fuller realization of equal freedom, nothing less than the flourishing of liberal justice. Let us examine in greater detail the moral psychology of this vital principle, and the relationship of this principle to the principle of utility.

CHAPTER 2

Social evolution and the moral psychology of equal freedom

As much as anything, Spencer's moral and political philosophy hinges on the principle of equal freedom, the primary decision procedure of his liberal utilitarianism. And being a stringent principle, equal freedom renders Spencer's utilitarianism authentically liberal and therefore rich in liberal ethical appeal.

This chapter opens by examining Spencer's evolutionary moral psychology of equal freedom in *Social Statics* with the aim of clarifying the relationship between the principle of equal freedom and utility. The second section does the same with respect to his writings after *Social Statics*.

The third section of this chapter compares T. S. Gray's with David Miller's interpretation of Spencer's principle of equal freedom. Essentially, the disagreement between Gray and Miller reduces to whether or not equal freedom or desert are more fundamental for Spencer. Although my view of this issue is closer to Miller's than Gray's interpretation, the former's interpretation is not without flaws, particularly because it underplays Spencer's utilitarianism.

The final section of this chapter addresses the sense in which virtue is constitutive of negative freedom for Spencer when special attention is paid to the role of moral self-restraint in his freedom theory. Spencer's liberal utilitarianism was not exclusively juridical and was not, therefore, quite so narrowly liberal. For many philosophers, including many contemporary communitarians and liberals, virtue and negative freedom are thought to be incommensurable.

This chapter, then, aims to show that although Spencer's conception of equal freedom was sometimes opaque, it nevertheless played a vital role in his moral and political theory. The principle of equal freedom was the centerpiece of Spencer's liberal utilitarianism. It was its cardinal decision procedure. If I successfully demonstrate at least this about his moral and political theory, then my study will have gone some small distance in contributing to the appreciation of Spencer's originality and to the rehabilitation of his importance.

THE EARLY MORAL PSYCHOLOGY OF EQUAL FREEDOM

The normative force of the principle of equal freedom is best appreciated by addressing the moral psychology behind it. Understanding this psychology is also crucial to grasping how Spencer's theory of freedom accommodates negative freedom with virtue. Moreover, this understanding is equally crucial in preparing for our subsequent analysis of the way in which moral rights foster utility.

As a first step in assessing Spencer's moral psychology of equal freedom, we must consider the relationship between the notions of "faculty," "faculty exercise" and happiness. In his first work, "The Proper Sphere of Government" (1842), Spencer claims that all animals possess "organs and instincts" or "external apparatus and internal faculties." When exercised, faculties necessary for survival strengthen, producing "health and happiness."[1] While humans possess physical faculties like animals, humans alone possess "moral and intellectual faculties" on whose exercise human happiness "essentially depends" (p. 251). Moreover, moral and intellectual faculty exercise improves character. Deprived of exercise, our intellectual and moral faculties degenerate and character deteriorates. Moral and intellectual self-development, and hence happiness, depends upon moral and intellectual faculty exercise.

In *Social Statics*, Spencer further develops these ideas. He contends that happiness is a "state of consciousness," caused by "action" upon consciousness whereby consciousness is modified by "certain affections." Spencer also refers to these modifications as "sensations." When our "faculties" are "exercised" with moderation and according to their "function," the "sensations of which happiness consists" are generated (p. 67). Faculty exercise, once again, produces happiness.

In *Social Statics*, however, Spencer never explicates his notions of "faculty" and "faculty exercise" with precision. The concept "faculty" is particularly equivocal. For instance, he sometimes

[1] Herbert Spencer, "The Proper Sphere of Government" in Spencer, *The Man Versus the State*, p. 250.

equates faculties with bodily and mental "functions" or "powers." Like the eyes, he contends, a faculty is "some power" by which humans "take in impression[s]" or "feelings and ideas" (p. 67). On this account, faculties seem to be bodily organs rather than instincts. Besides eyes, our organs of hearing, taste and digestion seem to be faculties as well. Parts of our nervous system and our brains are presumably faculties too for Spencer. At least they would seem to be the neurological side of faculties. Whether our other internal organs are faculties is unclear. According to Spencer, when such organs become pathological, discomfort usually ensues. Hence, they would seem partially to meet Spencer's criteria of a faculty. Yet such organs could not be said to "take in impressions." Nor, when functioning normally, could they be said to generate pleasure. Only by arguing that sound health was pleasurable could one plausibly maintain that such organs were, in any sense, "faculties."

Spencer's conception of faculty "exercise," and his explanation of how faculty exercise produces happiness, are just as equivocal as his conception of a faculty. On the one hand, Spencer holds that the "healthful" exercise of the faculties, in the sense of mere use, produces happiness. When the faculties are simply utilized, "pleasurable feeling" obtains. It "is from the *activity* of one or more of them that all gratification arises" (*Social Statics*, p. 67).

On the other hand, happiness from faculty exercise is sometimes said to derive from faculties being utilized at full capacity: "To be agreeable [and hence yield happiness], that exercise must be proportionate to the power of the faculty; . . . Hence, to have complete felicity is to have all the faculties exerted in the ratio of their several developments" (*Social Statics*, p. 6). In another passage, Spencer argues, furthermore, that unhappiness, or "evil," results when circumstances either thwart the exercise of developed faculties or overtax underdeveloped ones. He refers to such thwarting and overtaxing as the "non-adaptation of constitution to conditions" (pp. 55, 59). Yet, he also suggests that overtaxing underdeveloped faculties sometimes causes them to develop. In short, individuals experience intense pleasure when they exercise their faculties at their full potential. And the greater the number of faculties thus exercised, the happier the individual. When faculties are both underdeveloped and *severely* overtaxed, unhappiness follows. Yet *moderate* overexercise stimulates and improves faculties, enabling them to handle the formerly excessive demands placed upon them.

As faculties develop, they become capable of yielding still greater degrees of happiness. Faculty development, then, is sometimes paid in the coin of moderate discomfort.

Spencer offers numerous examples of faculty exercise and development meant to clarify his faculty psychology. For instance, he mentions the blacksmith's arm which increases in size and strength, the sailor's eye which becomes sharper in discerning distant objects, the blind man's sense of touch which becomes more delicate over time, the clerk's skills in writing and calculation which become more rapid with practice and the experienced musician's enhanced ability to detect subtle tonal errors in music (*Social Statics*, p. 60).

These examples clearly imply that faculty refinement and, hence, happiness result from moderate and habitual faculty exercise. Often strenuous and wearisome, like physical body-building, exertion strengthens faculties without injuring them.

Spencer's faculty theory and theory of faculty exercise suffers from conceptual imprecision. Still, happiness is plainly the normative end of faculty exercise for Spencer; and the above conceptual difficulties notwithstanding, freedom is just as plainly instrumental to this end. Let us see how Spencer defends freedom's instrumentality especially in terms of his theory of equal freedom.

In *Social Statics*, after having explained the way in which faculty exercise generates happiness, Spencer next affirms that since God wills human happiness, God therefore also wills that humans should exercise their faculties: "Now if God wills man's happiness, and man's happiness can be obtained only by the exercise of his faculties, then God wills that man should exercise his faculties; that is, it is man's duty to exercise his faculties, for duty means fulfillment of the Divine Will" (p. 69). The fulfillment of the latter, moreover, "presupposes freedom of action." More revealingly, "Man cannot exercise his faculties without certain scope. He must have liberty to go and to come, to see, to feel, to speak, to work, to get food, raiment, shelter, and to provide for each and all of the needs of his nature" (p. 68).

Spencer's early utilitarianism, then, was liberal in its instrumental justification of freedom and theological in its deeper justification of utility. It looked back to John Gay as much as it looked forward to Mill. It presaged Mill's justification of freedom as a necessary condition of happiness-generating faculty exercise. It looked back to Gay for whom God "could have no other design in creating mankind than their happiness; and therefore He wills their happiness; therefore the means of their happiness; therefore that my behavior, as far as it may be a means of the happiness of mankind, should be such."[2]

Having argued that freedom of action is instrumentally indispensable to the realization of happiness, Spencer asserts that *everyone* ought to have freedom of action, that *everyone* has a right to it (*Social Statics*, p. 69). Since all are endowed with faculties and are thus bound by Divine will to exercise them, all must be free to act. Furthermore, when, exercising their faculties, "two individuals clash, the movements of the one remain free only insofar as they do not interfere with the like movements of the other." Hence, "we arrive at the general proposition that every man may claim the fullest liberty to exercise his faculties compatible with the possession of like liberty by every other man" (p. 69). Or again:

> Liberty of action being the first essential to exercise of faculties, and therefore the first essential to happiness; and the liberty of each limited by the like liberty of all being the form which this first essential assumes when applied to many instead of to one, it follows that this liberty of each, limited by the like liberty of all, is the rule in conformity with which society must be organized. Freedom being the prerequisite to normal life in the individual, equal freedom becomes the prerequisite to normal life in society. (*Social Statics*, p. 79)

Throughout *Social Statics*, as well as in his subsequent writings, Spencer repeatedly refers to the principle of equal freedom as the "first principle," or as the "primary law," of justice. Equal freedom insures that all members of liberal utilitarian societies "shall have desires only as may be fully satisfied without trenching upon the ability of other individuals to obtain like satisfaction" (p. 58). It thus guarantees that all will enjoy meaningful opportunities to pursue happiness. As he says in the later *The Principles of Ethics*:

> But now if happiness itself cannot be cut up and distributed equally, and if equal division of the material aids to happiness would not produce greatest happiness, what is the thing to be thus apportioned? – what is it in respect of which everybody is to count for one and nobody for more than one?

[2] John Gay, *Concerning the Fundamental Principles of Virtue and Morality* [1731] in J. B. Schneewind (ed.), *Moral Philosophy From Montaigne to Kant*, 2 vols. (Cambridge University Press, 1990), vol. II. Spencer never mentions Gay though he was familiar with Paley's theological utilitarianism. After *Social Statics*, however, Spencer abandoned theological for secular utilitarianism explicitly repudiating (in the 1864 "Second Preface") the "theological implications" of the first edition of *Social Statics*.

> There seems but a single possibility. There remains to be equally distributed nothing but the conditions under which each may pursue happiness. The limitations to action – the degrees of freedom and restraint, shall be alike for all. Each shall have as much liberty to pursue his ends as consists with maintaining like liberties to pursue their ends by others; and one as much as another shall have the enjoyment of that which his efforts, carried on within these limits, obtain. But to say that in respect of these conditions everybody shall count for one and nobody for more than one, is simply to say that equity shall be enforced. (vol. 1, p. 253)

The principle of equal freedom is not unique to Spencer (though few philosophers have deployed this principle with such enthusiasm). Alan Gewirth has argued that the principle of equal freedom can be interpreted in three different ways and that these three versions are represented in the writings of Hobbes, Kant, Rousseau, J. S. Mill, H. L. A. Hart and, of course, Spencer. Gewirth also mentions Article 5 of the Declaration of the Rights of Man and Citizen as an example of the principle of equal freedom. He labels the first version the "specific act" version, according to which "a man is free to do any act so long as his doing it does not prevent other men from doing the same kind of act." Gewirth calls the second the "general libertarian" version by which "a man is free to do any act so long as his doing it does not infringe the freedom of others, i.e., so long as his doing it does not prevent others from doing (or being free to do so) whatever acts they may want to do." He refers to the third version as the "negative utilitarian" version according to which "a man is free to do any act so long as his doing it does not harm someone else." In Gewirth's view, Hobbes and Spencer are "specific act" proponents of equal freedom, Kant and Hart are "general libertarian" proponents and Mill and Rousseau are "negative utilitarian" proponents.[3]

Gewirth's classification of Spencer is surprising. Spencer is clearly *not* a "specific act" equal freedom theorist who, in Gewirth's words, "does not rule out physical assault, or cheating: A is free to cheat B or to assault B physically so long as this leaves B free (subsequently) to cheat or assault A or others" (*The Principles of Ethics*, p. 149). Indeed, Spencer is closer to being a "general libertarian" theorist for whom "A is not free to cheat or assault B at all, since this would diminish or infringe B's freedom to do other things" (p. 149). Spencer's principle of equal freedom emphasizes, as Gewirth goes

[3] Alan Gewirth, "Political Justice" in Richard B. Brandt (ed.), *Social Justice* (Englewood Cliffs: Prentice-Hall, 1962), pp. 141–54.

on to say of the "general libertarian" version, "the absolute value of freedom: the only limitation of the individual's freedom is to be the general freedom of others" (p. 150). And Spencer's approach to equal freedom also shares much with the "negative utilitarian" version insofar as his enthusiasm for freedom never overrides his commitment to utilitarianism.

A similar and much earlier misconstrual of Spencer's notion of equal freedom appears in George Lacy's *Liberty and Law* (1888). Lacy reconstructs Spencer's equal freedom principle as the "liberty of each to do as he likes . . . limited by the like liberty of all others to do as they like." He then condemns equal freedom as the "most outrageous jumble the mind of man ever conceived" because if each has the liberty to do as he likes then "it must be clear that no one with certainty can do as he likes, for others might like to prevent him, and others in their turn like to prevent these from preventing others, and so on, ad infinitum."[4] Lacy's reading of equal freedom is absurd and disingenuous and stems from his erroneous interpretation of equal liberty as each person's equal liberty to do as he or she *likes*. Thus wrongly understood, equal freedom justifies the kind of chaos befitting of Hobbes' state of nature.

Lacy also claims that Spencer's equal freedom principle reduces personal freedom to the narrowest parameters:

> If I may not do a thing that others may not do, I may not do it at all if by so doing I prevent others from doing it. Thus, I am actually prevented from doing anything at all, for it is quite certain that if I do it no one else can possibly do the same thing . . . In like manner, if I take a seat in a railway carriage no one else can take that particular seat, no matter how much they may want it. My act completely disables them from doing so. (*Liberty and Law*, p. 164)

Here, equal freedom means nothing less than the freedom to do the very same thing. Interpreting equal freedom this way is just as disingenuous as Lacy's previous reading. Moreover, this second absurd reading is incompatible with Lacy's first reading. Whereas the first permits everything, the second permits nothing. Lacy's misreading of Spencer is more unwarranted than Gewirth's.

Spencer's version of equal freedom has been given a bad name at the exegetical hands of both Lacy and Gewirth, a bad name that

[4] George Lacy, *Liberty and Law* (London: Swan Sonnenschein, Lowery and Co., 1888), p. 164. Lacy, a journalist and initially an admirer of Spencer, became a socialist and one of Spencer's harshest critics.

refuses to die thanks to Tim Gray's recent characterization of Spencer's equal freedom principle as indeterminate at best and as wholly destructive of freedom at worst. Following Lacy and Gewirth, Gray contends that, according to Spencer's equal freedom principle:

> Any particular restriction on liberty, and even a condition of general slavery, would be compatible with the specific interpretation, provided it applied equally to everyone . . . The only actions that it rules out are actions by A that prevent B from doing the same. Hence, provided A leaves B in a position to retaliate in kind, A is free to assault B. So, for example, while it rules out murder (since murder renders the victim incapable of retaliating in kind), it does not rule out assault, or fraud, or libel, or any other injury inflicted by A on B, provided B is left in a position to inflict the same injury on A.[5]

But Spencer did not understand equal liberty in such a preposterous way. His understanding of equal freedom was plainly not that version of it attributed to him by Lacy, Gewirth and Gray and summarily attacked by L. T. Hobhouse as well, when he observed: "My right to keep my neighbor awake by playing the piano all night is not satisfactorily counterbalanced by his right to keep a dog which howls all the time the piano is being played . . . Generally, the right to injure or take advantage of another is not sufficiently limited by the right of that other if he should have the power to retaliate in kind."[6]

Lacy, Hobhouse, Gewirth and Gray's misinterpretation of Spencer becomes plainer when one considers Spencer's "The Kantian Idea of Rights" which he appended to *The Principles of Ethics*. There, Spencer discusses Kant's "Universal Principle of Justice" from *The Metaphysical Elements of Justice* and acknowledges the close similarities between Kant's principle of justice and his own principle of equal freedom. Kant's principle of justice reads "So act

5 Tim Gray, *Freedom* (Atlantic Highlands: Humanities Press International, 1991), p. 164. Gray mentions Gewirth's interpretation of Spencer's equal freedom principle to support his own interpretation (p. 163).

6 L. T. Hobhouse, *Liberalism* [1911] (Oxford University Press, 1964), p. 36. See also D. G. Ritchie, "Law and Liberty: The Question of State Interference," *Studies in Political and Social Ethics* (London: Swan Sonnenschein, 1902), pp. 58–9, where Ritchie says that if Spencer's equal freedom principle means the liberty to do the very *same* act, then "I cannot occupy this spot of earth, on which at this moment I am standing, without interfering with the equal liberty of every one else to occupy this same spot at the same moment." Ritchie adds that if equal liberty means the liberty to do *similar* acts, then "No one has liberty to stand up and speak in his place [at a public meeting], unless every one else may stand up and speak in his place at the same time."

externally that the free use of your choice can coexist with the freedom of everyone in accordance with a universal law."[7]

Spencer also says that his principle of justice nonetheless differs from Kant's in two respects. First, according to Spencer, his principle is practical and utilitarian whereas Kant's is not. Kant's principle is to be conformed to "irrespective of beneficial ends." Second, Spencer says that with Kant's principle, the "negative element, or the obligation to respect the limits, is the dominant idea," whereas with his own principle, the "positive element – the right to freedom of action – is represented as primary, while the negative element, resulting from the limitations imposed by the presence of others, is represented as secondary."[8]

We can safely say that Spencer's grasp of Kant was flawed. Spencer appears not to understand that Kant's principle of justice is a restricted version of the categorical imperative. He does not seem to appreciate the sense in which the former is a principle of "external" freedom for Kant whereas the latter embodies fuller "internal" freedom in addition. For Kant, acting justly is acting so that one does not externally coerce the will of any other person. Moreover, one's motive in acting justly is typically fear of legal punishment. Hence, "external" freedom is a more impoverished kind of freedom than full moral "internal" freedom insofar as one is *externally* motivated to act with restraint. By contrast, acting freely in the "internal" sense is acting autonomously, is acting with a good will. It is being *internally* motivated to act by practical reasoning alone rather than because of merely external, prudential considerations. It is acting independently of causes external to one's own reasoning. It is acting with self-restraint as reason impels us rather than as fear compels us.

Despite Spencer's inadequate understanding of the relationship

[7] Immanuel Kant, "Metaphysical First Principles of the Doctrine of Right," *The Metaphysics of Morals* [1797] (Cambridge University Press, 1991), p. 231. Spencer's discussion of Kant relies on W. Hastie's problematic translation, *The Philosophy of Law* (Edinburgh: T. and T. Clark, 1887). Hastie translates Kant's principle of justice as "Act externally in such a manner that the free exercise of thy Will may be able to coexist with the Freedom of all others according to a universal Law."

[8] Spencer, "The Kantian Idea of Rights," *The Principles of Ethics*, vol. II, Appendix A, p. 453. Also see Spencer's "Filiation of Ideas" in Duncan (ed.), *The Life and Letters of Herbert Spencer*, pp. 539–40, for a similar contrast between himself and Kant. There, Spencer says that Kant's emphasis on restraint in equal freedom probably stems from the deeper reverence for authority in German culture whereas his emphasis on freedom of action stems from the greater concern for freedom and individuality in English culture.

between Kant's principle of justice and moral freedom, Spencer nevertheless understood Kant well enough to criticize Kantian ethical theory in typically utilitarian fashion. For instance, in his 1888 "The Ethics of Kant," Spencer condemns Kant's conception of good will for the way in which it eviscerates the meaning of good. In Spencer's words, "For neither Kant, nor any one else, ever has or ever can, frame a consciousness of a good will when from the word good are expelled all thoughts of those ends which we distinguish by the word good."[9]

Good will, then as far as Spencer is concerned, is meaningless unless it is understood consequentially. Indeed, it is necessarily utilitarian. Acting in accordance with the moral law alone entails acting in a way that is unavoidably utilitarian:

> The essential truth here to be noted, however, is that the Kantian principle, so much vaunted as higher than that of expediency or utilitarianism, is compelled to take expediency or utilitarianism as its basis. Do what it will, it cannot escape the need for conceiving happiness or misery, to self or others or both, as respectively to be achieved or avoided; for in any case what, except the conceived happiness or misery which would follow if a given mode of action were made universal, can determine the will for or against such mode of action? If, in one who has been injured, there arises a temptation to murder the injurer; and if, following out the Kantian injunction, the tempted man thinks of himself as willing that all men who have been injured should murder those who have injured them; and if, imagining the consequences experienced by mankind at large, and possibly on some occasion by himself in particular, he is deterred from yielding to the temptation; what is it which deters him? Obviously the representation of the many evils, pains, deprivations of happiness, which would be caused. If, on imagining his act to be universalized, he saw that it would increase human happiness, the alleged deterrent would not act. Hence the conduct to be insured by adoption of the Kantian maxim is simply the conduct to be insured by making the happiness of self or others or both the end to be achieved. By implication, if not avowedly, the Kantian principle is as distinctly utilitarian as the principle of Bentham. (*Essays*, pp. 215–16)[10]

9 Spencer, "The Ethics of Kant," *Essays*, vol. III, p. 203. In a footnote, Spencer candidly admits that his familiarity with Kant's writings was "extremely limited." Regarding Kant's *Critique of Pure Reason* in particular, he says, "In 1844 a translation of Kant's *Critique of Pure Reason* (then I think lately published) fell into my hands, and I read the first few pages enunciating his doctrine of Time and Space: my peremptory rejection of which caused me to lay the book down. Twice since then the same thing has happened; for, being an impatient reader, when I disagree with the cardinal propositions of a work I can go no further" (p. 206).

10 See, too, Spencer's assessment of Kant's supreme moral maxim where Spencer says, "It is that of considering what, in the particular case, would be the *result* if the suggested course of

In exposing Kant as a closet utilitarian, Spencer seems to abandon the implications of his assessment, in "The Kantian Idea of Rights," of Kant's principle of justice. In this assessment, recall, Spencer argued that Kant's version of equal freedom was, in contrast with his own version, anti-utilitarian.

Spencer's less-than-satisfactory treatment of Kant aside, Spencer nevertheless clearly understood equal freedom quite differently than Lacy, Hobhouse, Gewirth and Gray would have us believe. From the outset, Spencer held that individuals ought to pursue happiness by exercising their faculties within the parameters of equal freedom. "Presocial" and "militant" humans failed miserably in living happily because they failed so completely in respecting the principle of equal freedom. During the long twilight of "militancy" in particular, inter-societal conflict proscribes freedom for the sake of war-making efficiency. As warfare declines, equal freedom, faculty exercise and happiness begin flourishing.

Understanding Spencer's principle of equal freedom also requires examining his theory of the "moral sense," the centerpiece of his early moral psychology. In *Social Statics*, Spencer writes:

> The characteristics exhibited by beings in an associated state cannot arise from the accident of combination, but must be the consequences of certain inherent properties of the beings themselves. True, the gathering together may call out these characteristics; it may make manifest what was before dormant; it may afford the opportunity for undeveloped peculiarities to appear; but it evidently does not create them. (p. 17)

As with other inherent "characteristics," sociality awakens our "moral sense." The "moral forces upon which social equilibrium depends are resident in the social atom – man; and that if we would understand the nature of those forces and the laws of that equilibrium we must look for them in the human constitution" (*Social Statics*, p. 18). Moreover, as sociality stimulates our "moral sense," the intuitive importance of equal liberty to achieving happiness becomes clearer and clearer. Eventually, our "intellect" supplements our "moral sense" by conceptually refining our intuitions about equal freedom "into a scientific morality" (p. 84).

conduct were made universal: and then being deterred from willing such conduct by the badness of the conceived *result*" (p. 214; my italics). T. H. Green, who unlike Spencer, was well acquainted with Kant, criticized Kant's moral law on similar grounds. Like Spencer, Green held that the moral law veiled a hidden utilitarianism. See my "Between Kantianism and Consequentialism in T. H. Green's Moral Philosophy," *Political Studies*, 41 (1993).

Three mutually reinforcing phenomena promote our intuitive enthusiasm for equal freedom according to *Social Statics*. First, as discussed previously, habitual warfare eventually produces political integrity, stability and peace which, in turn, create opportunities for the evolution of our "moral sense." Second, Spencer also maintains that the "more essential" an action is, the "more powerful" our desire for it is and the "more intense the gratification derived therefrom" (p. 19).[11] In short, we desire more intensely those actions more essential to happiness. Thus, insofar as the principle of equal freedom is essential for happiness, we come to desire it intensely. Our "moral sense" intuitions, then, not only slowly encounter new opportunities for developing; they flourish because our desire to act as they recommend intensifies. The principle of equal freedom, in particular, remains a latent moral intuition until social conditions enable individuals to appreciate its importance for happiness. This appreciation, in turn, fosters a keen desire to practice equal freedom. Third, according to Spencer in *Social Statics*, God wills that we exercise and refine our "moral sense" and develop our fundamental moral intuitions including our intuitive zeal for equal freedom (p. 175).

In sum, in *Social Statics* Spencer regards our "moral sense" as a faculty that we desire to exercise because exercising it generates so much happiness. And as exercising this faculty is largely equivalent to practicing equal freedom, desiring to exercise our "moral sense" is largely equivalent to desiring to practice equal freedom. (That Spencer considers our moral sense a faculty is obvious when he says, "assuming the existence of such a [moral] faculty, there appears reason to think that its monitions afford a proper basis for a systematic morality" [p. 30].[12]) Practicing equal freedom, then, enhances our happiness which, in turn, intensifies our desire to practice equal freedom. The practice of equal freedom is a symbiotic dialectic of intensifying desire and growing satisfaction.

Spencer's "doctrine of the moral sense" seems indebted to the moral sense tradition of Shaftesbury and Hutcheson. Like Hutch-

[11] See, by comparison, J. S. Mill, *Considerations on Representative Government* [1861] in Robson (ed.), *Collected Works* (1977), vol. XIX, p. 403, where he says "whatever invigorates the faculties . . . creates an increased desire for their more unimpeded exercise."

[12] See also "The Proper Sphere of Government" where Spencer refers to the exercise of "moral and intellectual faculties" as being necessary to happiness. Spencer, *The Man Versus the State*, p. 251.

eson, the early Spencer was a moral sense utilitarian for whom moral judgements were essentially intuitive. However, unlike Hutcheson, Spencer held that moral approval and disapproval were more than just intuitions, more than just natural dispositions to treat others well or ill. For him, our moral sense generated elemental moral intuitions of approval and disapproval which our intellects subsequently refined. Furthermore, insofar as Spencer also regarded our moral sense as an exercisable faculty, he thought that it could be considerably strengthened if not perfected. Hutcheson, by contrast, was less sanguine about the growth potential of our moral intuitions.[13]

After *Social Statics*, Spencer left "moral sense" psychology behind. Let us now address the refurbished moral psychology of equal freedom in his more mature writings, particularly as he reformulated it in *The Principles of Psychology* and in *The Principles of Ethics*. We will return to Spencer's "moral sense" psychology in chapter 6 when we examine the extent to which Spencer's liberal utilitarianism was a priori or empirical.

THE MORAL PSYCHOLOGY OF EQUAL FREEDOM AFTER SOCIAL STATICS

In the chapter "Egoistic Sentiments" from the 1897 reprint of the 1880 third edition of *The Principles of Psychology*, Spencer recasts his moral psychology in Lamarckian terms. He now maintains that the egoistic sentiment of freedom (an inherited instinctive feeling that hindered faculty exercise results in frustrated gratification producing unhappiness while free faculty exercise generates happiness) accompanies our instinctive desires to exercise our faculties. Of this egoistic sentiment, Spencer writes:

> The emotional pain caused by bodily restraint does not consist of the represented loss of a pleasure about to be obtained. Interference arouses it when there is no immediate good to be pursued, and even when there is no desire to move. The consciousness of an imposed inability to act is a consciousness containing dimly-represented denials, not of one kind of gratification but of all kinds of gratifications. Power to use the limbs and senses unimpeded is associated in individual life with every kind of

[13] There is no way of determining how familiar Spencer was with the moral sense school of English moral philosophy. Spencer refers to Shaftesbury and Hutcheson only briefly in the "Introduction" of *Social Statics*.

pleasure; and it is similarly associated in the lives of all ancestry, human and pre-human. The body of the sentiment, therefore, is a vague and voluminous feeling produced by experiences organized and inherited throughout the whole past, to which a more definite, but still very general, form is given by the individual experiences received from moment to moment from birth upwards. And hence in the agitation excited by arrest of motions, there is a multitudinous re-representation of denials of all kinds, the individualities of which are mostly quite lost; while in the joy of liberty regained there are massed together the potentialities of gratifications in general.[14]

Being prevented from acting, then, is *naturally* frustrating and dissatisfying because such feelings about prevented action are so deeply rooted in our natures being inherited from previous generations. Acting freely is just as *naturally* satisfying for similar reasons. Moreover, these feelings are sharpened by the particular experiences of each of us. We, in turn, pass these sharpened feelings on to subsequent generations who sharpen them further through their own unpleasant experiences with prevented actions. As civilization matures, these feelings become robust cognitive sentiments. As the instrumental value of freedom becomes self-evident, the sentiment of "personal freedom" becomes "so highly re-representative" that "all ideas of concrete advantages are merged in the abstract satisfaction derived from securities against every possible interference with the pursuit of his ends by each citizen" (*The Principles of Psychology*, vol. II, p. 587).[15] Since Spencer surrounds this passage with examples of unfreedom, such as slavery and imprisonment, that are mostly human-caused physical restraints on intentional action, his reputation as an uncompromising negative freedom theorist seems, for the moment, intact. He makes no mention of some externally unhindered actions being worthier than others.[16]

14 Herbert Spencer, *The Principles of Psychology*, [1855], 2 vols. (New York: D. Appleton and Co., 1897), vol. II, pp. 585–6. *The Principles of Psychology* was first published in 1855. An expanded second edition was published in 1870 followed by another expanded third edition in 1880. The 1897 edition is a reprint of the 1880 edition.

15 See as well pp. 616–17 where Spencer states that the egoistic sentiment (for freedom) is a "love of personal freedom" which "delights in surrounding conditions that put no restraint on the activities – the feeling which is pained, even in inferior creatures, by whatever shackles the limbs or arrests locomotion, and which, in superior natures, is pained by whatever indirectly impedes the activities, and even by whatever threatens to impede them."

16 Spencer provides two examples of unfreedom that are preventions of non-purposive movements: covering a baby's mouth so that it is unable to breathe and grasping a dog's legs so that it can't move. However, neither breathing nor animal movement are what Richard Flathman calls "freedom evaluable." Neither breathing nor animal movement

In "Ego-Altruistic Sentiments," the next chapter in *The Principles of Psychology*, Spencer explains how our egoistic sentiments become moral sentiments as they encompass the interests and well-being of others. While "implying self-gratification," they "also imply gratification in others." (vol. II, p. 595) Ego-altruistic sentiments of approval and disapproval attach to actions that indirectly promote pleasure or pain in ourselves by directly promoting pleasure or pain in others. Such quasi-moral feelings stem from the "ulterior" benefits and drawbacks to ourselves which beneficial and harmful actions to others also entail. Hence, we learn to approve heartily of actions that gratify ourselves because they gratify others. And, hence, we also come to defend the freedom of action of others because we share in the satisfaction that they derive from acting freely. Ego-altruism, then, is a form of rational egoism grounded in our appreciation that sympathy pays.

Much of the chapter "Ego-Altruistic Sentiments" originally formed parts of Spencer's essay, "Morals and Moral Sentiments" (*Fortnightly Review*, 1871). Spencer condensed this essay and added it as a new chapter to the 1880 *Principles of Psychology*. Those parts Spencer chose not include in his revised chapter shed additional light on the role of sympathy in the development of ego-altruism. In one of these excluded parts, for instance, Spencer contends that his notion of sympathy is similar to Adam Smith's in *Theory of Moral Sentiments*.[17] Without discussing Smith's theory, Spencer argues that, as population growth causes regularized social interaction, sympathy inevitably arises from the display of feelings.[18] Secondly, this sympathy-generating display of feelings generates moral sentiments (notably respect for freedom) as follows: pain caused to others by

constitutes the kind of *purposive* behavior predicable of humans only. Therefore, mere breathing and animal movement can't be made unfree. Spencer offers these two examples in order to demonstrate that babies and animals supposedly possess rudimentary "egoistic sentiments" for freedom (Spencer, *The Principles of Psychology*, vol. II, pp. 584–5). Also see Spencer, *An Autobiography*, vol. I, p. 439, for the statement that "freedom in its absolute form is the absence of all external checks to whatever actions the will prompts."

17 See also Spencer, *An Autobiography*, vol. I, pp. 378–9 and "The Filiation of Ideas" in Duncan (ed.), *The Life and Letters of Herbert Spencer*, p. 537, for Spencer's contention that he arrived at his theory of sympathy independently of, and prior to, having become familiar with Smith's writings.

18 Also see Spencer, *An Autobiography*, vol. II, pp. 576–7, where Spencer observes, "During the progress from these types up to the highest types yet evolved, sympathy and sociality . . . have been acting and reacting, each as a cause and consequence – greater sympathy making possible greater sociality, public and domestic, and greater sociality serving to further cultivate sympathy."

one's actions causes pain in oneself. Repetition of such experiences produces an unconscious awareness of this causal relationship. As this awareness strengthens, each learns to "check himself" so that he doesn't indirectly harm himself by directly harming others. Eventually, such "checking" becomes consciously purposeful. Again, sympathy pays handsomely.[19] It doesn't so much, as with Adam Smith, make us impartial spectators favoring our own pleasures and pains no more than anyone else's. Sympathy leaves us partial to ourselves and, therefore, Spencer's conception of sympathy differs measurably from Smith's.

Respect for other's basic freedom is not the whole of self-restraint for self-restraint also comprises what Spencer calls "negative beneficence." Beyond actions that seriously harm others which equal freedom proscribes absolutely as punishable, "negative beneficence" proscribes, though not absolutely, less harmful actions. For example, "negative beneficence" stipulates that we ought to refrain from verbally insulting others. Sympathy also induces us to *assist* others, rather than merely refrain from harming them, because giving others pleasure rebounds on us. As with pain-producing actions, repetition of other-regarding, pleasure-producing actions causes us to value them intuitively at first and consciously afterwards. Gradually, individuals learn to *promote* the happiness of others consciously and enthusiastically. Spencer calls such assistance to others "positive beneficence."

Egoism and ego-altruism do not complete the entire spectrum of moral sentiments in *The Principles of Psychology*. In the chapter "Altruistic Sentiments," Spencer maintains that, as civilization advances, altruistic sentiments emerge alongside egoistic and ego-altruistic sentiments. Altruism, at first a dim feeling later becoming a vivid imperative, stems from our slow recognition that others experience unhappiness not just when we interfere with their actions but whenever *anyone* interferes with their actions. Sympathetically experiencing such unhappiness as our own, we not only demand freedom to act for ourselves (due to our egoism) but we begin demanding that others enjoy like freedom to act:

> The limit toward which this highest altruistic sentiment advances is tolerably clear. Its egoistic factor, finding satisfaction in surrounding conditions which put no immediate or remote restraint on the activities;

[19] Spencer, "Morals and Moral Sentiments," *Essays*, vol. I, pp. 346–4.

and its other factor, sympathy, by which it is made altruistic, ever tending as it grows more sensitive and comprehensive to excite a vivid fellow-feeling with this love of unrestrained activity in others; it results that the advance is towards a state in which, while each citizen will tolerate no other restriction on his freedom, he will tolerate that restriction on it which the like claims of fellow-citizens involve. Nay more – he will not simply tolerate this restriction, but will spontaneously recognize it and assert it – will be sympathetically anxious for each other citizen's due sphere of action as for his own; and will defend it against invasion while he refrains from invading it himself. This is manifestly the condition of equilibrium which the egoistic sentiment and the altruistic sentiment co-operate to produce. (*The Principles of Psychology*, vol. II, p. 618)

The emergence of our altruistic interest in equal freedom is equally a concern for equal rights. In becoming "more appreciative of the liberty of others, – more respectful of others' like claims," altruism becomes "desirous not to trench on the others' equal rights" (vol. II, p. 617). Moreover, like egoistic and ego-altruistic sentiments, altruistic sentiments strengthen as they evolve. Furthermore, altruism has replaced the "moral sense" faculty psychology of *Social Statics*. Finally, sympathy transforms egoism into altruism which suggests that altruistic sentiments are more refined, if not separate, modalities of egoism. Presumably, this transformation of egoism into full-blown altruism begins as ego-altruism.

Sympathy, therefore, plays as crucial a role in the evolution of altruism as it does in the evolution of ego-altruism. But how does sympathy work such marvels? How does witnessing the pain of others, whether inflicted by others or by ourselves, elicit pain in ourselves and motivate us to respect and defend their spheres of freedom? Here again, Spencer's discussion of sympathy in the chapter on "Altruistic Sentiments" is helpful. After observing that "even sympathy, and the moral sentiments resulting from sympathy, may be interpreted as caused by experiences of utility," Spencer continues:

The moral [ego-altruistic and altruistic] sentiments precede such recognitions of utility, and make them possible. The pleasures and pains that follow sympathetic and unsympathetic actions, have first to be slowly associated with these actions, and the resulting incentives and deterrents frequently obeyed, before there can arise the perceptions that sympathetic and unsympathetic actions are remotely beneficial or detrimental to the actor; and there must be a still longer and still wider registration and comparison of experiences, before there can arise the perceptions that they are socially beneficial and detrimental. When, however, the ultimate effects, personal and social, have gained general recognition, are expressed in current maxims, and lead to injunctions having the religious sanctions, the sentiments that prompt sympathetic actions and check unsympathetic ones, are immensely strengthened by their alliances. (*The Principles of Psychology*, vol. II, pp. 620–1)[20]

Sympathy, in short, flourishes because it works. Sympathetic feelings evolve because sympathetic actions redound to one's own happiness. Hence, individuals become increasingly ego-altruistic and altruistic as they learn that by making others happier, they sympathetically make themselves happier. In the case of ego-altruism, this primarily means enhancing the happiness of others by diligently respecting their rights. In the case of full-blown altruism, this means enhancing their happiness by insisting that everyone's rights are respected by everyone else. And the more that individuals act ego-altruistically and altruistically towards others, the more their sympathetic aptitude strengthens. So again, we see that, for Spencer, sympathy pays generously and that this reward stimulates, in turn, our sympathetic sensibilities all the more.[21]

Spencer's moral psychology of equal freedom reached maturity with *The Principles of Ethics*. Maturity, though, occasioned new difficulties. In *The Principles of Ethics*, particularly Part IV issued separately as *Justice* in 1891, Spencer introduces the "sentiment of justice" which is comprised of *both* egoistic and altruistic components. In a fashion that essentially parallels Spencer's explanation defended in *The Principles of Psychology* and in "Morals and Moral Sentiments," altruistic respect for equal freedom of others evolves, via sympathy, from the bosom of each person's egoistic claims to act freely. The "sentiment of justice," then, is really a relational sentiment by which egoistic and altruistic sentiments diverge from, compliment, and reinforce one another as they strengthen.[22]

Spencer also introduces the "protoaltruistic sentiment of justice" in *The Principles of Ethics*. The "protoaltruistic sentiment" refines psychological concepts first deployed in "Ego-Altruistic Sentiments"

[20] For a similar understanding of the development of sympathy in fostering virtuous conduct, see David Hume, *A Treatise of Human Nature* [1734–40] (Oxford University Press, 1978), pp. 498–501.

[21] Spencer is never clear as to whether sympathy is a sentiment like egoism, ego-altruism and altruism. However in *Social Statics* he refers to sympathy as a faculty.

[22] For the main discussions of the "sentiment of justice" in *The Principles of Ethics*, vol. II, see the chapter entitled "The Sentiment of Justice."

of *The Principles of Psychology* and in "Morals and Moral Sentiments." Protoaltruism temporarily reinforces the primitive emergence of sympathy as sympathy begins transforming egoism into ego-altruism and ego-altruism into full altruism. Like sympathy, protoaltruism makes us aware of the importance of restraint when interacting with others though differently. Beginning as primitive feelings for "revenge" and "retaliation" against physical aggression, these feelings evolve into vague desires to repay injuries suffered in equivalent kind. Spencer fails to explain, however, how our sense of equivalence first develops. As history advances, this "balancing of injuries" becomes more habitual and generates a general fear of retaliation. Individuals, fearing likely retaliation for their unrestrained actions, learn to put limits on their actions and simultaneously develop respect for these limits (*The Principles of Ethics*, vol. II, pp. 45, 65). As with Mill, as we shall see, retaliation plays a critical role in Spencer's theory of freedom.

The Principles of Ethics is sometimes perplexing. For example, Spencer suggests that altruism is composed of two kinds of conduct: that guided by justice (equal freedom) and that guided by beneficence. (Spencer also calls the former "primary altruism" and the latter "secondary altruism" [vol. II, p. 294].) These two kinds of altruistic conduct are, moreover, "distinguished from egoistic actions" (vol. II, p. 288). Hence, whereas these distinctions suggest that justice is a form of altruism which has nothing to do with egoism, we saw previously, by contrast, that egoism was a component of the "sentiment of justice." But mostly, *The Principles of Ethics* improves upon *Social Statics* by abandoning the latter's archaic moral faculty psychology. Spencer abandoned this faculty psychology because he became increasingly uncomfortable with the fuzziness of hypostatized concepts like faculty and faculty exercise. Both concepts are rooted in pre-evolutionary social theory, particularly phrenology, of which Spencer was, for a while, a youthful devotee.[23]

Phrenology originated in the work of Franz Joseph Gall and his pupil and colleague, J. C. Spurzheim, in Vienna at the end of the

[23] However, see Spencer, *The Principles of Ethics*, vol. I, pp. 334–5, where Spencer deploys the language of faculty exercise: "Inevitably . . . the tendency of peaceful conditions is to the continual increase in those faculties, that is, those nervous structures, which have for their spheres of activity, pleasure taken in the welfare of others." Altruism, in other words, is a physiological event involving palpable faculties.

eighteenth and beginning of the nineteenth centuries. George Combe became its principal English advocate soon afterwards. Gall's singular contribution to brain science was his contention that human behavior and brain functions were correlated and scientifically demonstrable. In marked contrast to the older sensationalist psychologies of Locke and Condillac, Gall held that our faculties and talents were not derived from our separate experiences but were inherited instincts conveyed by our cerebral organs. Though inheritable, these faculty instincts and their cerebral counterparts have remained relatively unchanged for innumerable generations. Gall held, in addition, that faculty activity nevertheless varied somewhat with the size of faculty organs within different brains. Size differences, furthermore, caused differing skull protuberances making it possible, according to Gall, to measure and compare faculty differences by measuring and comparing cranial bumps.

The faculty psychology of *Social Statics* is obviously much indebted to Gall. Like Gall, who believed that humans possessed an innate psychophysical "Moral Sense, Sentiment of Justice and Injustice," Spencer maintained that humans possessed a psychophysical, moral sense faculty.[24] According to R. M. Young, in *Mind, Brain and Adaptation in the Nineteenth Century*, Spencer's argument in *Social Statics* "adopts the form of the phrenological position while the resulting conception of the moral sense is put in the service of his own social theory."[25]

After *Social Statics*, Spencer took the combined associationist and social evolutionary turn leaving phrenological faculty psychology behind. With *The Principles of Psychology*, Spencer abandoned his belief that humans possessed an innate moral sense *qua* phrenological faculty. Our moral intuitions were simply inherited associational endowments rather than innate instincts fixed in us from birth. Like Mill and Alexander Bain, Spencer came to believe that our moral intuitions were acquired by the associations individuals made in

[24] See especially, Franz Joseph Gall, *On the Functions of the Brain and of Each of Its Parts: With Observations on the Possibility of Determining the Instincts, Propensities, and Talents, or the Moral and Intellectual Dispositions of Men and Animals, by Configuration of the Brain and Head*, transl. Winslow Lewis, 6 vols. (Boston: Marsh, Capen and Lyon, 1835).

[25] R. M. Young, *Mind, Brain and Adaptation in the Nineteenth Century* (Oxford University Press, 1970), p. 157. Though Young admits that "no obvious direct textual link" can be found between Spencer and Gall, he contends that Spencer's faculty psychology in *Social Statics* is remarkably similar to Combe's 1828 *Essay on the Constitution of Man and Its Relations to External Objects*, which sold over seventy thousand copies by 1838 (p. 158, note 4). My discussion of Gall and phrenology relies heavily on Young's impressive study.

their lives between their actions and pain and pleasure.[26] But unlike Mill and Bain, Spencer also held that these intuitions were passed from generation to generation becoming an accumulated endowment of our species. By blending pre-evolutionary associationism with evolutionary biology, Spencer developed a hybrid moral psychology that was a posteriori intuitionist yet unencumbered by the spurious faculty psychology of phrenology.

So by the time he wrote *The Principles of Ethics* Spencer unequivocally repudiated his once firmly-held view that equal freedom was a fixed moral-faculty intuition that we are each born with. Now he claims that:

> Only to those who are not by creed or cherished theory committed to the hypothesis of a supernaturally created humanity, will the evidence prove that the human mind has no originally implanted conscience. Though, as shown in my first work, *Social Statics*, I once espoused the doctrine of the intuitive moralists (at the outset in full, and in later chapters with some implied qualifications), yet it has gradually become clear to me that the qualifications required practically obliterate the doctrine as enunciated by them. It has become clear to me that if, among ourselves, the current belief is that a man who robs and does not repent will be eternally damned, while an accepted proverb among the Bilochs is that "God will not favor a man who does not steal and rob," it is impossible to hold that men have in common an innate perception of right and wrong.
>
> But now, while we are shown that the moral-sense doctrine in its original form is not true, we are also shown that it adumbrates a truth, and a much higher truth . . . And the implication is that if the life of internal amity continues unbroken from generation to generation, there must result not only the appropriate code, but the appropriate emotional nature, a moral sense adapted to the moral requirements. Men so conditioned will acquire to the degree needful for complete guidance, that innate conscience which the intuitive moralists erroneously suppose to be possessed by mankind at large. (*The Principles of Ethics*, vol. I, pp. 503–4)[27]

Moral principles like equal freedom, then, carry considerable survival efficacy for cultures that internalize them as seeming moral intuitions. As he argues in volume II, of *The Principles of Ethics*, the "sentiment of justice" (equal freedom) is "encouraged," becoming *seemingly* innate in those societies which, through conquest and

[26] For Mill, see J. S. Mill, *A System of Logic* [1843] in Robson (ed.), *Collected Works* (1973–4), vols. VII–VIII. For Bain, see Alexander Bain, *The Senses and the Intellect* (London: J. W. Parker, 1855) and Alexander Bain, *The Emotions and the Will* [1859] (London: J. W. Parker, 1875).

[27] Spencer's repudiation of moral intuitionism here accords with his repudiation of traditional natural rights theory after *Social Statics*.

expansion, begin enjoying internal concord and stability. As the "sentiment of justice" is passed from generation to generation, strengthening each time, it stimulates, in turn, greater concord and stability. Those societies where this dynamic commences tend to survive and prosper. Where, previously, societies characterized by militancy were more successful, societies enlivened with the "sentiment of justice" now succeed: "Conversely, conduct restrained within the required limits [of justice], calling out no antagonistic passions, favors harmonious cooperation, profits the group, and, by implication, profits the average of its individuals. Consequently, there results, other things being equal, a tendency for groups formed of members having this adaptation of nature, to survive and spread" (*The Principles of Ethics*, vol. II, p. 43). Spencer, moreover, extends this reasoning about the competitive efficiency of the "sentiment of justice" beyond it to other moral principles. Liberal societies where widespread beneficence supplements justice are even more likely to survive and flourish. They will be "those to [survive and grow, so as gradually to replace those societies] (*sic*) in which the individual nature is not so adapted to social requirements" (vol. I, p. 335).[28]

In sum, then, security and social tranquility foster the "sentiment of justice" which, in turn, further sustains security and social tranquility. And such furthering of security and tranquility only serves to nourish the "sentiment of justice" all the more. But "the sentiment of justice" needs to be cultivated if it is to thrive. Security and social tranquility do not insure that people will actually exercise and develop this sentiment. Security and tranquility merely create opportunities for people to do so.[29]

The Principles of Ethics also introduces the principle that individuals ought to reap the good and bad results of their conduct. Receiving the results of one's conduct whatever they may be presupposes that the relation between action and its results is as direct as possible because the more direct this relation, the more completely do the vigorous and talented reap the gains of their vigor and talents. The

[28] In *The Descent of Man*, Darwin explains how natural selection fashions altruism out of our primitive "social instincts." Like Spencer, he holds that tribes in which altruism is more widespread enjoy an "immense advantage" over their competitors. Charles Darwin, *The Descent of Man* [1871] in *The Origin of Species and the Descent of Man* (New York: The Modern Library, 1936), p. 500.

[29] Wiltshire calls this process a circular "causal conundrum." Cooperative stability promotes cooperative self-restraint which promotes cooperative stability. David Wiltshire, *The Social and Political Thought of Herbert Spencer* (Oxford University Press, 1978), p. 212.

more they reap these gains, the more they develop their talents. And the more they develop their talents, the happier and more successful they become *vis-à-vis* those less talented:

> Sentient beings have progressed from low to high types, under the law that the superior shall profit by their superiority and the inferior shall suffer from their inferiority. Conformity to this law has been, and is still, needful, not only for the continuance of life but for the increase of happiness; since the superior are those having faculties better adjusted to the requirements – faculties, therefore, which bring in their exercise greater pleasure and less pain. (*The Principles of Ethics*, vol. I, p. 227)

Inasmuch as Spencer also thought, not surprisingly, that vigor and talent were inheritable, he believed that successful "industrialized" societies were becoming populated by successive generations of increasingly vigorous and talented members.

The principle that individuals ought to receive the good and bad results of their actions is simply another version of the "sentiment of justice," a version that helps us better appreciate the critical role which equal freedom plays in Spencer's evolutionary moral psychology. Accordingly, the "sentiment of justice" can be regarded as a kind of talent, a talent more developed in some than in others. As the more gifted in this regard practice their talent for justice, they develop this moral talent, pass it on to their progeny who supplant the morally less talented over time. The preface to "Factors of Organic Evolution" explains how this pivotal moral talent evolves: "Of course there are involved the conceptions we form of the genesis and nature of our higher emotions; and by implication, the conceptions we form of our moral intuitions. If functionally-produced modifications are inheritable, then the mental associations habitually produced in individuals by experiences of the relations between actions and their consequences, pleasurable or painful, may, in the successions of individuals, generate innate tendencies to like or dislike such actions."[30] Hence, because respecting equal freedom is such a vital practice, talent in this practice commands our most enthusiastic moral approval. This approval masks itself as a potent moral intuition as each generation passes it along the next. Slowly, the principle of equal freedom becomes a self-evident moral axiom.

We can now better appreciate why the sentiment of equal freedom

[30] Herbert Spencer, "Factors of Organic Evolution," *Essays*, vol. I, p. 464.

is so crucial. As the commitment to equal freedom grows, as those talented in its practice dominate, the linkage between action and results in non-ethical behaviors becomes more unfettered. Individuals begin developing myriad talents, whatever they happen to be. The evolution of moral talents fosters the evolution of all talents and this fostering of talents is no less than the practice of happiness.

But are all talents worthy of being cultivated? Spencer assumes that the evolution of the sentiment of equal freedom fosters only laudable talents and sentiments. Ironically, the growth of equal freedom might expose society to those in whom this talent is weak. The wicked and depraved might take advantage of emerging liberal sentiments and institutions in order to destroy them. Moreover, given Spencer's Lamarckianism, they might succeed in passing on their anti-talents to subsequent generations thereby insuring liberalism's permanent defeat.

Nevertheless, the role of freedom in linking result to action is transparent. Just as Spencer deemed equal freedom conditionally necessary to faculty exercise in his earlier writings, he deemed it conditionally necessary to harmonizing actions and results and developing talents in his later works. As he contends in *The Principles of Ethics*:

> The formula [of equal freedom] has to unite a positive element with a negative element. It must be positive in so far as it asserts for each that, since he is to receive and suffer the good and evil results of his actions, he must be allowed to act. And it must be negative in so far as, by asserting this of everyone, it implies that each can be allowed to act only under the restraint imposed by the presence of others having like claims to act. Evidently the positive element is that which expresses a prerequisite to life in general, and the negative element is that which qualifies this prerequisite in the way required when, instead of one life carried on alone, there are many lives carried on together.
>
> Hence, that which we have to express in a precise way, is the liberty of each limited only by the like liberties of all. This we do by saying: Every man is free to do that which he wills, provided he infringes not the equal freedom of any other man. (vol. II, pp. 61–2)[31]

We must be free if we are to reap from our actions the good and evil results that we deserve. Practically speaking, this means that we must be equally free, which means, in turn, that we must exercise our

[31] See, as well, vol. II, p. 45, where Spencer writes that the results of one's "own nature and consequent actions" cannot be "gained or suffered" unless the "faculties of all kinds have free play."

moral skills of self-restraint. We must all cultivate equal freedom, we must all nourish the "sentiment of justice" that resides within us.

Spencer's moral psychology of freedom after *Social Statics* was not unproblematic and not always easy to interpret. Still, as in *Social Statics*, Spencer continued to justify equal freedom instrumentally. Spencer continued to stress that freedom of action *per se* was necessary for pursuing and realizing happiness. Happiness requires that faculties, talents, or whatever we choose to call them, be freely exercised. However, owing to sociality, realizing happiness also requires equally free action. The exercise and perfection of our "sentiment of justice" *qua* commitment to equal freedom maximizes the extent to which all can earn the results of their actions through exercising their talents and thus achieve happiness. Therefore, equal freedom's instrumentality is *indirect* because general happiness is not a goal that society *directly* attempts to serve up to its members but is rather a function of each member's equally free activity. General utility is best cultivated by each exercising his or her own talents within the parameters of equal freedom. The principle of equal freedom, after *Social Statics*, remains Spencer's paramount decision procedure on behalf of general utility, which he never forswears as his overriding criterion of right action. Moreover, according to Spencer, we have come to revere the principle of equal freedom as an incomparably vital decision procedure because social evolution favors societies in which such moral principles have taken root and flourished.

THE PRIORITY OF EQUAL FREEDOM VERSUS THE PRIORITY OF DESERT

We have seen that desert is central to Spencer's conception of justice in *The Principles of Ethics.* We have seen, furthermore, that his principle of desert is a version of his principle of equal freedom. For individuals to develop their talents, they must be able to reap *only* what their actions sow. They must, in short, be equally free.

Two recent interpreters of Spencer, David Miller and T. S. Gray, have disagreed sharply over the place of equal freedom compared to the place of desert in Spencer's moral and political theory. Whereas Miller argues that Spencer's fundamental principle of justice stipulates distribution according to desert, Gray holds that, "for Spencer social justice is satisfied, not when everyone receives reward in accordance with his personal deserts, but when everyone receives that reward to which he is entitled under the rules laid down by the law of equal freedom."[32] For Gray, desert (or what he prefers to call "the principle of efficiency") is of secondary importance. Gray, not unexpectedly, also sees great similarities between Spencer and Nozick insofar as he regards both as entitlement theorists.

I wish to argue principally against Gray and only marginally against Miller. As we saw earlier in this chapter, desert figured prominently in *The Principles of Ethics*. Indeed, contrary to Gray, it commanded more than secondary importance.

Gray's claim that desert is secondary is related to his interpretation of Spencer's conception of desert as a principle of efficiency. In Gray's words, "Clearly the word 'desert' is regarded by Spencer as interchangeable with the words 'merit' and 'worth,' and these words are in turn defined in terms of biological fitness or efficiency."[33] Thus, because desert allegedly means efficiency, it is secondary to justice – for efficiency makes little sense, according to Gray, as a credible principle of justice. Gray's interpretation is difficult to sustain, particularly when we consider the other meanings for efficiency that Gray attributes to Spencer. Gray says that, by biological efficiency, Spencer also means: "earning," "invention," "nature," "capacity," "ability," "strength," "skill," "ingenuity," "effort," "better," "superiority," "virtue," "achievement" and "conduct." For Gray, "conduct" is particularly "quite neutral: no injunction of the principle that each 'shall take the consequences of its own conduct,' carries any connotation of reward in accordance with personal desert, unless it can be established that the 'conduct' in question is fully within the agent's control and responsibility."[34] Naturally, conduct must be free for an agent to deserve its consequences. But it doesn't follow that conduct therefore means desert or efficiency. Moreover, many of the other above terms can't possibly mean biological efficiency either. Hence, Spencer can't have meant biological efficiency by desert.

If desert does not mean biological efficiency and is not a secondary principle for that reason, then how prominent a principle

[32] T. S. Gray, "Herbert Spencer's Theory of Social Justice – Desert or Entitlement?", *History of Political Thought* 2, (1981), 163. For Miller's position, see David Miller, *Social Justice* (Oxford University Press, 1976), pp. 180–208.

[33] Gray, "Herbert Spencer's Theory of Social Justice," p. 168.

[34] Ibid., pp. 169–70.

is it? Is Miller right that desert is Spencer's fundamental principle of justice and not equal freedom as Gray maintains?

Gray rests his claim that the principle of equal freedom is Spencer's primary principle of justice in *The Principles of Ethics* on one of the closing paragraphs from Spencer's intellectual autobiography, "The Filiation of Ideas." Gray cites the following portions of this paragraph:

> In "The Ethics of Social Life – Justice," there is at length a return to the topic with which the whole series of my writings commenced. In "The Proper Sphere of Government," and then in *Social Statics*, endeavours were made to reach definite ideas concerning the just regulation of private conduct and the just relations of individuals to the social aggregate, represented by its government. And now, after all the explorations made in an interval of forty years, this topic came up once more to be dealt with in the light of the results which had then been reached. No essential changes of the views set forth in *Social Statics* proved needful; but there came to be recognized a deeper origin for its fundamental principle. The assertion of the liberty of each limited only by the like liberties of all, was shown to imply the doctrine that each ought to receive the benefits and bear the evils entailed by his actions, carried on within these limits; and Biology had shown that this principle follows from the ultimate truth that each creature must thrive or dwindle, live or die, according as it fulfills well or ill the conditions of its existence . . . And thus, this ultimate principle of social conduct was affiliated upon the general process of organic evolution.[35]

In saying that equal freedom "impl[ies]" in a "deeper" sense that "each ought to receive the benefits and bear the evils entailed by his actions," Spencer is not suggesting that equal freedom is superior to, or even distinct from, desert.

Furthermore, Gray's citation omits the following portion of this important paragraph which contravenes his interpretation: "a principle [that each ought to receive benefits and bear evils of his action] which, in the case of social beings, implies that the activities of each must be kept within the bounds imposed by the like activities of others. So that, while among inferior creatures survival of the fittest is the outcome of aggressive competition, among men as socially combined it must be the outcome of nonaggressive competition: maintenance of the implied limits, and insurance of the benefits gained within the limits, being what we call justice" ("The Filiation

[35] Spencer, "The Filiation of Ideas" in Duncan (ed.), *The Life and Letters of Herbert Spencer*, pp. 575–6. For T. S. Gray's interpretation of this passage, see Gray, "Herbert Spencer's Theory of Social Justice," pp. 178–9.

of Ideas," p. 576). In claiming that desert "implies" equal freedom as well as the reverse (the sole "implies" quoted by Gray), Spencer is suggesting that the principle of desert and the principle of equal freedom are identical principles with equal freedom being the form which desert takes in sociality.

In addition, Gray offers a passage from *The Principles of Ethics* where Spencer explicitly states that if one of the two principles is primary at all, then it is the principle of desert and not the principle of equal freedom. Gray explains away this admission arguing that equal freedom applies only to humans whereas the principle of benefits and evils applies to non-humans as well. Hence, Gray concludes, the former principle is "more civilized" and consequently superior. However, Spencer says only that the principle of equal freedom applies to "gregarious creatures." This claim is ambiguous making Gray's extrapolation unwarranted. Moreover, the final sentence of the passage in question asserts that the principle of equal freedom is "simply a specification of that form which the primary law [the principle benefits and evils] takes under the conditions of gregarious life . . ." (vol. II, p. 32).[36] For one concept to specify another implies that first merely reformulates the second entailing that neither is more basic than the other.

We might nevertheless insist, following Spencer's admission just noted, that one of our two principles must be more fundamental. To the extent that the principle of equal freedom is the form which the principle of benefits and evils apportioned to conduct takes in sociality, then, if anything, the latter principle is more rudimentary.

Thus, Miller's interpretation of the relationship between desert and equal freedom in Spencer is more perspicacious than Gray's. Desert best captures what Spencer means by justice. Justice is "the obtainment by each of as much benefit as his efforts are equivalent to – no more and no less . . . justice requires that individuals shall severally take the consequences of their conduct, neither increased nor decreased."[37] But because we live socially, the principle of desert entails, if it is not actually equivalent to, the principle of equal freedom.

What is prior, of course, to the principles of desert and equal freedom is happiness, which both principles instrumentally promote.

[36] Also see Spencer, *The Principles of Ethics*, vol. II, p. 279, where Spencer equates desert with respect for equal freedom and basic rights.

[37] Spencer, *The Principles of Sociology*, vol. II, p. 610.

Remember that in *Social Statics*, Spencer argues that freedom *per se* is instrumentally necessary to happiness-generating faculty exercise. Equal freedom is instrumentally necessary to happiness-generating faculty exercise given sociality. Thus, inasmuch as the principle of equal freedom is also a social version of the principle of desert, desert is identically instrumental.

The principle of desert, like the principle of equal freedom, is an action-guiding decision procedure for Spencer. Insuring that individuals reap the results of their actions is the best way of maximizing happiness. They must act *for* and *by* themselves. Happiness is a function of activity but the activity must produce for each person only those results that he or she deserves. Hence, our action-guiding maxim should be: "Act such that you receive what you deserve." But this maxim is practically inadequate and must be fortified in a way that takes account of the constraints that sociality imposes. Our enriched, action-guiding maxim must therefore be: "Act such that you receive what you deserve without denying others the like freedom to receive what they deserve." As our criterion of right and wrong, general happiness commends the principle of equal freedom as our fundamental decision procedure.

EQUAL FREEDOM, VIRTUE AND POWER

Negative theories of freedom are not irrevocably unconcerned with the cultivation of selfhood. Some negative freedom theorists value the cultivation of selfhood but leave its content mostly to each person. Berlin, for one, seems to adopt this position at times.[38] Spencer adopts it as well.

First of all, Spencer cares deeply about the quality of human action. Developing one's faculties, cultivating one's individuality and exercising self-restraint are worthy ways of acting. In *Social Statics*, he expressly links these valued ways of acting with the realization of equal freedom: "That condition of things dictated by the law of equal freedom, that condition in which the individuality of each may be unfolded without limit save the like individualities of others; that condition toward which, as we have just seen, mankind is progressing, is a condition toward which the whole of creation

[38] Isaiah Berlin, "Introduction," *Four Essays on Liberty* (Oxford University Press, 1982), p. lxi. Berlin states that he will not object if the "value of a field of free choice amounts to a doctrine of self-realization."

tends"(p. 391).[39] The "ultimate man" will be that manner of man in which perfect "morality," "individuation" and "life" coincide in all members of society (p. 396). In such societies, all will embrace the "salutary truth that no one can be *perfectly free till all are free*; no one can be perfectly moral till all are moral; no one can be perfectly happy till all are happy" (my italics) (p. 409).

Spencer's conception of freedom is subtly though distinctly perfectionist. Each individual's freedom depends upon all others acting freely *qua* acting morally; and all others act morally insofar as they exercise self-restraint. Thus, freedom is not simply unimpeded action but is equally *virtuous* action. It is a *kind* of action, namely the action of moral individuality, of self-control.[40]

Spencer's theory of freedom is perfectionist in a deeper sense. Individuals only become fully equally free when all act freely by exercising perfect self-control. When everyone exercises perfect self-control, everyone is perfectly positioned to cultivate all their other faculties and talents (and hence their happiness) to the full. The role of virtue in Spencer's theory of freedom is considerable.

Spencer also holds that freedom as virtuous self-restraint is best promoted by negative freedom. (As Kantians might say, right makes for virtue.) In the language of faculty exercise, freedom *from* external restraint *to* exercise faculties promotes freedom as a cluster of political virtues of which the principle of equal freedom is the most important. The practice of this master virtue, in turn, enables other virtues to be practiced and perfected. Spencer's idiosyncratic linkage of negative freedom and virtue, it seems to me, is original and intriguing.[41]

[39] Also see p. 389 where Spencer maintains: "There is another form under which civilization can be generalized. We may consider it as a progress toward that constitution of man and society required for the complete manifestation of everyone's individuality. To be that which he naturally is – to do just what he would spontaneously do – is essential to the full happiness of each, and therefore to the greatest happiness of all." And see p. 395 where Spencer says that "what we call the moral law – the law of equal freedom – is the law under which individuation becomes perfect and that ability to recognize and act up to this law is the final endowment of humanity – an endowment now in the process of evolution."

[40] When we keep in mind that, for Spencer, acting freely is also a matter of "spontaneously" developing one's individuality, then moral freedom as acting with forbearance is equally acting "spontaneously."

[41] T. S. Gray has also noted that Spencer sometimes speaks the language of positive freedom *qua* self-determination. However, Gray contends that negative freedom remains the dominant freedom motif in Spencer's theorizing. Gray also maintains that, contrary to many of Spencer's twentieth-century critics, his commitment to negative freedom is not incompatible with his social organicism. For Gray, Spencer defended a version of individualism that was opposed to "collectivism" though not to the kind of decentralized

Wiltshire, then, unfairly says of Spencer that he "ignored the now commonplace distinction between 'freedom from' and 'freedom to' " and that his "preoccupation with external limitations of liberty neglects its more 'positive' requirements, and demands a statement of criteria relating to the *value* and *purpose* of liberty, the *conditions* and *ways* in which liberty is *beneficially exercised* and the state of mind with which liberty is used" (my italics).[42] Clearly, Spencer was cognizant of the "value and purpose" of freedom in terms of promoting both moral individuality and, of course, happiness. We might *even* say of Spencer's liberalism what Hobhouse later said of his own improved liberalism:

> Liberalism is the belief that society can safely be founded on this self-directing power of personality, that it is only on this foundation that a true community can be built, and that so established it foundations are so deep and so wide that there is no limit that we can place to the extent of the building. Liberty then becomes not so much a right of the individual as a necessity of society. It rests not on the claim of A to be let alone by B, but on the duty of B to treat A as a rational being.[43]

As to Wiltshire's conceptually distinct charge that Spencer also ignored the "conditions and ways" necessary to the beneficial utilization of freedom, we should first clarify what Wiltshire means in making it. Wiltshire appears, at first, to be criticizing Spencer for failing to recognize the distinction between freedom and power which W. L. Weinstein makes in "The Concept of Liberty in Nineteenth Century English Political Thought."[44] Simply put, Weinstein argues that freedom must be distinguished from the power to use freedom and that freedom is thus best understood negatively.[45] Yet insofar as Wiltshire sympathetically invokes T. H. Green

"social organicism" characterizing advanced industrial societies. See Gray, *The Political Philosophy of Herbert Spencer*, pp. 219–33.

42 Wiltshire, *The Social and Political Thought of Herbert Spencer*, p. 188.

43 Hobhouse, *Liberalism*, p. 66.

44 W. L. Weinstein, "The Concept of Liberty in Nineteenth Century English Political Thought," *Political Studies*, 13 (1965).

45 Weinstein argues that lack of power is itself not a lack of freedom. Nonetheless, he makes some wide-ranging concessions to this claim. He says, for instance, that deliberate conditioning of people, or a ruling elite's deliberate failure to eliminate illiteracy by comprehensive schooling, may constitute coercion as much as a lack of power to utilize freedom. But surely it is just as reasonable to suggest that deliberate policies aimed at keeping wages low, health costs high and housing substandard amount to interferences with freedom no less than to inabilities to use freedom. In short, the distinction between freedom and power may less sharp than Weinstein believes. For Weinstein's concessions, see Weinstein, "The Concept of Liberty in Nineteenth Century English Political Thought,"

(for whom he says "positive liberty means power") and other new liberals such as Hobhouse (for whom he says freedom without power is really "no freedom at all, or a lower form of freedom for all"), he is not blaming Spencer for failing to distinguish between two logically distinct concepts. Rather, he is suggesting that Spencer failed to appreciate that freedom *is* power.

Spencer, however, sometimes tacitly characterized freedom as power in the new liberal sense of equal opportunity. For instance, in *Social Statics*, Spencer says of equal freedom:

> Our first principle requires, not that all shall have like shares of the things which minister to the gratification of the faculties, but that all shall have like freedom to pursue those things – shall have *like scope*. It is one thing to give to each an *opportunity* of acquiring the objects he desires; it is another, and quite a different thing, to give the objects themselves, no matter whether due endeavor has or has not been made to obtain them. (my italics) (pp. 118–19)

And in an early essay entitled "Over-Legislation," Spencer writes, "It is one thing to secure to each man the *unhindered power* to pursue his own good; it is a widely different thing to pursue the good for him" (my italics).[46]

Spencer's characterization of equal freedom as equal opportunity was not limited to occasional suggestive generalizations. He advocated controversial reforms such as nationalizing land and free legal assistance for the poor; reforms which new liberals also championed. For Spencer (as will be seen in chapter 7), private property in land undermined equal opportunity to exercise faculties and talents and thereby undermined the pursuit of happiness. Land nationalization, by contrast, would restore equal opportunities. In effect, it would help guarantee "like scope" to "pursue" those things "which minister to the gratification of the faculties," would help secure to "each man the unhindered power to pursue his own good." Similarly, providing the poor with tax-supported, free legal counsel would empower them with greater equal opportunity before the law.

In sum, Spencer's theory of freedom occasionally invoked the new liberal battle cry of empowerment. Because his theory of freedom championed empowerment, albeit selectively, his theory highlighted

p. 161. See also Alan R. White, *Rights* (Oxford University Press, 1984), pp. 139–42, for another unavailing attempt to make the same kind of distinction. And see Berlin, "Two Concepts of Liberty," *Four Essays on Liberty*, p. 125.

46 Spencer, "Over-Legislation," *Essays*, vol. III, p. 235.

the difficulties in distinguishing sharply between freedom as securing each individual "the unhindered power to pursue his own good" and freedom as pursuing "the good for him." As we shall subsequently see, Spencer's later disavowal of much of his land reform scheme suggests that he recognized the difficulties of maintaining this distinction.[47]

Power and virtue were central to Spencer's theory of freedom. At times, Spencer saw clearly that the meaning of freedom was impoverished when unfortified by a concern for power. Moreover, though it would be imprudent to claim that Spencer understood himself as defending what we would call a virtue theory of freedom, acting freely was nonetheless, for him, implicitly acting virtuously. Acting virtuously meant acting as the principle of equal freedom, our most sacred decision procedure, commands. Acting virtuously meant acting procedurally. Procedural virtue, as constitutive of equal freedom, was a condition of happiness.

This chapter has tried to demonstrate the utilitarian instrumentality of Spencer's principle of equal freedom via his evolutionary moral psychology. We have seen that the principle of equal freedom was the primary decision procedure of his liberal utilitarianism. It, more than anything, provided his utilitarianism with its liberal credentials, with its liberal ethical appeal.

Moreover, we have seen how Spencer explained how equal freedom has become such a potent moral sentiment. In *Social Statics*, while still laboring in the shadows of phrenology, he deemed equal

[47] W. L. Weinstein would, no doubt, object that equating equal freedom with the power of equal opportunity confuses two contingently related concepts, namely freedom and power. The latter, he would say, is simply a condition for exercising equal freedom.

This likely response also raises a related objection brought to my attention by Richard Flathman. It might be said that equating freedom with self-restraint again confuses two contingently associated concepts, freedom and virtue. It might be argued that self-restraint is simply a condition of another sort for exercising equal freedom. This objection, however, drives too sharp a wedge between the notions of freedom and self-restraint. These two concepts are more internally interwoven than the notion of "condition" allows. Perhaps I am offering a variation on John Gray's contention that "while the distinction between social freedom and power or ability is an important one, it is one which is difficult or impossible to make where the powers and abilities in question have to do with the subjective conditions of choice." By these subjective conditions, Gray means, in particular, the reasonableness of the choices facing an agent. For an available choice to be a free choice, it must be one which a "reasonable man" might make. Surely, part of acting as a "reasonable man" is acting with a measure of restraint. Self-restraint is constitutive of freedom as rational action. For Gray's discussion of freedom and reason, see Gray, "On Negative and Positive Liberty" in Gray and Pelczynski (eds.), *Conceptions of Liberty in Political Philosophy*, pp. 335–9.

freedom an innate moral-faculty intuition. However, by the time he wrote *The Principles of Ethics*, he had abandoned this outmoded faculty psychology in favor of an evolutionary associationist account of how our basic moral sentiments, including the principle of equal freedom, have emerged and have become so intuitively self-evident. Like any moral sentiment, equal freedom owes its saliency to the happiness-generating, competitive favors it bestows on societies that espouse it. Wherever the "sentiment of justice" enlivens the hearts of humans, they are happier being able to enjoy the fruits of their talents as well as the pleasures that come from cultivating them. And wherever humans are happier, wherever they become whatever they deserve to become, societies thrive driving their illiberal rivals to the wall. Liberal utilitarianism is history's favored philosophical child.

This chapter has also tried to show how Spencer's negative theory of freedom was equally a virtue theory of freedom. For Spencer, equal freedom was more than freedom from external constraint. It was, in addition, the practice of a special kind of freedom, of equal freedom as self-restraint. Being equally free is, then, a matter of what Berlin calls "positive self-mastery", of exercising and cultivating this virtue. Thus, it is also an "exercise concept" in Charles Taylor's sense of positive freedom.[48] Spencer's theory of freedom, therefore, supports rather effectively Gerald MacCallum's thesis that all "freedom from" propositions are always, in addition, "freedom to" propositions.[49]

Finally, insofar as acting equally freely is acting virtuously and insofar as the principle of equal freedom is the fundamental decision procedure of his liberal utilitarianism, acting virtuously is just as necessary to maximizing happiness as the principle of equal freedom. Being disposed to follow rules is just as instrumentally crucial as the rules themselves. Rule following presupposes the disposition to follow rules. Thus, Spencer's liberal utilitarianism is as critically dispositional as it is rigorously juridical.

[48] Charles Taylor, "What's Wrong with Negative Liberty," *Philosophy and the Human Sciences, Philosophical Papers*, 2 vols. (Cambridge University Press, 1985), vol. II, pp. 211–29.

[49] Gerald C. MacCallum, Jr., "Negative and Positive Freedom," *The Philosophical Review*, 76 (1967).

CHAPTER 3

Equal freedom and moral rights

At least since Bentham, most philosophers have regarded moral rights and utility as incommensurable. For instance, David Lyons has forcefully argued that they are incompatible despite having once embraced J. S. Mill's attempt to reconcile them. C. L. Ten as well seems to share this assessment, particularly with respect to Mill. Even R. B. Brandt, who views rights and utility as compatible and Mill's version of their compatibility as promising, holds that utilitarianism nevertheless allows "no place" for rights which are "secured to one absolutely, though the heavens fall."[1]

Herbert Spencer was a rare utilitarian who thought otherwise. He was an indirect utilitarian for whom moral rights were as pivotal as the principle of equal freedom. Whereas equal freedom constituted Spencer's fundamental principle of justice, moral rights followed from equal freedom as secondary derivations. Like their parent principle, moral rights indirectly promoted happiness. Like the principle of equal freedom, Spencer took them seriously. Chapters 3, 4 and 5 will explore the plausibility of Spencer's accommodation of stringent moral rights with utility.

Chapter 3 is more modest than chapter 4 and chapter 5 insofar as Spencer's utilitarian justification of moral rights is kept comfortably in the background. That is, chapter 3 focuses on Spencer's conception of moral rights as derivations of equal freedom and argues, in essence, that they are meant to provide substance to the otherwise empty formalism of equal freedom. Moral rights are prudential strategies that mature by becoming increasingly well defined as human history unfolds. They emerge as inviolable conditions (or nearly inviolable ones in the later Spencer) for

[1] Lyons, "Utility and Rights"; C. L. Ten, *Mill on Liberty* (Oxford University Press, 1980), especially p. 49; and R. B. Brandt, "Utilitarianism and Moral Rights," *Canadian Journal of Philosophy*, 14 (1984).

harmonizing everyone's pursuit of happiness. Hence, moral rights are indirectly instrumental in promoting happiness no less crucially than equal freedom.

In addition, chapter 3 investigates what Spencer means by claiming that moral rights are logical "corollaries." However, contrary to what Spencer seems to believe, moral rights cannot possibly be deductions from the principle of equal freedom in a strict logical sense. Rather, their true nature becomes clearer as we begin analyzing, within the context of his larger theory of social evolution, Spencer's contention that they are "conditions" for achieving happiness.

Chapter 3 concludes by briefly assessing the significance of one particular right, namely the basic right to freedom. We shall see that the principle of equal freedom is nothing less than a reformulation of this basic right. This conclusion bolsters claims made previously about the relationship between freedom *per se* and equal freedom.

Moral rights, then, are elemental for Spencer. They provide his principle of equal freedom, the centerpiece of his liberal utilitarianism, with normative substance. By specifying the principle of equal freedom, they render it a more serviceable decision procedure.

RIGHTS AS COROLLARIES OF EQUAL FREEDOM

Spencer's theory of rights was no traditional theory of natural rights although it resembled one in his early writings. Though stringent "corollaries" of equal freedom, moral rights were never, for Spencer, metaphysical prerogatives of right reason. On the other hand, Spencer never subscribed to Bentham's sweeping deprecation of natural rights as perilous nonsense either.[2]

His first published essay, "The Proper Sphere of Government," says little about basic rights, though what it does say is largely unimaginative and seems firmly rooted in the natural rights tradition. There, Spencer links the "preservation of man's natural rights" to the maintenance of "justice" (although not to the principle of

[2] W. R. Inge argues that Spencer's ambivalence about natural rights stemmed from Thomas Hodgskin's influence on him when both worked at *The Economist* during the 1840s and 1850s. See W. R. Inge, "Liberty and Natural Rights," The Herbert Spencer Lecture (Oxford University Press, 1934), p. 5.

equal freedom which he had yet to develop).[3] Next, he provides several examples of the kinds of natural rights which the maintenance of justice serves. These include "natural rights" of consumers to purchase food at competitive prices (hence Spencer's early endorsement of the repeal of the Corn Laws); natural "rights of conscience" (hence his support for the disestablishment of the Anglican church); and "natural rights" not to be taxed to maintain the poor (hence his support for eliminating the 1834 Poor Law) ("The Proper Sphere of Government," pp. 189–201).

Spencer, then, seems to have been initially attracted to the idea of traditional natural rights. Still, the attractiveness of this idea did not displace the appeal which underlying utilitarian considerations always held for him even from the outset. Respect for natural rights was eminently "expedient." Respect for them furthered "general happiness" which was the "great end in view" (p. 207).

By contrast, *Social Statics* provides a more fully developed treatment of rights. Not only are rights deemed important but they are also explicitly and repeatedly treated as deductive corollaries of equal freedom. After criticizing the "empty" arbitrariness of Bentham's "doctrine of expediency" in the "Introduction," Spencer adds:

> We seek a system that can return a definite answer when we ask, "Is this act good?" and not, like yours, reply, "Yes, if it will benefit you." If you can show us such a one – if you can give us an axiom from which we can develop successive propositions until we have with mathematical certainty solved all our difficulties – we will thank you. If not, we must go elsewhere. (*Social Statics*, p. 4)

Presumably, by "axiom," Spencer means the principle of equal freedom (or justice in the terminology of "The Proper Sphere of Government"). And by "successive propositions," he presumably means basic rights.

In subsequent chapters, Spencer deploys similar language which we can also safely interpret as referring to rights as deductive specifications of the principle of equal freedom. For instance, Spencer writes:

3 Spencer, "The Proper Sphere of Government," p. 188. See also p. 187, where Spencer writes that the purpose of government is to "defend the natural rights of man . . . in a word, to administer justice."

The realization of the divine idea being reduced to the fulfillment of certain conditions, it becomes the office of a scientific morality to make a detailed statement of the mode in which life must be regulated so as to conform to them. On each of these axiomatic truths it must be possible to build a series of theorems immediately bearing upon our daily conduct; or, inverting the thought, every act stands in a certain relationship to these truths, and it must be possible in some way or other to solve the problem, whether that relationship is one of accordance or discordance . . .

Each of these axioms, however, may have its own set of consequences separately deduced, or indeed, as already hinted, *must* have them so deduced . . . It is with the several inferences to be drawn from that primary condition to greatest happiness, the observance of which is vaguely signified by the word *justice*, that we have now to deal. Our work will be to unfold that condition into a system of equity; to mark out those limits put to each man's proper sphere of activity by the like spheres of other men; to delineate those relationships that are necessitated by a recognition of those limits; or, in other words, to develop the principles of Social Statics. (*Social Statics*, pp. 65–6)

Insofar as "axiomatic truths" in the above refers to our fundamental principles like the principle of justice, the "series of theorems" deducible from these principles surely refers to rights. Phrases like "set of consequences" and "limits" surely refer to basic rights as well.

Moreover, by claiming that justice "vaguely" signifies "that primary condition to happiness," Spencer is also suggesting that happiness only flourishes where equal freedom is satisfied. Secondly, by saying justice "vaguely" signifies the principle of equal freedom, he means that justice (and hence equal freedom) remains ambiguous unless it is reduced to its constituent rights. Furthermore, by concluding that deriving these constituent rights amounts to developing the "principles of Social Statics," he implies that a proper theory of basic rights is a theory of *static* rights. As a title, then, *Social Statics* refers to nothing less than indefeasible fundamental rights.

Elsewhere in *Social Statics*, Spencer is more explicit:

The process by which we may develop this first principle into a system of equity is sufficiently obvious. We have just to distinguish the actions that are included under its permit from those which are excluded by it – to find what lies inside the sphere appointed for each individual and what outside. Our aim must be to discover how far the territory of *may* extends and where it borders upon that of *may not*. We shall have to consider every deed, whether, in committing it, a man does or does not trespass upon the ordained freedom of his neighbor – whether, when placed side by side, the shares of liberty the two parties respectively assume are equal. And by thus separating that which can be done by each without trenching on the privileges of others from that which cannot be so done, we may classify actions into lawful and unlawful. (p. 100)

These borders of "may not" are what Spencer thereafter labels corollaries of equal freedom or rights; and in the phraseology of faculty exercise, "it is this freedom to exercise the faculties within specific limits which we signify by the term 'rights' " (p. 182).[4]

Now, given that Spencer regards rights as so many specifications of the principle of equal freedom, it should be unsurprising that the emergence of the sentiment of equal freedom is tantamount to the emergence of, and respect for, individual rights (*Social Statics*, p. 178).[5] Furthermore, in the early *Social Statics*, it should also be unsurprising that Spencer continues to embrace a traditional-sounding theory of natural rights. Recall from our previous discussions that, in this work, he maintained that all humans possess a moral sense in which the principle of equal freedom resides as intuition. From the beginning of human history, this intuition has been emerging as a conscious moral imperative via the exercise of the moral sense. Inasmuch as rights are specifications of equal freedom, they are similarly intuitions which moral sense exercise awakens. This is why Spencer also refers to rights as instincts in *Social Statics*.[6]

The last chapter of *The Man Versus the State*, entitled "The Great Political Superstition," is Spencer's most systematic discussion of

[4] See also "The Filiation of Ideas" where Spencer says about *Social Statics*, "Dissatisfaction with that condition of thought led to the search for an ultimate principle from which the limitations were deducible, and this when found proved to be a principle from which were also deducible the various so-called rights. The whole ethical scheme, in so far as justice is concerned, had been reduced to a completely deductive, and consequently quite coherent, form satisfying the love of ideal completeness." Spencer, "The Filiation of Ideas" in Duncan (ed.), *The Life and Letters of Herbert Spencer*, p. 540.

[5] See as well pp. 84–5 where Spencer maintains that there is a growing assertion of "human rights" in those societies which value equal freedom.

[6] Without employing the term "natural," Spencer also sharply criticizes Bentham for denying the existence of rights "antecedent" to government (*Social Statics*, p. 86). Note also that Spencer's theory of rights in *Social Statics* anticipates his theory of sympathy in "Morals and Moral Sentiments." Foreshadowing his later claim that the sentiment of equal freedom develops as we become more sympathetic, Spencer asserts that sympathy promotes respect for rights.

rights.[7] This discussion is particularly intriguing because, in it, his thinking about rights shifts. Near the beginning of this unusual chapter, Spencer first seems to defend traditional natural rights. He suggests rather foolishly that natural rights must be taken seriously because German jurisprudence has long taken them seriously (p. 137). Spencer next criticizes Bentham's rejection of natural rights on two accounts. First of all, he argues, when Bentham says that government creates rights, "two meanings may be given to the word creating." It means either that government creates "something out of nothing," which is absurd, or it means that government simply gives "form and structure to something which already exists." This latter alternative simply "begs the whole question" for we can't help wondering just what that pre-existing something is (*The Man Versus the State*, p. 139).

Spencer's second criticism of Bentham is confusing. According to Spencer, Bentham supposedly concedes that "something" indeed "already exists" from which rights are derived. This "something" is the "powers and rights" that society as a whole possesses to everything useful to humans. Spencer finds it absurd that government somehow reallocates this collective right as individual rights. Though absurd, this reasoning is not Bentham's.

Spencer's defense of natural rights now becomes quite unconventional. He asserts that sociological analysis of tribal societies demonstrates particularly well how "universally recognized customs" and "usages" successfully regulate interpersonal conduct. He then adds, "Now, among the customs which we thus find to be pre-governmental, and which subordinate governmental power when it is

[7] By "great political superstition," Spencer means the principle of unchecked majority rule. He defends strong rights in order to contain what he regards as the socialistic perils of this principle. In a November 13, 1883 letter to E. L. Youmans, Spencer says that he has decided to write a series of articles for *The Contemporary Review* (later reprinted as *The Man Versus the State*). He adds, "I shall probably commit myself to a series of four articles. For some time past I have been getting more and more exasperated at the way in which things are drifting towards Communism with increasing velocity: and though I fear little is to be done I am prompted to make a vehement protest, and am intending to say some very strong things." Spencer to E. L. Youmans, 13 November 1883 in Duncan (ed.), *The Life and Letters of Herbert Spencer*, p. 238. Wiltshire, in *The Social and Political Thought of Herbert Spencer*, p. 93, says that Spencer was offered, but turned down, the Liberal candidacy of Leicester because of the public impact of *The Man Versus the State*. He also claims that the essay "sums up Spencer's political creed" and that the editor of *The Contemporary Review* proposed the idea of the essay in early 1883. However, though acerbic, *The Man Versus the State* does not reflect the subtlety of Spencer's views and is, therefore, no "summing up." Moreover, Spencer was not approached in early 1883 to write the essay as the November 13th letter to Youmans goes on to say that he had only recently been contacted by the editor of *The Contemporary Review*.

established, are those which recognize certain individual rights – rights to act in certain ways and possess certain things" (*The Man Versus the State*, p. 142). Furthermore, "But even without seeking proofs among the uncivilized, sufficient proofs are furnished by early stages of the civilized. Bentham and his followers seem to have forgotten that our own common law is mainly an embodiment of 'the customs of the realm'" (p. 143).

These claims suggest that Spencer's theory of natural rights was nontraditional. To claim that rights are natural in the sense of naturally arising out of "customs" and "usages" is not to understand them as timeless metaphysical principles. It is to understand them as human artifacts.[8]

Spencer next says that comparative analysis of civilized societies also reveals striking uniformity in the kinds of rights that arise out of "custom" and "usage." For instance, modern societies generally forbid, as violations of rights, acts like homicide, theft, adultery, breach of contract, libel, and false witness. This uniformity is not fortuitous because "the alleged creating of rights was nothing else than giving formal sanction and better definition to those assertions of claims and recognitions of claims which *naturally* originate from the individual desires of men who have to live in presence of one another" (*The Man Versus the State*, p. 144; my italics). Furthermore, "the insuring to each individual the unhindered pursuit of the objects of life, within limits set by others' like pursuits, is increasingly recognized as a duty of the State. In other words, along with social progress, there not only goes a fuller recognition of these which we call natural rights, but also a better enforcement of them by Government. Government becomes more and more the servant to these essential prerequisites for individual welfare" (pp. 145–6).

Thus, for Spencer, rights are natural insofar as the record of historical progress reveals that certain "customs" and "usages" constitute natural responses to the antagonisms of sociality. Only those societies, in which a fixed array of "customs" and "usages" happen to flourish under the banner of immutable rights, survive

[8] In "Natural Rights: Bentham and John Stuart Mill," H. L. A. Hart says that, in attacking natural rights theory, Bentham understood natural rights in three senses. For their proponents according to Bentham, natural rights were "not artifacts," they "did not depend for their existence on social convention or recognition," and they "reflected or were adapted to certain features of human nature." H. L. A. Hart, *Essays on Bentham* (Oxford University Press, 1982), p. 84.

and flourish themselves. Moreover, social progress vouchsafes a *single* pattern of basic rights. In this respect, equal freedom's corollaries are traditional natural rights yet their discovery is not guaranteed to any particular society. Many societies never institutionalize basic rights and therefore founder. Such societies never become "industrial" societies, never become competitive. In this respect, Spencerian rights are natural in a non-traditional, evolutionist sense. They are also natural in a non-traditional sense insofar as they are a practice, insofar as they are emergent usages and conventions. Humans *make* them even if it so happens that only a fixed pattern of stringent rights promises general felicity.[9]

Besides appealing to the "court of politics" in order to explain and justify basic rights, Spencer insists that we dare not ignore the "court of science" either:

> But if we adopt either the optimist view or the meliorist view – if we say that life on the whole yields more pleasure than pain; or that it is on the way to become such that it will yield more pleasure than pain; then these actions by which life is maintained are justified, and there results a warrant for the freedom to perform them. Those who hold that life is valuable, hold, by implication, that men ought not to be prevented from carrying on life-sustaining activities. In other words, if it is said to be "right" that they should carry them on, then, by permutation, we get the assertion that they "have a right" to carry them on. Clearly the conception of "natural rights" originates in recognition of the truth that if life is justifiable, there must be a justification for the performance of acts essential to its preservation; and therefore, a justification for those liberties and claims which make such acts possible.
>
> But being true of other creatures as of man, this is a proposition lacking ethical character. Ethical character arises only with the distinction between what the individual *may* do in carrying on his life-sustaining activities, and what he *may not* do. This distinction obviously results from the presence of his fellows . . . The non-ethical form of the right to pursue ends, passes into the ethical form, when there is recognized the difference between acts which can be performed without transgressing the limits [imposed by the presence of one's fellow citizens], and others which cannot be so performed. (*The Man Versus the State*, pp. 149–50)

This passage is striking because it couples together so clearly the notions of pleasure, freedom and basic rights. Insofar as life tends to

[9] See also Spencer's equally unorthodox analysis of "a priori beliefs" in Spencer, *The Principles of Ethics*, vol. II, pp. 70–7. There, such beliefs are products of social evolution and are necessary.

be more pleasurable than painful, freedom of action is warranted since free action better maintains life and, hence, promotes pleasure. Rights delineate those "essential" specifications ("liberties and claims") of free action given our sociality. Hence, rights are morally warranted as well. Moreover, they are "natural" precisely because they are so "essential," so warranted. Their naturalness does not stem from their place in natural law but from their inestimable service on behalf of utility.[10]

The differences, then, between Bentham and Spencer on the relationship between freedom, rights and utility may be less than Spencer realizes, notwithstanding the genuine differences between them regarding the existence of natural rights. For instance, in his criticism of Article IV of the "Declaration of the Rights of Man and Citizen" decreed by the French Constituent Assembly in 1791, Bentham says, "Accordingly, the exercise of the rights allowed to and conferred upon each individual ought to have no other bounds set to it by the law than those which are necessary to enable it to maintain every other individual in the possession and exercise of such rights as the regard due to the interests or greatest possible happiness of the whole community taken together admit of his being allowed."[11] In other words, like Spencer, Bentham sees basic rights as mutually limiting specifications of freedom grounded in the principle of utility.

J. S. Mill's theory of rights was even closer to Spencer's theory of rights than Bentham's theory was. In chapter 4 we shall compare Mill and Spencer's respective versions of liberal utilitarianism at length including their respective theories of moral rights in relation to utility. However, we should note here that Spencer's view of natural rights as customary practices appears in Mill too. In "Austin on Jurisprudence," Mill praises John Austin's view that natural law represented that "portion of systems [of law], which arose from the wants and feelings of human nature generally."[12] According to Mill

[10] One recent interpreter of Spencer contends that the final chapter of *The Man Versus the State* defends traditional natural rights. According to John Offer, "Once again [in the last chapter of *The Man Versus the State*], the theme is the legitimate sphere of government action, and, once again, an appeal is made to 'natural rights', a concept which he enjoyably but not satisfactorily defends in the essay against Bentham." John Offer, "Introduction" in John Offer (ed.), *Herbert Spencer: Political Writings* (Cambridge University Press, 1994), pp. xxv–xxvi.

[11] Jeremy Bentham, "Anarchical Fallacies" [1843] in Jeremy Waldron (ed.), *Nonsense Upon Stilts* (London: Methuen, 1987), p. 61.

[12] J. S. Mill, "Austin on Jurisprudence" [1863] in Robson (ed.), *Collected Works*, (1984), vol. XXI.

following Austin, Roman *jus gentium* arose from the need that Roman jurists saw to craft common laws for the disparate cultures that came under Roman rule as their empire expanded. Furthermore, for Mill:

> it was this Roman idea of a *jus gentium*, or portion of law common to all nations, which grew insensibly into the modern idea of Natural Law. "Thus *Jus Naturale*, or law of nature," as Mr. Maine observes, "is simply the *jus gentium* seen in the light of a peculiar theory." That theory, as both he and Mr. Austin remark, was derived from the precept "Live according to Nature" of the Greek philosophical schools. ("Austin on Jurisprudence," pp. 185–6)[13]

Likewise, according to Michael Freeden, J. A. Hobson also understood the naturalness of natural rights unconventionally much the way I have suggested that Spencer did. Hobson, though arguably not a utilitarian, "discarded 'natural' in the sense of 'innate' or 'self-evident' and adopted it instead in the sense of physiologically and psychologically necessary to the adequate functioning of the human being."[14]

In Spencer, bad arguments often accompany compelling ones. For instance, Spencer says that the "non-ethical form of the right to pursue ends" only becomes an ethical form with sociality. Yet the notion of a "non-ethical" right is incoherent. How can a right be "non-ethical" and still be a right? Labelling such a right a "form" of a right is unsatisfactory. A "non-ethical form" of a right is no less incoherent.[15]

In Spencer's defense, one might think that "non-ethical" rights exist unrecognized in presociality. Given the rarity of social interaction and friction, individuals would seldom notice the existence of

[13] Mill continues: "Being observed or recognised universally, these principles were supposed to have a higher origin than human design, and to be (we quote Mr. Austin) 'not so properly rules of human position or establishment, as rules proceeding immediately from the Deity himself, or the intelligent and rational Nature which animates and directs the universe.' This notion, once formed, was, by an obvious process, so enlarged as to include merely moral or merely customary rules which had obtained general acceptance" ("Austin on Jurisprudence" p. 186) I would like to thank Jonathan Riley for calling my attention to Mill's account of natural law in his essays on Austin.

[14] Michael Freeden, *The New Liberalism* (Oxford University Press, 1978), pp. 216–17.

[15] See also Spencer, *The Man Versus the State*, p. 153, where Spencer writes, "Thus it becomes clear, alike from analysis of causes and observation of facts, that while the positive element in the right to carry on life-sustaining activities, originates from the laws of life, that negative element which gives ethical character to it, originates from the conditions produced by social aggregation."

such rights. They would have no need to notice them. Rights become "ethical," or moral rights, once sociality begins and humans need moral rules to govern their interactions. Thus, need-driven recognition transforms "nonethical" rights into moral rights. However, if the "presocial" state is thoroughly asocial, how can there be any rights whatsoever (including "forms" of rights)? Asociality would prelude the genesis of normative concepts such as rights and proto-rights.

Finally, Spencer confuses right in the sense of *ought* with right in the sense of *a* right. He slides from the former to the latter "by permutation." Bentham, of course, contemptuously ridiculed this kind of not-so-subtle sleight of hand. For Bentham, right as ought was the "adjective shape" of right and was conceptually distinct from the "substantive" right as a noun. Whereas the adjectival form of right was meaningful, the nominative form was, for Bentham, pernicious gibberish.[16]

The Principles of Ethics contains Spencer's last systematic treatment of moral rights. In "Justice" (Part IV) of *The Principles of Ethics*, he continues to define rights as corollaries of the principle of equal freedom. After discussing equal freedom in several early chapters of "Justice," he treats rights in relation to the principle of equal freedom in a compact chapter entitled "Its Corollaries." The chapter opens as follows:

> Men's activities are many in their kinds and the consequent social relations are complex. Hence, that the general formula of justice may serve for guidance, deductions must be drawn severally applicable to special classes of cases. The statement that the liberty of each is bounded only by the like liberties of all, remains a dead letter until it is shown what are the restraints which arise under the various sets of circumstances he is exposed to.
>
> Whoever admits that each man must have a certain restricted freedom, asserts that it is *right* he should have this restricted freedom. If it be shown to follow, now in this case and now in that, that he is free to act up to a certain limit but not beyond it, then the implied admission is that it is *right* he should have the particular freedom so defined. And hence the several

16 See, in particular, Bentham, "Anarchical Fallacies," p. 68, where Bentham observes: "In its adjective shape, it [right] is as innocent as a dove: it breathes nothing but morality and peace. It is the shape that, passing in at the heart, it gets possession of the understanding; it then assumes its substantive shape, and joining itself to a band of suitable associates, plants the banner of insurrection, anarchy, and lawless violence." See also Taylor, *Men Versus the State*, p. 242.

particular freedoms deducible may fitly be called, as they commonly are called, his *rights*. (*The Principles of Ethics*, vol. II, p. 79)[17]

By maintaining that equal freedom "remains a dead letter" unless specific restraints are deduced from it, Spencer is making the familiar claim that the principle of equal freedom remains formalistic when it is not supplemented by the normative density that rights bring to it. Equal freedom must be juridically specified for it to "serve for guidance." (We should also notice the logical sleight of hand which we encountered previously. As before, Spencer slides from right *qua* ought to its nominative form.)

Several chapters later, Spencer defends his theory of moral rights a final time. Following *The Man Versus the State*, Spencer continues distancing himself from traditional natural rights theory. Rights are not abiding, moral sense intuitions or revelations of abstract reasoning. They are neither transcendental nor presocial. Rights are emergent *social* practices. They are strategies for coping with sociality which are natural only to the extent that the evolution of society is natural. Governments only recognize what prudential reason requires:

If, as we have seen, rights are but so many separate parts of a man's general freedom to pursue the objects of life, with such limitations only as result from the presence of other men who have similarly to pursue such objects, then, if a man's freedom is not in any way further restricted, he possesses all his rights . . . Many times and in various ways we have seen that rights, truly so called, originate from the laws of life as carried on in the associated state. The social arrangements may be such as fully recognize them, or such as ignore them in greater or smaller degrees. The social arrangements cannot create them, but can simply conform to them or not conform to them. (*The Principles of Ethics*, vol. II, p. 195)[18]

Spencer's theory of natural rights was unconventional, though it wasn't entirely original in that Mill and Austin shared elements of his view that moral rights were "natural" conventions. Spencer began as a traditional natural rights theorist and modified his

[17] See also the "General Preface," *The Principles of Ethics*, vol. I, pp. 24–5, in which Spencer treats rights as corollaries of equal freedom. Written in 1893, when *The Principles* was issued in its complete, two-volume form, the "General Preface" was Spencer's last sustained discussion of moral rights and equal freedom.

[18] For another less systematic discussion of the emergence of equal freedom and its derivative rights written at approximately the same time as "Justice," see Spencer, "Absolute Political Ethics," *Essays*, vol. III. However, instead of the term "rights," Spencer uses expressions like "special restrictions," "definite sets of restraints" and "corollaries."

approach once he embraced social evolutionary theory. He became persuaded that rights arose from the customs and usages of societies. They were neither metaphysical absolutes accessible only to natural reason nor artifacts of positive law, and yet they were to be taken extremely seriously.[19]

THE BASIC RIGHT TO FREEDOM

Spencer early on rejected traditional natural rights theory though he was slower in discarding the language of natural rights. The same conclusion stands when we focus upon the basic right to freedom which we first encounter in *Social Statics* where Spencer says that each individual has a "right to that liberty" to do "all that his faculties naturally impel him to do" (p. 69). But due to sociality, everyone's efforts to exercise this basic right are bound to produce conflicts making the principle of equal freedom a natural remedy. In short, given thickening sociality, the basic right of freedom engenders the principle of equal freedom and all its derivative rights. Furthermore, if freedom prior to sociality is a basic right, then freedom after sociality must also be a basic right. Of course, if freedom remains a basic right for socialized humans, then it follows that equal freedom is a basic right for them as well. Insofar as *Social Statics* defends quasi-traditional natural rights, we may infer that equal freedom was, in *Social Statics*, nothing less than a natural right.[20]

The underlying importance of the basic right to freedom for Spencer was not lost on his contemporaries. George Lacy, for instance, in *Liberty and Law*, resolves that Spencer, "derives all his conceptions of natural rights from the fundamental conception of the right to liberty, and they might, indeed, all be embraced in that right" (p. 122). D. G. Ritchie as well, in *Natural Rights*, suggests that a rudimentary right to freedom undergirds Spencer's principle of equal freedom.[21]

More recently, Michael Taylor has also maintained that a basic

[19] Recall that in his later works, Spencer held that equal freedom was an emergent practice rather than an abiding intuition.

[20] Recall Spencer's claim in "The Kantian Idea of Rights" that, in contrast to Kant's equal freedom formula, his formula placed greater stress on the "right to freedom of action." See also "The Filiation of Ideas" in Duncan (ed.), *The Life and Letters of Herbert Spencer*, p. 539, where Spencer says that the "primary assertion" contained in the principle of equal freedom is the "claim" or "right" of every individual "to free action."

[21] D. G. Ritchie, *Natural Rights* [1894] (London: George Allen and Unwin, 1952), p. 142.

"natural right to liberty" was central to Spencer's theory of freedom because, according to Taylor, Spencer held that "certain activities are necessary for the maintenance of life" (*Men Versus the State*, p. 241).[22] Taylor approvingly cites Ritchie's criticism that Spencer's evolutionary theory of rights merely established that there were "certain conditions *necessary* for the life of *any* society" and not that traditional natural rights, in fact, existed (p. 241; my italics). That is, for Taylor following Ritchie, Spencer's theory of natural rights was not really a theory of natural rights though Spencer mistakenly thought that it was. Taylor, however, ignores Ritchie's added comment that "Mr. Spencer himself really says the same thing, giving it as the ultimate 'secret'." By Spencer's own admission in other words, his theory of natural rights was *secretly* no traditional theory.

Usually, though, Ritchie reproves Spencer for defending traditional natural rights. Generally speaking, as far as Ritchie was concerned, Spencer was just another intuitionist advocate of natural rights who clothed his intuitionism in the dress of evolutionary theory in order to justify *laissez-faire* more effectively. According to Ritchie, Spencer wrongly held that natural rights existed simply because all modern societies have come to recognize the same inventory of rights. On the contrary, in Ritchie's view, this congruity merely establishes that certain "conditions" are essential for any society to thrive.[23] Proponents of natural rights mistake the essentiality of these conditions for their ostensibly elevated metaphysical status and consequently swathe these conditions in the language of natural rights.

Moreover, for Ritchie, whereas ancient societies that happened to institutionalize these conditions as custom, habit and tradition

[22] Taylor also holds that in *The Methods of Ethics*, Sidgwick meant Spencer in claiming that "All natural rights, on this view, may be summed up in the Right to Freedom." However, it is unclear whether Sidgwick is specifically thinking of Spencer here. See Henry Sidgwick, *The Methods of Ethics* [1907], 7th edition (Indianapolis: Hackett Publishing Co., 1981), p. 274.

[23] D. G. Ritchie, *The Principles of State Interference*, [1891] (London: Swan Sonnenschein and Co., 1896), p. 39. In this book, two of whose four chapters are devoted to criticizing Spencer's *The Man Versus the State*, Ritchie also accuses Spencer of abstract individualism for supposing that individuals have "meaning and significance" apart from their communal relations with others. In addition, according to Ritchie, Spencer conceives the relationship between citizens and the state as a zero-sum liberty game according to which more liberty for the former means less for the latter and vice-versa. Moreover, Ritchie charges that Spencer's abstract individualism conflicts with his social organicism, an accusation often made by interpreters of Spencer. See especially pp. 11–13 and 23.

tended to flourish in the past, modern societies that began justifying and consciously refining these conditions with a *deliberate* eye to their utility-generating power now thrive as never before. Thus, utilitarian practical reasoning constitutes a turning point in moral theorizing. And by revealing that these "essential conditions" of well-being are not really natural rights, modern utilitarianism also "makes what one may call a 'Copernican' change in our way of considering the question of rights."[24] So-called natural rights are nothing more than those moral rights which "ought to be recognized" by society as socially useful.[25]

But as we have seen, and as Ritchie concedes on one occasion by acknowledging Spencer's "ultimate secret," Spencer likewise came to view natural rights as merely those rights that "ought to be recognized." The present chapter has shown just how nuanced Spencer's "secret" theory of rights was especially in his post-*Social Statics* writings. Spencer may well have often spoken in the tongue of traditional natural rights. But he spoke this venerated tongue in a cryptic idiosyncratic way.

This chapter has shown that Spencer viewed rights as corollaries, or specifications, of the principle of equal freedom. Hence, Wiltshire wrongly asserts that the "formula of equal freedom is a safe enough introductory gambit for any theoretical system, yet no limits are specified for it. The absence of such a specification throws the interpretation of equal freedom open to whim" (*The Social and Political Thought of Herbert Spencer*, p. 160). Spencer *did* specify the principle of equal freedom. For him, interpreting equal freedom properly is not open to whim.

However, in one sense, the principle of equal freedom and its derivative corollaries are an empty "introductory gambit." Spencer seems to believe that rights are corollaries of the principle of equal freedom in a genuine logical sense. He seems convinced that moral rights follow from the meaning of equal freedom the way that corollaries in formal logic follow from their axioms.

[24] Ritchie, *Natural Rights*, p. 101.

[25] Ritchie, *The Principles of State Interference*, p. 43. Also see Sandra M. Den Otter, *British Idealism and Social Explanation* (Oxford University Press, 1996), pp. 160–6 and 196–8 for a valuable discussion of Ritchie's theory of rights. Den Otter's study is a first-rate examination of the relationship between British idealism and nineteenth-century evolutionary theory and sociology.

Clearly, the relationship between the principle of equal freedom and moral rights cannot possibly be purely logical. Transforming the principle of equal freedom into a serviceable decision procedure by specifying its juridical content is not a matter of logical entailment. What Spencer actually means by the relationship between equal freedom and moral rights will become clearer in the next chapters.

Furthermore, we should now better appreciate the unconventional sense in which Spencer came to regard fundamental rights as natural. Hence, modern interpreters of Spencer such as Offer, Wiltshire, Machan and Asirvatham err insofar as they uniformly maintain that Spencer defends traditional natural rights *throughout* his works.[26] Moreover, if I am right in insisting that Spencer understood rights as customary practices, then we are further warranted in concluding that they can't be strict logical corollaries.

With Spencer's account of rights as corollaries of the principle of equal freedom behind us, we need to address next how he understood rights in relation to utility. We need to assess how his utilitarianism was a hybrid of deontological and consequentialist moral reasoning. We need, in short, to take up the challenge of his liberal utilitarianism.

[26] For Wiltshire, see his contention that Spencer founded his "individualism" on a "theory of natural rights" and that he embraced the long-since controvertible "notion that liberty . . . could derive from individual rights extraneous to society." Wiltshire, *The Social and Political Thought of Herbert Spencer*, pp. 178–80. And in his *Herbert Spencer's Theory of Social Justice* (Lucknow: The Upper India Publishing House, 1936), p. 168, E. Asirvatham maintains that Spencer "to the end of his life, firmly believed in the theory of natural rights." Also see Tibor Machan's "Introduction" to Spencer, *The Principles of Ethics*, vol. 1, p. 18, where he asserts that Spencer believed that "we all have natural rights." But note that Machan suggestively adds that Spencer "took a utilitarian perspective on rights." Offer's characterization of Spencer as an advocate of traditional natural rights was discussed in note 10.

CHAPTER 4

Moral rights and utility

> Now all these men, to whatever party they might belong, Godwin no less than Burke, Malthus no less than Godwin, were supporters of the principle of utility. It is clear that the doctrine of utility was becoming the universal philosophy in England, and that reformers were forced to speak the language of utility if they wanted to make their opinions accepted or even understood by the public to which they were addressed.[1]

Perhaps there is something anodyne in opening this chapter with this uncontrovertible remark from Elie Halévy's *The Growth of Philosophic Radicalism.* But insofar as this chapter is as much about utility in Spencer as it is about rights, we must not underestimate the historically obvious concerning Spencer's intellectual context lest we also ignore the analytically intriguing in his moral theory. We dare not forget that Spencer, when speaking in the juristic idiom of rights, continued speaking that same "language of utility" of his intellectual predecessors and peers. It is precisely this mix of conceptual languages that makes his liberalism so historically interesting and even provocative.

This chapter builds on themes begun in the previous two chapters. Whereas those chapters demonstrated Spencer's indirect, liberal utilitarianism in terms of the principle of equal freedom and then related his theory of moral rights to this principle, chapter 4 reinvestigates his indirect, liberal utilitarianism by focusing exclusively on his theory of moral rights. We shall see that moral rights, as specifications of equal freedom, indirectly promote utility as does their parent principle.[2] Like the principle of equal freedom, they too

[1] Elie Halévy, *The Growth of Philosophic Radicalism* [1928] (London: Faber and Faber, 1972), pp. 153–4.

[2] Direct utilitarianism holds that the principle of utility should serve both as a standard for assessing actions and institutions and as a direct source of moral obligation. Indirect

are critical decision procedures. Spencer's attempt to accommodate strong moral rights and utility will be a focus of this chapter.

Chapter 4 begins by examining Spencer's conviction that, as specifications of the principle of equal freedom, moral rights are particularly valuable devices for promoting utility indirectly. No other strategies, as far as Spencer was concerned, outperform their maximizing fecundity. In order to underscore the indirect utilitarian role that moral rights play for Spencer, we shall compare his theory of moral rights to that of J. S. Mill. Doing so will not only enhance our grasp of the strong similarities between them but will also show that both participated in a distinctive mode of Victorian, liberal utilitarian theorizing which may not have been, after all, quite so unusual. Spencer's friendship with Mill, and their admiration for each other, will be discussed as well in order to contextualize the continuities between their respective versions of liberal utilitarianism.

MORAL RIGHTS AND INDIRECT UTILITY

The relationship between fundamental rights and utility is a little examined yet markedly important dimension of Spencer's moral theory. Some recent interpreters of Spencer have ignored this facet of his thought entirely. Wiltshire, for one, offers no sustained analysis of Spencer's utilitarianism although he does, as we have seen, discuss Spencer's conception of rights superficially. In *Herbert Spencer*, James Kennedy insists that Spencer was "at odds" with utilitarianism.[3] And R. M. Young, despite his appreciation, in *Mind, Brain and Adaptation in the Nineteenth Century*, of the utilitarian nature of Spencer's

utilitarianism, by contrast, maintains that the principle of utility merely functions as a standard for evaluating actions and institutions and not as a source of direct obligation. In the liberal version of indirect utilitarianism, basic moral rights function as the source of the latter. Hence, indirect utilitarians hold that general utility is best maximized over the long run when people assiduously fulfill their moral and legal obligations. Direct utilitarianism, then, is arguably synonymous with act utilitarianism whereas indirect utilitarianism is a variety of rule utilitarianism where, in its liberal utilitarian variety, rights serve as stringent rules constraining the direct pursuit of utility.

[3] James G. Kennedy, *Herbert Spencer* (Boston: Twayne Publishers, 1978), p. 111. Kennedy writes: "Natural rights were the heart of Spencer's political philosophy. He could illustrate social relations and social development by organic analogies, but he never could allow that the social organization made the general welfare an end in itself. Each individual had a prior claim to happiness. Such a stand put Spencer at odds with the utilitarians, who recognized no natural rights and aimed to calculate the general welfare."

associationist psychology, has more recently suggested that Spencer was essentially anti-utilitarian.[4]

Others, such as Asirvatham and Miller, fare somewhat better. Asirvatham notes that Spencer never wavered in believing that happiness ought to be the ultimate aim of action even though he denied that it ought to be an immediate aim. In Asirvatham's words, Spencer emphasized "obedience to certain abstract and unbending principles under which alone greatest happiness is to be realized" (*Herbert Spencer's Theory of Social Justice*, p. 152). Yet Asirvatham also contends that Spencer's principle of justice, the most essential of these principles, is of limited practical use because of its vagueness and generality (p. 164).[5] Asirvatham is correct as far as he goes. Yet he fails to appreciate that rights, as corollaries of equal freedom, lessen its vagueness and generality. He fails to appreciate the practical power of moral rights as guides for indirectly maximizing utility. Asirvatham's insensitivity to Spencer's utilitarian justification of moral rights is surprising insofar as he recognizes the utilitarian instrumentality of equal freedom for Spencer and insofar as he also correctly understands that Spencer regarded rights as corollaries of the principle of equal freedom.

David Miller, too, recognizes the indirect nature of Spencer's utilitarianism. Miller contends that Spencer "accused other utilitarians of making the general happiness the direct object of pursuit, of demanding that people should act with perfect [utilitarian] altruism on all occasions." Hence, according to Miller, Spencer held that "general happiness could only be attained indirectly" by adherence to certain principles of justice (*Social Justice*, p. 182).[6] Despite the accuracy of his characterization of Spencer, Miller says precious little about how Spencer sought to accommodate his theory of strong rights with his commitment to the principle of utility.

Of all of Spencer's modern interpreters, Michael Taylor best captures the contending juridical and utilitarian poles of Spencer's liberalism. Yet as we shall shortly see, Taylor does not sufficiently explore the logical tensions of this curious theoretical amalgam nor

[4] R. M. Young, "Herbert Spencer and 'Inevitable' Progress," *History Today*, 37 (1987), 18. For Young's discussion of Spencer's relationship to utilitarianism in *Mind, Brain and Adaptation in the Nineteenth Century*, see pp. 153–9 and 169.

[5] Also see p. 153. Recall Wiltshire's similar inability to appreciate how rights infused equal freedom with content for Spencer.

[6] Miller's remarks about Spencer's indirect utilitarianism are limited to a single, though suggestively rich, paragraph.

does he make Spencer out to be the thoroughgoing liberal utilitarian that I am convinced he is.

Let us return to those conceptual features that make Spencer's utilitarianism so thoroughly liberal as well as utilitarian. For Spencer, moral rights, like the principle of equal freedom, promote happiness indirectly. Happiness, as we have seen, requires equal freedom and equal freedom, in turn, remains nonsubstantive unless specified by rights. Condemned to increasingly complex patterns of social interaction, we can succeed in maximizing happiness only by confining our actions to boundaries delineated by basic rights. Rights are necessary but not sufficient conditions for maximizing happiness. Respect for them is the best possible strategy.

In *Social Statics* and in *The Principles of Ethics*, Spencer repeatedly attacks attempts to legislate happiness directly as, in his view, Benthamite utilitarians advocate. For instance, in *Social Statics*, he asserts:

> The expediency philosophy, however, ignores this worldful of facts. Though men have so constantly been balked in their attempts to secure, by legislation, any desired constituent of that complex whole, "greatest happiness," it nevertheless continues to place confidence in the unaided judgment of the statesman. It asks no guide; it possesses no eclectic principle; it seeks no clue whereby the tangled web of social existence may be unraveled and its laws discovered. But, holding up to view the great desideratum, it assumes that, after an inspection of the aggregate phenomena of national life, governments are qualified to concoct such measures as shall be "expedient." (p. 12)

Moreover, the principle of utility is remarkably obscure:

> And as the world yet contains none [omniscient humans], it follows that a specific idea of "greatest happiness" is for present unattainable. It is not, then, to be wondered at if Paleys and Benthams make vain attempts at definition. The question involves one of those mysteries which men are ever trying to penetrate and ever failing. It is the insoluble riddle which Care, Sphinx-like, puts to each newcomer, and in default of answer devours him. And as yet there is no Oedipus, nor any sign of one. (*Social Statics*, p. 7)

In a very revealing footnote later in the text, Spencer fortifies his grounds for discarding this "great desideratum" as a direct guide for social policy. He says, "We do not here debate the claims of this maxim [the greatest happiness of the greatest number]. It is sufficient for present purposes to remark that were it true it would be utterly useless as a first principle; both from the impossibility of determining specifically what happiness is, and from the want of a measure by which to mete it out, could we define it" (*Social Statics*, p. 87).

Furthermore, as the following hypothetical dialogue with an imaginary adversary also makes plain, happiness results only from free faculty exercise *within* boundaries delimited by rights:

> "Does not happiness consist in the due satisfaction of all the desires? In the due exercise of all the faculties?"
>
> "Yes."
>
> "And this exercise of the faculties is impossible without freedom of action. The desires cannot be satisfied without liberty to pursue and use the objects of them."
>
> "True."
>
> "Now it is this freedom to exercise the faculties within specific limits which we signify by the term 'rights,' is it not?" (*Social Statics*, p. 182)[7]

The Principles of Ethics also defends basic rights because they so effectively promote happiness indirectly. In volume I, Spencer says quite unambiguously: "When alleging that empirical utilitarianism [Benthamism] is but introductory to rational utilitarianism [Spencer's improved variety], I pointed out that the last does not take welfare for its immediate object of pursuit, but takes for its immediate object of pursuit conformity to certain principles which in the nature of things, causally determine welfare" (vol. I, pp. 194–5). In volume II, he makes much the same distinction between "rational" indirect utilitarianism and vulgar "empirical" direct utilitarianism when he says that "empirical utilitarianism, which makes happiness the immediate aim, stands in contrast with the rational utilitarianism, which aims at fulfillment of the *conditions* to happiness" (vol. II, p. 260; my italics).

Spencer next explains why "rational" utilitarianism is so preferable. Its superiority stems from its acknowledgement that the conditions to happiness are intelligible and demonstrable whereas,

[7] And see p. 395 where Spencer says that respect for rights is no less than the realization of equal freedom. Equal freedom is the "law under which individuation becomes perfect, and that ability to recognize and act up to this law is the final endowment of humanity – an endowment now in process of evolution. The increasing assertion of personal rights is an increasing demand that external conditions needful to a complete unfolding of individuality shall be respected." For an instance of the utility-promoting function of rights coming between *Social Statics* and *The Principles of Ethics*, see Spencer, *The Principles of Psychology*, vol. II, p. 617.

happiness itself is not. Bentham's opposite mistaken belief leads him to believe erroneously that happiness can be promoted directly. In Spencer's words:

It is not then self-evident, as Bentham alleges, that happiness is an intelligible end while justice is not; but, contrariwise, examination makes evident the greater intelligibility of justice as an end. And analysis shows why it is the more intelligible. For justice, or equity, or equalness, is concerned exclusively with *quantity* under stated conditions; whereas happiness is concerned with both *quantity* and *quality* under conditions not stated. When, as in case of theft, a benefit is taken while no equivalent benefit is yielded – when, as in case of adulterated goods bought or base coin paid, that which is agreed to be given in exchange as of equal value is not given, but something of less value – when, as in the case of broken contract, the obligation on one side has been discharged while there has been no discharge, or incomplete discharge, of the obligation on the other; we see that, the circumstances being specified, the injustice complained of refers to the relative amounts of actions, or products, or benefits, the natures of which are recognized only so far as is needful for saying whether *as much* has been given, or done, or allowed, by each concerned, as was implied by tacit or overt understanding to be *an equivalent.* But when the end proposed is happiness, the circumstances remaining unspecified, the problem is that of estimating both quantities and qualities, unhelped by any such definite measures as acts of exchange imply, or as contracts imply, or as are implied by the differences between the doings of one aggressing and one aggressed upon (*The Principles of Ethics*, vol. 1, p. 198; my italics).

In addition, by erroneously believing that utility can be directly promoted legislatively, Bentham devalues the conditions of utility maximization:

But now passing over this assertion of Bentham that happiness is a more intelligible end than justice, which we find to be the reverse of truth, let us note the several implications of the doctrine that the supreme legislative body ought to make the greatest happiness of the greatest number its immediate aim.

It implies, in the first place, that happiness may be compassed by methods framed directly for the purpose, without any previous inquiry respecting the conditions that must be fulfilled; and this presupposes a belief that there are no such conditions. For if there are any conditions without fulfillment of which happiness cannot be compassed, then the first step must be to ascertain these conditions with a view to fulfilling them; and to admit this is to admit that not happiness itself must be the immediate end, but fulfillment of the conditions to its attainment must be the immediate end. (*The Principles of Ethics*, vol. 1, p. 199)

These passages are not unproblematic. For instance, in the first passage, if justice is more "intelligible" because it rests upon the exchange of quantifiable equivalents, then in what sense is physical aggression or the threat of physical aggression a nonequivalent exchange? If justice is desert, if it is a matter of receiving quantitatively no more nor no less than the good and bad results of one's actions, then how is assault receiving less than one deserves? And how can we quantify assault and rectify it accordingly? Quantifying justice is sometimes no less problematic than quantifying happiness.

Justice, then, may not always be easily understood as a quantifiable market exchange. Still, Spencer may be correct in concluding that happiness is unmeasurable with any precision and that, therefore, all attempts to directly legislate utility are futile. He may be quite right to insist that if utility is to be fostered at all, then it must be fostered indirectly.[8] Ascertaining and respecting certain juridical "conditions" may be the most promising strategy for maximizing happiness.

So the legacy of *Social Statics* remains implacable. The principle of equal freedom and its juridical specifications as well as the criterion, greatest happiness, continue to comprise the conceptual nucleus of Spencer's mature moral theory. Maximizing the happiness requires strict adherence to decision rules like moral rights. Because happiness "cannot be cut up and distributed equally," there "remains to be equally distributed nothing but the conditions under which each may pursue happiness." Each "shall have as much liberty to pursue his ends as consists with maintaining like liberties to pursue their ends by others" and thus, everybody will truly "count for one and nobody for more than one." In short, "equity shall be enforced" (*The Principles of Ethics*, vol. I, p. 253).

In sum, equity stipulates that the essential "conditions" to happiness must be unflinchingly upheld. Basic moral rights must be vigorously enforced. Whereas the meaning of happiness is ambiguous, the meaning of justice and its juridical specifications are not. Though standards of happiness may vary, "certain general conditions" must be firmly established if general happi-

[8] See also vol. I, p. 200, where Spencer oddly remarks, "If, then [for Bentham], we may properly skip justice, and go directly to the end happiness, we may properly skip Bentham's polity, and go directly to the end happiness. In short, we are led to the remarkable conclusion that in all cases we must contemplate exclusively the end and must disregard the means."

ness, however conceived, is to be attained. We have to show "respect for one another's claims: there must be neither those direct aggressions which we class as crimes against person and property, nor must there be those indirect aggressions constituted by breaches of contracts. So that maintenance of equitable relations between men is the condition to attainment of greatest happiness in all societies; however much the greatest happiness attainable in each may differ in nature, or amount, or both" (*The Principles of Ethics*, vol. I, p. 202). Maintaining equitable relations between individuals as a universal condition to general happiness is nothing less than achieving a "social equilibrium" which "does not admit of *variation*" (vol. I, p. 203; my italics). Furthermore, Spencer admits that this "universal requirement" of happiness was what he had in mind in calling his first book *Social Statics* (vol. I, p. 203) Again, we see that by this title Spencer meant "indefeasible moral rights."

Volume II, of *The Principles of Ethics* buttresses Spencer's views on justice in volume I leaving little doubt that by "conditions," he means basic rights. For example, in his analysis of the "right to physical integrity," he states that "considered as the statement of a condition by conforming to which the greatest sum of happiness is to be obtained, the law [of equal freedom] forbids any act which inflicts physical pain or derangement" (vol. II, p. 81).

Because by "conditions" Spencer means moral rights, the meaning of "corollary" now becomes clearer. As corollaries of the principle of equal freedom, moral rights are simply causally necessary conditions for maximizing utility. They do not follow logically from the meaning of equal freedom as Spencer often seems to think. This is why I have used expressions like "strategies" and "specifications of equal freedom" as alternatives for describing his conception of moral rights.

The meaning of corollaries as conditions makes even deeper sense when we again take account of Spencer's later marriage, after *The Principles of Psychology* especially, of use-inheritance, association psychology, moral intuitionism and utility. Actions which typically produce pleasure or pain tend to generate fixed mental associations between types of action, pleasure and pain, and approval and disapproval. These mental associations, in turn, tend to get inherited as moral intuitions of approval and disapproval. In addition, sympathy extends these intuitions of approval and disapproval to actions affecting others. Finally, these intuitions tend to become stronger and more self-evident over time.

Moreover, societies in which these associations are comparatively more widespread are more successful *vis-à-vis* rival societies. Moral societies are also happier societies because moral intuitions such as mutual respect and forbearance are comparatively more deeply entrenched in them. Their members are freer and, therefore, enjoy more fully the conditions of happiness.

Moral rights, then, constitute refinements of our most important, acquired moral intuitions, that is, mutual respect and forbearance. They commend and protect what we gradually come to recognize as our most essential pleasure-producing activities. Hence, as corollaries of equal freedom, they are strategies that we gradually sanctify as our best decision rules.

To summarize thus far, and to borrow from Jan Narveson, we might say that Spencer understands moral rights as identifying "important sources of utility."[9] Moreover, they are non-arbitrary as they identify such vital, permanent sources of utility. Yet, as has been stressed previously, they are artificial in as much as they are historical practices.

With these clarifications of Spencer's theory of rights in mind, we can begin to appreciate the spuriousness of Spencer's attempt to distinguish "rational" from "empirical" utilitarianism. Because Spencer held that moral rights were *logical* deductions from the principle of equal freedom, he characterized his brand of utilitarianism as "rational" utilitarianism in contrast to Benthamism which eschewed logical deduction and was therefore merely "empirical." But, as we shall see in chapter 6, Spencer's conception of deduction proves to be other than logical entailment. It proves to be what it was for Bentham and what it has been for all utilitarians ever since. The only difference is that in Spencer's case, he was convinced that an emerging, unchanging set of juridical strategies best maximized general happiness. By contrast, Bentham and most subsequent utilitarians have been less dogmatic, believing that utilitarian justice requires strategic flexibility.

In other words, where most utilitarians have welcomed the importance of such strategic flexibility, Spencer saw only hazards

[9] Jan Narveson, "Rights and Utilitarianism" in Wesley E. Cooper, Kai Nielsen and Steven C. Patten (eds.), *New Essays on John Stuart Mill and Utilitarianism* (Guelph: Canadian Association for Publishing in Philosophy, 1979), p. 160.

liable to undermine the entire utilitarian enterprise. For Spencer, such flexibility risked degenerating into a "new Toryism" of self-defeating state interference. "Philosophic radicalism," as far as Spencer was concerned, was anything but radically liberal and was, therefore, anything but successfully utilitarian.

MILL, SPENCER AND THE EMERGENCE OF LIBERAL UTILITARIANISM

The indirect instrumental role which moral rights play for Spencer can be better understood and therefore better assessed by comparing Spencer and J. S. Mill on fundamental rights and utility. The similarities between them in this regard are quite profound, particularly if John Gray's earlier interpretation of Mill as well as Fred R. Berger's and Jonathan Riley's Mill are the genuine Mill.[10] And, if we are to believe Gray, "It seems that neither Mill nor Spencer noticed the striking family resemblance between their respective theories."[11]

The continuities between Spencer and Mill ought not to be terribly surprising. Nor did these two theorists fail to notice these salient continuities, as Gray suggests. Spencer and Mill were friends who respected each other and knew each other's work well.

Spencer's admiration for Mill, his senior by fourteen years, began when Spencer was a young man and never waned. For instance, soon after the publication of *Social Statics* in 1850, Spencer wrote to his father of his "evident satisfaction, that his name was being coupled with that of Mr. J. S. Mill."[12] And when Mill died, Spencer wrote an obituary notice for the *Examiner* (May 17, 1873) proclaiming his respect for Mill, as well as his sense of irreparable loss. Among other things, Spencer says that he especially prized those occasions in which their respective philosophical positions converged.[13]

[10] For Gray, see John Gray, *Mill on Liberty: A Defence* and John Gray, "Indirect Utility and Fundamental Rights," *Social Philosophy and Policy*, 1 (1984). For Berger, see Fred Berger, *Happiness, Justice and Freedom* (Berkeley: University of California Press, 1984). For Riley, see Riley, *Liberal Utilitarianism*.

[11] John Gray, *Hayek on Liberty* (Oxford University Press, 1984), p. 106. See also John Gray, "Spencer on the Ethics of Liberty and the Limits of State Interference," *History of Political Thought*, 3 (1982).

[12] Duncan (ed.), *The Life and Letters of Herbert Spencer*, p. 60.

[13] For the full text of Spencer's obituary notice, see Spencer, *An Autobiography*, vol. II, pp. 506–8. Spencer's impressions of Mill in the obituary notice are interesting. Spencer writes, for example, that Mill was excessively concerned with learning and work, which

The heartfelt mutual regard which Spencer and Mill shared is further illustrated by an unusual gesture on Mill's part. Early in 1866, Spencer decided to cease the serial publication of his writings. He had been issuing serialized installments of his books to subscribers for some time and, due to declining subscriptions, decided to abandon further publication. Mill responded to Spencer's predicament by offering to guarantee profitability to Spencer's publishers. When Spencer declined Mill's offer, Mill persisted by arranging for some of Spencer's wealthy admirers to buy up any unsold copies of future works. Spencer reluctantly consented though this scheme became unnecessary as Spencer soon afterwards received $7,000 in public securities purchased in his name by a group of Americans.[14]

In the final chapter of *Utilitarianism*, entitled "Of the Connection Between Justice and Utility," Mill says that justice is composed of "two essential ingredients." These are the "desire to punish" someone for harming others (including oneself) and the "belief that there is some definite individual or individuals to whom harm

hastened his death. Spencer also says of Mill: "Though, being a Utilitarian, knowledge and action must have been regarded by him as subordinate to the gaining of happiness, immediate or remote; yet, practically, this ultimate purpose seemed to be ignored. But though in him the means to happiness had come to occupy the foreground of consciousness, almost to the extent of thrusting out the end, just as it does in the man of business who thinks only of making money, and almost forgets the uses of money" (*An Autobiography*, vol. II, p. 122). For additional evidence of Spencer and Mill's friendship and mutual respect, see Spencer to J. S. Mill, April 3, 1864 in Duncan (ed.), *The Life and Letters of Herbert Spencer*, pp. 114–15. See, as well, from J. S. Mill to Spencer, March 11, 1865 in Duncan (ed.), *The Life and Letters of Herbert Spencer*, pp. 118–19, where Mill informs Spencer of his forthcoming "Auguste Comte and Positivism" in the *Westminster and Foreign Quarterly Review*. He adds: "In forming an estimate of him, I have necessarily come in collision with some of your opinions – a thing for which I should never think of apologizing to you or any advanced thinker; but it has so happened that though our points of agreement very greatly exceed in number and importance those of difference, the latter are those respecting which, accidentally, most has been said to the public, on my side at least. What I have now written, however, will give a very false impression of my feelings, if it raises any idea but that of minor differences of opinion between allies and fellow-combatants. In a larger volume which I shall soon have the pleasure of offering to you, there will be very little or nothing to qualify the expression of the very high value I attach to your philosophic labours." The "larger volume" promised to Spencer was Mill's *Examination of Sir William Hamilton's Philosophy*. Spencer responded in the July 1865 issue of *The Fortnightly Review* with "Mill Versus Hamilton – The Test of Truth," which was republished in *Essays*, vol. II.

14 For Mill's initial rescue proposal and Spencer's response, see Spencer, *An Autobiography*, vol. II, pp. 134–6. Earlier, in 1858, Spencer asked Mill to help him obtain a position at India House. See ibid., vol. II, pp. 22–4. Mill and Spencer also participated in an ill-fated attempt to salvage *The Reader*. *The Reader*, devoted to scientific thought, literary criticism and, in Spencer's words, "the advance of liberal opinion," was sold to Spencer, Mill and others in 1865. Within a year, it was resold and died.

has been done."[15] Let us first compare Spencer and Mill with respect to the latter "ingredient" and then with respect to punishment.

Mill's analysis of the second ingredient of justice is bound up with his notion of a right. While discussing this ingredient, Mill holds that, in most cases, rights are claims to be legally protected (by punishment or the threat thereof) from harm. Moreover, rights and their correlative duties of "perfect obligation" are to be contrasted with non-right claims and their duties of "imperfect obligation." Finally, this contrast is no less than that between justice and beneficence (*Utilitarianism*, pp. 247-8).[16]

As with Mill, Spencer contrasts the conceptual family of justice, rights and enforceable obligation with that of beneficence, non-right claims and unenforceable obligation.[17] Furthermore, both Mill and Spencer attempt to accommodate the former conceptual family with utility in a similar fashion.

[15] J. S. Mill, *Utilitarianism* [1861]in Robson (ed.), *Collected Works* (1969), vol. x, p. 248.

[16] In effect, "duties of imperfect obligation" are weaker duties. They are not, to borrow from P. J. Kelly's analysis of Bentham, "conclusive reasons" for action in the way "duties of perfect obligation" are. See Kelly, *Utilitarianism and Distributive Justice*, p. 68. Regarding my understanding of Mill on the relationship between utility and moral rights, I owe a great deal to Gray's *Mill On Liberty: A Defence* and to Jonathan Riley's *Liberal Utilitarianism*. Riley would remind us that Mill also holds that rights can be enforced by custom and conscience. Moreover, for Riley, "an individual's permanent interests include not only vital interests secured by rights but also important interests not secured thus . . . If someone fails to satisfy those customary expectations [of beneficence], Mill implies, then he harms others, and society legitimately punishes him by opinion though not by law." Jonathan Riley, "One Very Simple Principle," *Utilitas*, 3 (1991), 21. Indeed, Mill does not always sharply differentiate between the conceptual family of justice, rights and *legally* enforceable obligation and the conceptual family of beneficence, non-right claims and unenforceable obligation. For example, "perfect obligation" overlaps with "imperfect obligation" where he says, "When we call anything a person's right, we mean that he has a valid claim on society to protect him in the possession of it, either by the force of law *or* by that of education and opinion." Mill, *Utilitarianism*, p. 250 (my italics). Mill's equivocation reflects the deeper and controvertible distinction between self-regarding and other-regarding interests of his liberty principle. Whereas self-regarding interests fall outside the domain of enforceable obligation, other-regarding interests fall within it. Mill probably inherited the distinction between "perfect" and "imperfect" obligation from Bentham's distinction between "probity" and "beneficence."

[17] For Spencer, beneficence consists in self-restraint and action on behalf of others outside the requirements of the principle of equal freedom. Whereas justice concerns "things which are to be claimed as rights," both kinds of beneficence "concern things which are to be accepted as benefactions." Justice, in short, exemplifies "primary altruism" while beneficence exemplifies "secondary altruism." This distinction is blurred wherever the state tries to furnish its citizens "with the means to happiness" rather than merely securing them the "unhindered pursuit of happiness." Spencer, *The Principles of Ethics*, vol. II, pp. 289–94. Parts V and VI of *The Principles of Ethics*, entitled "Negative Beneficence" and "Positive Beneficence," treat both kinds of beneficence.

Near the close of *Utilitarianism*, Mill carefully addresses the relation of justice and rights to utility. He says, for instance, "Justice is a name for certain *classes of moral rules*, which concern the essentials of human well-being more nearly, and are therefore of more *absolute obligation* than any other rules for the guidance of life; and the notion which we have found to be of the essence of the idea of justice, that of a *right* residing in an individual, implies and testifies to this more binding obligation" (p. 255; my italics). And as the last sentence of *Utilitarianism* concludes, "Justice remains the appropriate name for certain social utilities which are vastly more important, and therefore more *absolute and imperative*, than any others are as a *class* (though not more so than others may be in particular cases); and which, therefore, ought to be, as well as naturally are, guarded by a sentiment not only different in degree, but also in kind; distinguished from the milder feeling which attaches to the mere idea of promoting human pleasure or convenience, at once by the more definite nature of its commands, and by the sterner character of its sanctions" (p. 259; my italics).[18] Moreover, in a letter to George Grote, Mill writes: "human happiness, even one's own, is in general more successfully pursued by acting on *general rules*, than by measuring the consequences of each act; and this is still more the case with the general happiness, since any other plan would not only leave everybody uncertain what to expect, but would involve perpetual quarrelling: and hence *general rules* must be laid down for people's conduct to one another, or in other words *rights and obligations* must, as you say, be recognized" (my italics).[19]

As these passages suggest, and as revisionist interpreters of Mill have argued, Mill was an indirect utilitarian who viewed rights as second-order devices for promoting utility. As a long-term utility strategy, Mill considered strong rights superior.[20]

When Mill was about to issue *Utilitarianism* in book form in early

[18] See, as well, pp. 250–1 where Mill says that "general utility" understood as our "most important and impressive kind[s] of utility," as our "most vital" interests, is the ultimate justification of rights. This justification gives rights their "character of absoluteness."

[19] Mill to George Grote, January 10, 1862 in F. E. Mineka and D. N. Lindley (eds.), *Collected Works*, (1972), vol. xv, p. 762. And see J. S. Mill, "Bentham" [1838] in Robson (ed.), *Collected Works*, (1969), vol. x, pp. 110–11.

[20] I do not wish to join the controversy over whether Mill was what we would term an act-utilitarian or a rule-utilitarian. Alan Ryan suggests that "it is impossible to tie Mill down to a particular view of the relationship between rules and morality." Ryan, *The Philosophy of John Stuart Mill*, p. xviii.

1863, Spencer wrote to Mill in order to remove what he considered a serious misunderstanding on Mill's part. As Spencer saw it, Mill wrongly implied, in a footnote near the end of *Utilitarianism*, that Spencer was anti-utilitarian.[21] The seriousness with which Spencer took this improper characterization is borne out by the fact that Spencer reprinted his letter of clarification to Mill virtually in full in his *An Autobiography* and partially in *The Principles of Ethics*. In his letter, Spencer writes:

> The note in question greatly startled me by implicitly classing me with the Anti-utilitarians. I have never regarded myself as an Anti-utilitarian. My dissent from the doctrine of Utility as commonly understood, concerns not the object to be reached by men, but the method of reaching it. While I admit that happiness is the ultimate end to be contemplated, I do not admit that it should be the proximate end. The Expediency-Philosophy having concluded that happiness is the thing to be achieved, assumes that morality has no other business than empirically to generalize the results of conduct, and to supply for the guidance of conduct nothing more than its empirical generalizations.
>
> But the view for which I contend is, that Morality properly so-called – the science of right conduct – has for its object to determine *how* and *why* certain modes of conduct are detrimental, and certain other modes beneficial. These good and bad results cannot be accidental, but must be necessary consequences of the constitution of things; and I conceive it to be the business of moral science to deduce, from the laws of life and the conditions of existence, what kinds of action necessarily tend to produce happiness, and what kinds to produce unhappiness. Having done this, its deductions are to be recognized as laws of conduct; and are to be conformed to irrespective of a direct estimation of happiness or misery.[22]

Spencer makes two claims in his letter to Mill that warrant emphasis. First, Spencer asserts that he is not an opponent of

[21] Spencer read the earlier 1861 version of *Utilitarianism* that was published in *Fraser's Magazine*. When he learned that Mill was about to publish the essay as a book, he wrote to Mill asking him to delete the offending footnote. Mill replied that it was too late to alter the footnote in proof but that he would append a second footnote acknowledging Spencer's concerns. The two footnotes have been preserved in all subsequent editions of *Utilitarianism*. Mill's second footnote accurately reflects Spencer's position at the time, because Mill allowed Spencer to see the proof of the second footnote and correct it. For Mill's response, see Mill to Herbert Spencer, 25 February, 1863 in Duncan (ed.), *The Life and Letters of Herbert Spencer*, pp. 108–9. For Spencer's follow-up thanking Mill for permitting him to see and correct the second footnote, see Spencer to J. S. Mill, March 1, 1863 in Duncan (ed.), *The Life and Letters of Herbert Spencer*, p. 109.

[22] Spencer, *An Autobiography*, vol. II, pp. 88–9 and Spencer, *The Principles of Ethics*, vol. I, p. 91. See, as well, Spencer, "Morals and Moral Sentiments," *Essays*, vol. I, p. 333; Spencer, "Replies to Criticisms," *Essays*, vol. II, p. 263 and Alexander Bain, *Moral Science* (New York: D. Appleton and Co., 1880), pp. 307-8, where this same letter to Mill is quoted either partially or in full.

utilitarianism; rather he is merely an opponent of utilitarianism as it is "commonly understood" implying that he *is* a utilitarian as "uncommonly understood." The kind of uncommon utilitarianism that he recommends is one which acknowledges that happiness is the final end of human action but denies that it is the "proximate" or intermediate end.

Second, the proper utilitarian "method" of "proximate end[s]" is one that deduces from the "laws of life and the conditions of existence, what kinds of actions necessarily tend to produce happiness, and what kinds to produce unhappiness." These "kinds of actions" are to be adopted as "laws of conduct." They are to be adopted even if alternative strategies of "direct estimation" turn out to maximize happiness better in exceptional cases. That is why such "kinds of action" are "proximate" ends and the utilitarian method which they embody is an indirect one. Moreover, we may surmise that these "kinds of action," or "laws of conduct," refer to specifications of the principle of equal freedom. In short, they refer to strong moral rights.

In *An Autobiography*, after reprinting his letter to Mill, Spencer adds that the immature nature of Bentham's utilitarianism was not unconnected with the fact that, during Bentham's time, scientific "causation" was incompletely understood and that the search for it to explain empirical phenomena had not yet become a "mental habit." Hence, "That the connexions between conduct and consequence in every case are causal, and that ethical theory remains but rudimentary until the causal relations are generalized, was a truth not recognized by them [the Benthamites]" (p. 90). In other words, until utility-causing classes of behaviors are generalized scientifically and protected by stringent moral rights, utilitarian theory will remain impoverished. As he says in his letter to Mill, only when certain "kinds of action" are recognized as "laws of conduct," as "proximate" ends, will happiness best be maximized.

Spencer justifies moral rights in the same indirect utilitarian way in *The Principles of Ethics* where he again discusses his letter to Mill. After noting that he long ago repudiated Mill's suggestion in *Utilitarianism* that he was anti-utilitarian, and after quoting passages from his letter to Mill, Spencer again claims that traditional utilitarians inadequately understand practical causality. They fail to see the "possibility of knowing by deduction from fundamental principles, what conduct *must* be detrimental and what conduct *must* be beneficial" (*The Principles of Ethics*, vol. 1, p. 92). By "fundamental principles," Spencer presumably means the principle of equal freedom and the laws of moral psychology. By "what conduct," he presumably means conduct that ought to be protected by moral rights.[23]

As in his letter to Mill, Spencer reemphasizes that his brand of indirect utilitarianism represents a perfected form of Benthamism. Unfortunately, Benthamites have "disregarded the fact that empirical utilitarianism is but a transitional form to be passed through on the way to rational utilitarianism" (*The Principles of Ethics*, vol. 1, p. 90).

Revisionist interpreters of Bentham would dispute Spencer's characterization of Benthamism as a form of what we would call crude act-utilitarianism. Recently, several scholars have spent much interpretative capital unmasking Bentham for the sophisticated utilitarian that he supposedly was. For instance, P. J. Kelly argues that Bentham cobbled together a largely successful hybrid of indirect as well as direct utilitarianism. According to Kelly, Bentham's utilitarian "system of obligations provides a framework within which individual agents can act on direct utilitarian reasons, without their actions undermining the conditions of social interaction on which the most important sources of utility depend. In this way Bentham combines aspects of a direct and indirect utilitarian theory" (*Utilitarianism and Distributive Justice*, p.69). And insofar as this system of obligations was nothing less than a system of fundamental rights, "Bentham was able to accommodate liberal values such as liberty, equality, and personal inviolability within his theory of distributive justice" (p. 11).[24]

Notwithstanding the accuracy of Spencer's grasp of the dissimilarities between Bentham and himself, the similarities between Mill

[23] Also see Spencer, *The Principles of Ethics*, vol. 1, p. 92. Spencer's discussion and partial citation of his letter to Mill in Part 1 (first published separately as "The Data of Ethics" in 1879) of *The Principles of Ethics* occurs sixteen years after this letter was originally drafted (1863). The complete citation and endorsement of the same letter in *An Autobiography* (1894) occurs thirty-one years later. The continuity of Spencer's indirect utilitarianism is unmistakable. See also Spencer's unpublished "About Carlyle" (1883) where he defends utilitarianism (particularly Mill's version) from Carlyle's "contemptuous condemnation" of it as a "pig philosophy." As far as Spencer was concerned, Carlyle was a crude moral intuitionist for whom "talking Ethics is much like an anatomist dissecting the human body with a hatchet." Herbert Spencer, "About Carlyle," *The Herbert Spencer Papers*, MS. 791/355/4, University of London Library, pp. 18–23.

[24] Also see Ross Harrison, *Bentham* (London: Routledge and Kegan Paul, 1983) pp. 238–41.

and Spencer are, as we have seen, palpable. Indeed, they are more palpable than many imagine. Mill, as some interpreters have stressed, held that direct strategies for maximizing utility, which appeal immediately to aggregate utility in judging policy alternatives, thereby devaluing rights, are self-defeating. They are self-defeating because general happiness is generated when individuals think and act for themselves. General happiness can never be maximized by the state thinking and acting *for*, or on *behalf of*, its citizens. Happiness cannot be served up to people. Those who try, serve up a paltry gruel instead. Happiness is generated by activity, by doing, by striving and by achieving. "Experiments in living," and not administrative distribution from above, produces far more long-term happiness. Second, direct strategies are self-defeating because of human fallibility. No one, particularly government officials, can possibly anticipate all the intertwining consequences of alternative policies. No one is intelligent enough to know how best to promote general welfare directly, how to *make* others happy.[25] The direct pursuit of utility is simply beyond the capacity of human good will and intelligence and would collapse under the weight of its own complexity. Spencer too, as we have seen, voiced similar reservations about the inherently self-defeating dangers of unsophisticated Benthamism. According to Spencer, in *Social Statics*, Benthamism was vaingloriously naive:

> And now, in the midst of his admiration and his awe, the student shall suddenly see some flippant redtapist get upon his legs and tell the world how he is going to put a patch upon nature! Here is a man who, in the presence of all the wonders that encompass him, dares to announce that he and certain of his colleagues have laid their heads together and found out a way to improve upon the Divine arrangements! Scarcely an idea have these meddlers got of what underlies the facts with which they propose to deal, as you shall soon find on sounding their philosophy; and yet, could they carry out their pretensions, we should see them self-appointed nurses to the universe! They have so little faith in the laws of things, and so much faith in themselves, that, were it possible, they would chain earth and sun together, lest centripetal force should fail! Nothing but a Parliament-made agency can be depended upon; and only when this infinitely complex humanity of ours has been put under their ingenious regulations and provided for by

[25] For fine analyses of why Mill thinks that direct utilitarianism is self-defeating, see Gray, *Mill On Liberty: A Defence*, p. 35 and Gray, "Indirect Utility and Fundamental Rights," pp. 79–80. See also Berger, *Happiness, Justice and Freedom*, p. 248.

their supreme intelligence will the world become what it ought to be! Such, in essence, is the astounding creed of these creation menders. (pp. 263–4)

For Spencer, as for Mill, direct utilitarianism was self-defeating because happiness flourishes best where individuals act for themselves. And for Spencer, as for Mill, direct utilitarianism was self-defeating because, in any developed society, the seamless web of individual actions is so complex that no central authority could possibly manage these actions in an optimally maximizing way. In Spencer's words, "Evidence thrust before us every morning shows throughout the body polity a fructifying causation so involved that not even the highest intelligence can anticipate the aggregate effects".[26]

Thus far, we have seen that Mill and Spencer judged direct utilitarianism unsatisfactory principally because it is self-defeating. We have seen why both *rejected* direct utilitarianism. Yet we still need to understand better why both also *embraced* indirect utilitarianism so enthusiastically. For Mill, happiness is ultimately a function of the use and development of "elevated faculties." Humans experience greatest happiness when they exercise and strengthen their higher faculties. Furthermore, as Mill writes in *On Liberty*:

The human faculties of perception, judgement, discriminative feeling, mental activity, and even moral preference, are exercised only in making a choice. He who does anything because it is the custom makes no choice. He gains no practice either in discerning or in desiring what is best. The mental and moral, like the muscular powers, are improved only by being used.[27]

Clearly, for Mill, happiness not only presupposes faculty exercise but it also presupposes *choice* in exercising faculties. Truly exercising faculties means choosing to exercise them. Only when we live autonomously do we have a chance to develop our capacities and be happy. Hence, like Spencer, Mill viewed happiness as an exercise concept, as something that can only be achieved and not provided. And like Spencer, especially in the early *Social Statics*, Mill compared faculty exercise to muscular development.

Both Mill and Spencer, then, bestowed pride of normative place to critical choice-making. But because of the strains of thickening

[26] Spencer, *The Principle of Ethics*, vol. II, p. 269. "Fructifying causation" exemplifies Spencer's "Law of the Multiplicity of Effects" discussed in chapter 1.

[27] J. S. Mill, *On Liberty* [1859] in Robson (ed.), *Collected Works*, (1977), vol. XVII, p. 262.

sociality, both also conferred pride of normative place to their respective liberty principles as well as to their respective theories of moral rights which each thought followed from these principles. Both theorists, that is, deployed their respective liberty principles and systems of moral rights as decision procedures for ensuring the widest possible scope for exercising our talents, for structuring sociality so that everyone enjoys similar basic opportunities for maximizing his or her happiness as best he or she can. If all individuals are to have the same fair chance to choose their happiness as best they can, then all must live within the same juridical restraints on freedom.

Many modern, sympathetic interpreters of Mill might wish to maintain a healthy distance between Mill's and Spencer's versions of liberal utilitarianism for fear that Spencer's ignominious reputation (for us) might sully Mill's liberal credentials. Such fears, however, are unwarranted.

Let us further compare the basic components of Mill's and Spencer's indirect utilitarian strategies to see why such fears are exaggerated. For Mill, good is "utility in the largest sense" of which security, freedom and individuality are the foremost kinds of utilities. They are our "most important and impressive kind[s] of utility," our "most vital of all interests," with security and freedom lexically outranking individuality and deserving the protection of basic moral rights.[28] Hence, "utility in the largest sense" is generated when everyone cultivates his or her individuality (becomes "autonomous" according to John Gray) on the condition that no one's interests in security and freedom are harmed.[29] As long as no one's rights to security and freedom are violated, each is free to make the best of himself or herself as best he or she can. Each is free, that is, to exercise and develop his or her talents and capacities.[30]

[28] For Mill's discussion of security and freedom as being our "most important and impressive kind[s] of utility," as our "most vital of all interests," again see Mill, *Utilitarianism*, pp. 250–1. For Mill's discussion of individuality as being a vital kind of utility, see Mill, *On Liberty*, pp. 260–1.

[29] "I regard utility as the ultimate appeal on all ethical questions; but it must be utility in the largest sense, grounded on the *permanent* interests of man as a progressive being. Those interests, I contend, authorise the subjection of individual spontaneity to external control, only in respect to those actions of each, which concern the interests of other people." Mill, *On Liberty*, p. 224 (my italics). By "permanent interests of man as a progressive being," I take Mill to mean security and freedom.

[30] Remember again the following passage from *Utilitarianism* cited earlier: "Justice is a name for certain classes of moral rules which concern the essentials of human well-being more

Insofar as security and freedom are our most important utilities, they are, as has been suggested, protected by rights. To violate one of these basic rights is to harm someone. To violate these rights is to infringe upon others' "most vital of all interests," to do things which deeply "concern others." For instance, physical assault violates our vital interest in security. Such harms, such violations of rights, are what Mill principally has in mind by harm in his celebrated liberty principle.[31] For Mill, rights are specifications, or "corollaries" as Mill sometimes calls them like Spencer, of this principle. They infuse Mill's liberty principle with practical guidance. When one abides by the liberty principle, one violates no one's fundamental rights. One fulfills one's cardinal "duties of perfect obligation." Moreover, and more importantly, one *empowers* others by providing them equal opportunities to develop as moral individuals in hopes that they will, as a result, respect everyone else's like freedom.

I say "more importantly" deliberately because while Mill regards security and freedom as our most crucial utilities, he nevertheless does not regard them as "higher" utilities or pleasures. The development of individuality, especially moral individuality, is a "higher" pleasure. Security and freedom are so crucial because individuality presupposes them. They are *conditions* that promote individuality indirectly. The different senses in which these three kinds of utilities are important may account for Jonathan Riley and John Gray's disagreement, noted in the "Introduction," over which kind of utility is most vital for Mill. Riley claims that security is more important whereas Gray claims that the development of individuality is more important.[32] However, both Gray and Riley are correct though differing in their emphasis. Security may be more important in the sense that without it individuality is nothing. But individuality is more important because, in the last analysis, it is everything.

The "symbiotic relationship" between security and freedom on

nearly, and are therefore of more absolute obligation than any other rules for the guidance of life; and the notion which we have found to be of the essence of the idea of justice, that of a right residing in an individual, implies and testifies to this more binding obligation." Mill, *Utilitarianism*, p. 255. Rights, that is, are stringent moral rules that protect our essential interests of security and freedom.

[31] Recall that, according to the liberty principle, society is entitled to restrict those individual actions which "concern the [permanent] interests of other people."

[32] For Riley, see again Riley, *Liberal Utilitarianism*, p. 329. For Gray, see John Gray, *Mill On Liberty: A Defence*, p. 117.

the one hand, and individuality on the other, is clear in what has just been said. The rights-protected security of person and property, as well as the rights-protected freedom to choose and act, *enable* individuals to exercise and refine their moral faculties. Morally refined individuality, in turn, causes individuals to behave more justly by respecting one another's basic moral rights. In other words, justice and individuality consolidate one another and "utility in the largest sense" flourishes.[33]

We saw earlier how Spencer's principle of equal freedom, like Mill's liberty principle, comprises the primary decision procedure of his indirect utilitarian strategy. And as with Mill, we saw how moral rights, as second-order derivations of his principle of liberty, function as more detailed decision procedures.

The similarities between their respective versions of liberal utilitarianism go deeper. For Spencer, as we have seen, utilitarians are not only compelled to embrace an indirect strategy due to the psychological fact that happiness results only when faculties, or talents as he reconceptualizes faculties in his later writings, are freely exercised. Utilitarians are also compelled, as we have seen, to embrace an indirect strategy which is rights-oriented because our pleasure-producing interests invariably conflict due to the fact that we live socially. Embracing an indirect, liberal strategy entails, furthermore, that we can differentiate between our most essential pleasure-producing interests and our less essential ones. As specifications of the principle of equal freedom, rights distinguish between these two kinds of interests just as they do as specifications of Mill's liberty principle. Rights mark the bounds of the legitimate exercise of our talents, of legitimate self-development. They identify, protect and harmonize, to borrow Mill's terminology, our most "essential sources of utility." They protect sources of utility which are akin to security and liberty in Mill.[34]

The practice of equal freedom, then, is for Spencer no less than

[33] For an excellent discussion of the symbiosis between security, freedom and individuality in Mill, see Riley, *Liberal Utilitarianism*, pp. 186–90. See also Berger's claim that "Mill began his account and defense of individuality with his claim that it is both an *ingredient* of the good life and a *necessary condition* for the achievement of the other components of well-being." Berger, *Happiness, Justice and Freedom*, p. 233. And see Wendy Donner, *The Liberal Self* (Ithaca: Cornell University Press, 1991), pp. 125 and 186.

[34] In *Social Statics*, Spencer refers to these two most important kinds of rights as the rights to "life" and "personal liberty." In *The Principles of Ethics*, he calls them rights to "physical integrity" and "free motion and locomotion." Unlike Mill, though, Spencer also defends other less rudimentary moral rights. These include rights to the "use of the earth," to

the practice of respect for moral rights. It is no less than the practice of the virtue of self-restraint. Hence, we have returned to a central theme from chapter 2. We now also see that Spencer's liberal utilitarianism is symbiotic like Mill's. By having the state enforce basic rights, Spencer believes that individuals will enjoy a baseline from which to develop their talents, particularly their moral talents. Insofar as they exercise and strengthen their moral talents, insofar as they learn self-restraint, they come to respect basic rights willingly. They come to respect equal freedom willingly. Furthermore, individuals come to enjoy ever-widening opportunities to develop their non-moral talents as well. In short, with Spencer as with Mill, justice and moral individuality reinforce one another. Justice and rights-respecting virtuosity consolidate one another. And as with Mill, this mutually reinforcing symbiosis increases overall utility.

Spencer, then, was as *self-consciously* utilitarian as Mill was, and like Mill (if we follow Berger, Riley and the earlier Gray), he makes a compelling case for rights-oriented, indirect utilitarianism. Given sociality, utilitarians must adopt an indirect strategy because happiness is best maximized when all individuals develop their moral, mental and physical capacities by "exercising" them. The only way to exercise them effectively, especially with regard to moral and mental capacities, is by choosing to exercise them. The only way to improve them is by *deciding for ourselves* as we struggle to resolve the moral and intellectual dilemmas we face. This is why freedom is so sacrosanct for Spencer no less than for Mill. Utilitarians must *also* adopt an indirect strategy which is rights-oriented because individual utilities invariably conflict, making it necessary to distinguish between more and less crucial utilities. As practical decision procedures, Mill's liberty principle and Spencer's equal freedom principle cannot make the requisite subtle distinctions. Their theories of moral rights play this role. Moral rights pick out and protect our baseline interests. They shelter and harmonize our most vital avenues for developing our personalities and making ourselves happy as best we can.

There are, however, two important dissimilarities between Spencer's and Mill's respective efforts to reconcile strong moral rights

"property" and to "free exchange and free contract." We shall examine these additional rights in chapter 6.

with utility. First, Mill's and Spencer's moral rights possess different degrees of stringency. For Mill, rights are stringent but not so stringent that they can never be overridden or subject to critical revision.[35] They are, to employ Richard Flathman's terminology, "moderated" rights.[36]

Spencerian moral rights are less "moderated" than their Millian counterparts. As we have seen, Spencer held that rights issued from practices, customs and usages. Yet, as we have also seen, he held that those that were emerging were indefeasible or *static*. This difference in juridical stringency was not lost on either Spencer or Mill. Both saw this difference as the fundamental difference in their respective versions of liberal utilitarianism.

Let us return to Spencer's 1863 letter to Mill. Recall that, in this letter, Spencer says that the proper science of utility should seek to determine "what kinds of action *necessarily* tend to produce happiness, and what kinds to produce unhappiness" (my italics). That is, as has been stressed previously, only one set of practices promote happiness best with only a critical sub-set of these deserving the protection of rights. Yet, by saying "necessarily tend" and not simply "necessarily," Spencer means that, while only a fixed set of rights-shielded practices maximize happiness, such practices do not always do so. What matters is what happens in most cases over the long run.

As just noted, this difference in rights stringency was not lost on Mill. In response to Spencer's 1863 letter, Mill observed:

> Your explanation narrows the ground on which we differ, though it does not remove our difference; for, while I agree with you in discountenancing a purely empirical mode of judging of the tendencies of human actions, and would on that subject, as well as on all others, endeavour to reach the widest and most general principles attainable, I cannot admit that any of these principles are *necessary*, or that the practical conclusions which can be drawn from them are even (absolutely) universal.[37]

[35] Of Mill's kind of indirect utilitarianism, Gray writes, "The indirect view, inasmuch as its net is cast wider than the scope of social rules, can consistently treat social rules as more than rules of thumb and less than absolutist requirements." See Gray, "Indirect Utility and Fundamental Rights," p. 84. Isaiah Berlin, by contrast, claims that, for Mill, rights are "absolute" and "inviolable." But he adds that, for Mill, rights are also "defined in terms of rules so long and widely accepted that their observance has entered into the very conception of what it is to be a normal human being." This claim implies that rights are consensus-driven and therefore defeasible artifacts. Berlin, "Two Concepts of Liberty," *Four Essays on Liberty*, p. 165.

[36] Richard E. Flathman, "Moderating Rights," *Social Philosophy and Policy*, 1 (1984).

[37] Mill to Herbert Spencer, February 25, 1863 in Duncan (ed.), *The Life and Letters of Herbert Spencer*,

John Gray has suggested that Spencer's moral rights are more moderate than my portrayal of them claims. Gray mentions Spencer's support of military conscription and moderate taxation as concessions to generous defeasibility.[38] However, we should not forget that Spencer held that liberal utilitarian utopia, in which moral rights would be perfectly respected, was a genuine possibility. This would make the state unnecessary, causing it to wither away. Hence, conscription and taxation would wither away as well. In fairness to Gray, by the time he wrote *The Principles of Ethics*, Spencer had become less sanguine about the prospects of liberal utilitarian utopia arriving any time soon. And as he became less sanguine, he became less insistent that moral rights, as corollaries of equal freedom, be respected *now* whatever the cost.

In any case, moral rights always remain ideally indefeasible for Spencer. They eventually become indefeasible, in practice, as liberal societies evolve towards perfection. Again, Spencer means to underscore this indefeasibility by the term "statics" in *Social Statics* and by the expression "absolute ethics" in *The Principles of Ethics*. Of course, should liberal progress cease, as Spencer worried that it had in his later years, defeasibility would reemerge as a feature of moral rights.

Gray also says that it "seems that neither Mill nor Spencer noticed the striking family of resemblance between their respective theories."[39] As we have seen, both were quite aware of these resemblances insofar as both acknowledged the limited differences between them resting on the question of rights stringency.

The limited differences between Mill's and Spencer's versions of liberal utilitarianism are probably related to their differing attitudes towards socialism. Whereas Mill, as is well known, became favorably disposed towards socialism, Spencer remained mostly hostile to it.

p. 108. See also the second footnote of Mill, *Utilitarianism*, p. 258: "With the exception of the word 'necessarily,' I have no dissent to express from this doctrine; and (omitting that word) I am not aware that any modern advocate of utilitarianism is of a different opinion."

[38] John Gray, "Spencer on the Ethics of Liberty and the Limits of State Interference," pp. 476–8. In "Egoism, Obligation, and Herbert Spencer," *Utilitas*, 5 (1993), Martin Wilkinson argues, for similar reasons as Gray, that rights are defeasible for Spencer. See especially pp. 73–4.

[39] John Gray, "Spencer on the Ethics of Liberty and the Limits of State Interference," p. 473. See, as well, T. S. Gray, "Is Herbert Spencer's Law of Equal Freedom a Utilitarian or a Rights-Based Theory of Justice?", *Journal of the History of Philosophy*, 26 (1988). There, T. S. Gray concurs with John Gray in asserting that Spencerian rights are not "doctrinaire" (p. 278). But he also inconsistently claims that, for Spencer, the "right is prior to the good" because Spencer had a "fixed and preconceived view" of the limits of equal freedom (p. 266).

This difference, in turn, is surely related to the stringency differences in their respective theories of rights. A more "moderated," defeasible theory of moral rights, like Mill's, is logically more compatible with socialism. A more moderated theory of rights is friendlier to reconceptualizing freedom as positive power. We should not be surprised, then, that Mill's liberal utilitarian strategy became more welfarist pushing Mill closer to new liberals who followed him such as Green and Hobhouse. Therefore, Wendy Donner may be correct in classifying Millian rights into two kinds, namely "negative" and "positive" rights. For Donner, insofar as Mill holds that basic rights protect our most "important and impressive" kinds of interests (security and liberty), he is led to endorse "positive" as well as "negative" liberal rights. According to Donner, "Positive rights are part of an egalitarian theory of justice, and to leave them out is to miss the core of Mill's liberalism."[40] Liberty, on her interpretation, entails positive rights because "liberty of self-development" is a vital liberty for Mill. Hence, we are perfectly obligated to promote it.[41]

The issue of whether or not Mill's right to liberty includes the liberty of self-development is the heart of Donner's disagreement with Gray about Mill. In Donner's words, "This is one reason why libertarian interpretations of Mill such as that offered by John Gray are so misguided." (*The Liberal Self*, p. 162). They render Mill an elitist for whom the right to liberty applies only to "those who have attained a threshold of autonomy" (p. 182).[42]

The second fundamental difference between Mill's and Spencer's respective theories of moral rights lies in how humans acquire their sense of morality, including their belief in the sanctity of moral rights. For Mill, moral feelings are acquired by each of us during our lifetimes. Each of us must start fresh exercising and developing our moral sentiments through the educative guidance of our cultural milieus. Each of us must relearn the utilitarian value of respecting basic rights. For Spencer, by contrast, moral sentiments were

[40] Donner, *The Liberal Self*, p. 162. We might note T. H. Green's classification of moral rights into "negative rights" and "positive equality of conditions." For an analysis of the juridical similarities in Mill, Spencer and Green, see my "The Discourse of Freedom, Rights and Good in Nineteenth-Century English Liberalism," *Utilitas*, 3 (1991).

[41] See especially Donner, *The Liberal Self*, chapter 8.

[42] For Gray's discussion of Mill's right to liberty as a right to autonomy, see especially Gray, *Mill On Liberty: A Defence*, pp. 52–7. However, if Donner's Mill is the correct Mill, then why did Mill and Spencer fail to appreciate this formidable and obvious difference between them?

acquired inheritances which each generation of individuals strengthened, in turn, through exercise before passing them along to the next generation. As Spencer wrote to Mill, "I believe that the experiences of utility organized and consolidated through all past generations of the human race, have been producing corresponding nervous modifications, which, by continued transmission and accumulation, have become in us certain faculties of moral intuition – certain emotions responding to right and wrong conduct, which have no apparent basis in the individual experience of utility."[43] Thus, given that respect for moral rights is our most vital moral emotion, it is fundamentally an accumulated species experience rather than exclusively an individual experience as it is with Mill.

Whereas Gray discounts these limited though important differences between Mill and Spencer, holding, furthermore, that neither appreciated how similar their versions of liberal utilitarianism were, Jonathan Riley prefers to emphasize their differences. For Riley, contrary to Berger, Gray and myself, Mill's liberty principle is not an equal freedom principle from which basic moral rights are derived. Rather, Mill's liberty principle stipulates that all individuals possess a basic moral right to liberty with respect to self-regarding actions only. In Riley's words, "Mill's liberty principle says each person has a *moral right* to liberty in that sense [acting as he desires] if and only if his conduct is purely self-regarding."[44] As I understand Riley, all other basic rights – like property rights – are, for Mill, defined in terms of other-regarding actions with the aim of establishing security of expectations. The latter, in other words, are not based on the liberty principle.

In any case, for Riley, Mill's liberty principle is not an equal freedom principle. Riley holds that such a principle is "fundamental to all liberal doctrines that subscribe to the rule of law" adding that "Mill's doctrine would be nothing new" if his liberty principle amounted to nothing more than that. Rather, Mill is "defending far

[43] Quoted in Bain, *The Emotions and the Will*, p. 722. Also cited in Young, *Mind, Brain and Adaptation*, pp. 177-8. Darwin, likewise, faulted Mill's moral theory for the same reason: "Mr. Bain (see, for instance, 'The Emotions and the Will,' p. 481) and others believe that the moral sense is acquired by each individual during his lifetime. On the general theory of evolution this is at least extremely improbable. The ignoring of all transmitted mental qualities will, as it seems to me, be hereafter judged as a most serious blemish in the works of Mr. Mill." Darwin, *The Descent of Man*, p. 472, note 5.

[44] Riley, "One Very Simple Principle," p. 33. I am also indebted to personal correspondence from Jonathan Riley for his views on the differences between Mill's and Spencer's liberty principles.

more than" the rule of law "insisting that legal and moral rules (however impartial) do not properly extend to purely self-regarding conduct. Society has no legitimate authority (whether in the form of law or customary opinion) within self-regarding spheres." Equal liberty *qua* the rule of law, in short, "offers the individual no protection whatsoever from majority despotism in his private affairs."[45]

One might concede that Mill's liberty principle is no equal freedom principle especially on Riley's understanding of equal freedom. In effect, Riley understands equal freedom in the same way that Wiltshire understands it leading him to condemn it for similar reasons. For Wiltshire, remember, "no limits are specified" by the principle of equal freedom throwing its interpretation "open to whim." In other words, for Wiltshire as for Riley, the principle of equal freedom does not *guarantee* a moral right to liberty with respect to our self-regarding actions. But, we saw that Spencer's version of equal freedom was not "open to [interpretative] whim" insofar as it enshrined the freedom to choose as a basic, universal right. Moreover, in Spencer's case, the principle of equal freedom was no empty, and therefore no dangerously illiberal, gesture. Thus, the principle of equal freedom can be fully compatible with protecting self-regarding action, depending on how we specify the principle's derivative rights.[46]

At least one of Mill and Spencer's contemporaries seems to have understood them as liberal utilitarians whose conceptions of freedom were nearly identical. In his 1879 review in *Mind* of Spencer's "The Data of Ethics," Alexander Bain correctly concludes that both prized guaranteeing every individual a sphere of free choice though he wrongly underplays Spencer's awareness of the powerful similarities between himself and Mill. Bain observes:

> How the greatest happiness of mankind is to be arrived at remains open for discussion. There is a general agreement at the present day that the best course is for each individual to occupy a *limited sphere* without thinking of the universal happiness. Mr. Spencer seems to me to be arguing for several pages without an opponent. The expressions that he quotes from Bentham

[45] Ibid., pp. 35–6.

[46] Despite wanting to maintain a healthy distance between Mill's and Spencer's version of liberal utilitarianism, Riley has suggested to me that Mill's right to liberty in self-regarding matters is indefeasible. Therefore, it is as strong as any of Spencer's moral rights. If Riley is correct about the indefeasibility of the right to liberty for Mill, then the distance between Mill and Spencer may be even smaller than I have suggested.

and Mill need to be taken along with their whole system, which is, to my mind, not so very far from Mr. Spencer's own. They would say that Society should confine itself to *protecting each man and woman in the pursuit of their own happiness in their own way.* This is the text of Mill's *Liberty.* I admit that they are not able to prove beyond dispute, that the greatest Happiness will be attained in this form; but as far as the needful computation can be carried, they think it is in favour of such an arrangement. (my italics)[47]

This section began by promising to compare Mill and Spencer with respect to both of Mill's "two essential ingredients" of justice. Thus far, we have focused upon the extensive similarities and limited but significant dissimilarities with respect to Mill's first ingredient, namely the "belief that there is some definite individual or individuals to whom harm has been done." Let us now compare Spencer to Mill's second ingredient of justice in *Utilitarianism,* namely the "desire to punish" someone for causing harm to others. Here again, the similarities between Mill and Spencer are formidable and surprising.

Regarding the "desire to punish," Mill holds that it is the outgrowth of two instincts. These are self-defense and sympathy. We are naturally inclined to retaliate against those who harm or attempt to harm us, and our natural capacity to sympathize with others inclines us to retaliate on their behalf when they too are harmed or threatened. This natural capacity to sympathize is supplemented, furthermore, by the powers of human intelligence which lead individuals to see that their own self-defense is bound up with that of their community. Insofar as the "desire to punish" remains selfish, insofar as sympathy and intelligence cause us to retaliate on behalf of others merely because we feel that harm to them rebounds upon us, it "has nothing moral in it." (Mill, *Utilitarianism,* p. 249). Punishment (and pain avoidance) only becomes moralized when the desire to do it stems from a normative concern for the general good. Moralized punishment only arises when persons resent a "hurt to society, though not otherwise a hurt to themselves" or when they do not resent a "hurt to themselves however painful, unless it be of the kind which society has a common interest with them in the repression of" (p. 54).

Now Spencer, as we should recall from chapter 2, defends a similar theory of punishment and retaliation in *The Principles of Ethics.* There, we saw how Spencer viewed retaliation as reinforcing

[47] Alexander Bain, "Critical Notices, The Data of Ethics," *Mind,* 4 (1879), 566.

the emergence of sympathy and how he viewed sympathy as a sentiment that causes individuals to experience the unhappiness of others stemming from interference with their actions. This, in turn, causes individuals to affirm not simply their own egoistic claims to happiness-producing free action but to affirm altruistically like claims on behalf of others. As with Mill, sympathy moralizes pain avoidance. With Spencer, though, sympathy does not arise from a normative concern for the general interest as it does with Mill. Consequently, Spencer's psychology of sympathy is not moralized in Mill's precise sense. Mill might say that Spencer's later moral theory ultimately remains egoistic and thus "has nothing moral in it."[48]

The following schema illustrates the similarities between Mill and Spencer (in *The Principles of Ethics*) on punishment:

Spencer
- Two rudimentary sentiments of justice
  - egoistic sentiment
  - altruistic sentiment
- Sympathy generates altruism out of egoism
- Proto-altruistic sentiment of retaliation separately reinforces this generation

Mill
- Two instincts comprising "desire to punish"
  - instinct of self-defense
  - instinct of sympathy
- Sympathy extends self-defense to defense of others
- Intelligence contributes to this extension

For Spencer, sympathy transforms egoistic sentiments into altruistic ones by extending the range of our opportunities for experiencing pleasure and pain. In Mill, sympathy transforms self-defense instincts into sincere claims on behalf of others.

There are other differences between Mill's and Spencer's psychologies of punishment. For instance, whereas Mill sees punishment as part of the meaning of justice and as evolving from our instincts of

[48] Spencer admits as much when he says that though "altruistic pleasure, as being a part of the consciousness of one who experiences it, can never be other than egoistic, it will not be consciously egoistic." Spencer, *The Principles of Ethics*, vol. I, p. 279. See, too, Spencer's remark on p. 283 that: "In its ultimate form, then, altruism will be the achievement of gratification through sympathy with those gratifications of others which are mainly produced by their activities of all kinds successfully carried on – sympathetic gratification which costs the receiver nothing, but is a gratis addition to his egoistic gratifications."

self-defense and sympathy, Spencer does not regard punishment as part of the meaning of justice. Rather, for him in *The Principles of Ethics*, punishment is a "proto-altruistic" sentiment separate from sympathy which buttresses the latter during its formative emergence. Punishment *qua* "revenge" or "retaliation" begins as an impulse to repay injuries with rough equivalents leading early humans to behave more circumspectly.

So if Spencer's psychology of sympathy is not fully moralized in Mill's sense, should we concede that Spencer's utilitarianism is not genuinely utilitarian? Is it possible that Spencer is simply an egoistic hedonist? Though an important question, it is best to postpone answering it until chapter 6 which takes up Spencer's methods of moral reasoning in detail.

Spencer, plainly enough, understands moral rights much as Mill understood them. For Spencer as well as for Mill, moral rights indirectly foster utility. They best promote general happiness on balance and over the long run but not necessarily in each short-term case. This is because maximizing general happiness requires that all individuals exercise their talents (or "faculties" in Mill's terminology and in Spencer's early terminology). This, in turn, entails that all have the freedom to exercise their talents which further entails that all enjoy extensive rights-secured opportunities. Hence, Spencer was a liberal utilitarian, much as Mill was. Nevertheless, Spencer's theory of rights differs from Mill's in two significant respects. First, in contrast to Mill, Spencerian moral rights are indefeasible. Overriding them, or extending their reach as later liberals advocated, is never justified (at least insofar as liberal societies begin approaching liberal perfection). For Spencer, only a fixed array of moral rights tends to maximize general utility. Second, compared to Mill, Spencer held that respect for moral rights was an inheritable talent tending to grow stronger over time as each generation cultivated this talent passing it along strengthened to the next. For Mill, moral individuality was not an inheritable characteristic. Rather, moral sentiments, including our sense of justice, were acquired by each individual during his or her lifetime only.

Both Mill and Spencer, then, were utilitarians who also took moral rights seriously (although Spencer took them more seriously). And precisely because they took moral rights so seriously, precisely because they regarded them as second-order, decision procedures "imposing constraints on utilitarian policy," to borrow from Gray, Spencer was just as much of an indirect liberal utilitarian as Mill.

CHAPTER 5

The logical coherence of Spencer's liberal utilitarianism

Liberal utilitarianism, so it now seems, has a rich historical tradition of its own that is neither unsophisticated nor meager. R. B. Brandt, R. M. Hare, John Gray, L. W. Sumner and Jonathan Riley may have provided it with a twentieth-century analytic voice, but Spencer, *as much as* Mill, fathered it in order to rescue Victorian utilitarianism from what he viewed as the troubled legacy of Bentham. Spencer, *as much as* Mill therefore, deserves our critical attention and maybe even our homage. But to pay Spencer the homage that he deserves as one of liberal utilitarianism's founders is not to suggest that his version of it fares any better than Mill's version of it or, for that matter, later analytical versions. Though liberal utilitarianism may exhibit considerable ethical appeal precisely because of its zest for strong moral rights and respect for individual integrity while remaining faithful to the maximization of utility, it nevertheless may be incurably flawed. Indeed, its ethical appeal may be the very source of its failure. By endeavoring to accommodate liberal values with a consequentialist theory of good, liberal utilitarianism, in the eyes of its critics, tries to reconcile the irreconcilable. Utilitarianism, according to these critics, cannot be made ethically appealing in the liberal sense without forgoing its systematic coherence. It supposedly cannot cherish moral rights and individual integrity without abandoning its commitment to systematizing morality according to one *exclusive* criterion of good. Utilitarianism, it is argued, cannot be made sufficiently liberal. Since the logic of moral reasoning supposedly does not allow for this possibility, one must choose between liberalism and utilitarianism. Only the philosophically naive and foolhardy dare cross the Rubicon of liberal utilitarianism.

Spencer nevertheless crossed this Rubicon although he seems not to have appreciated that he was doing anything of the kind. Spencer, like Mill, felt that utilitarianism could be improved and made liberal without risking what seems so obviously perilous to many of us today.

So where accommodating stringent moral rights and utility seems sufficiently unpromising for modern critics of liberal utilitarianism, Spencer believed, like Mill, that utilitarianism could be improved by making it attractively liberal as well as systematically coherent. Yet, on one level, Spencer's rights theory did not logically jeopardize his utilitarianism. With respect to political, as opposed to moral rights, consequentialist considerations were *always* overriding for Spencer. Hence, any treatment of the logical coherence of Spencer's liberal utilitarianism must address his theory of political rights as well as his theory of moral rights.

The first section of this chapter examines what Spencer refers to as "political rights." For Spencer, such rights are not genuine derivations of the principle of equal freedom and, hence, are not genuine moral rights. According to him, as respect for authentic moral rights deepens, political rights become redundant, withering into irrelevance with the withering away of the state. Yet, insofar as societies remain normatively immature, such rights are necessary for protecting genuine moral rights.

My analysis of Spencer's theory of political rights includes an extended discussion of his defense of universal suffrage which he modified in his later writings. But the starting point of my treatment of Spencer's theory of political rights will be his "right to ignore the state" of *Social Statics.* This right deserves special attention because of its implications, some of which are confusing, for Spencer's theory of political rights and for his theory of the state. This right also deserves special attention because of the way in which Spencer's defense of it anticipates core ideas of modern philosophical libertarians like Robert Nozick.

In the second section of this chapter, we shall return to the larger issue of the logical compatibility between strong moral rights and utility. If moral rights as robust as Spencer's prove incompatible with consequentialist reasoning, then liberal utilitarianism has distinct logical limits.

POLITICAL RIGHTS

In order to assess fully Spencer's marriage of strong rights and the principle of utility, a crucial distinction needs to be drawn, namely that between what he refers to as "rights properly so-called" and "political rights." "Rights properly so-called" are authentic specifications of equal freedom. Only such rights are necessary conditions of happiness and are, as a consequence, genuine moral rights. "Political rights," by contrast, are impermanent and defeasible. They are interim devices made necessary by our provisional moral imperfection. Insofar as our imperfection continues to make government necessary, they help insure that government does not degenerate into an enemy of justice by threatening moral rights proper. As a necessary evil, government can too easily lose sight of its liberal utilitarian purposes unless "political rights" are sustained. The "right to ignore the state" and the right of universal suffrage are the most interesting and most important of Spencer's political rights.[1]

Spencer's only sustained argument for the "right to ignore the state" occurs in a chapter by the same name in the original 1851 edition of *Social Statics*. Near the beginning of this unusual chapter, Spencer remarks:

> Hence, there is a certain inconsistency in the attempt to determine the right position, structure, and conduct of a government by appeal to the first principles of rectitude. For, as just pointed out, the acts of an institution which is in both nature and origin imperfect cannot be made to square with the perfect law. All that we can do is to ascertain, firstly, in what attitude a legislature must stand to the community to avoid being by its mere existence an embodied wrong; secondly, in what manner it must be constituted so as to exhibit the least incongruity with the moral law; and thirdly, to what sphere its actions must be limited to prevent it from multiplying those breaches of equity it is set up to prevent.
>
> The first condition to be conformed to before a legislature can be established without violating the law of equal freedom is the acknowledgment of the right now under discussion – the right to ignore the state. (*Social Statics*, pp. 186–7)[2]

The spadework for this "first condition" of moral legislation occurs in the chapter, "Political Rights," which immediately precedes "The Right to Ignore the State." Essentially an attack on social contract

[1] Inasmuch as "political rights" are not full moral rights, they lack the intuitive force of moral rights whether considered as moral sense intuitions in *Social Statics* or as inherited intuitions in Spencer's later writings. Their lack of intuitive force reflects their weaker normative status and helps account for Spencer's disenchantment with them after *Social Statics*.

[2] Of three dimensions in which we can "ascertain" the morality of government, Spencer puts the "attitude" which a "legislature must stand to the community" first. That is, he puts the "right to ignore the state" first.

theory, "Political Rights" also defends the indefeasibility of fundamental moral rights. In order to demonstrate that social contract theorists err in supposing that individuals, in the state of nature, compromise the inviolability of their fundamental moral rights when they contract themselves into the advantages of political society, Spencer offers a hypothetical dialogue between himself and a proponent of social contract theory.

After first getting his hypothetical opponent to concede that guaranteeing essential rights, for the sake of promoting faculty exercise and happiness, is the purpose of a social contract, Spencer quickly shepherds him into a tangle of absurdities. First, Spencer says that both surely agree that individuals form communities for the "preservation of their rights." After his adversary readily concurs, Spencer retorts that his adversary also claims that "men give up their rights on entering the social state." When the latter concurs again, Spencer accuses him of nonsensically implying that "on becoming members of a society men give up what by your own showing they joined it the better to obtain" (*Social Statics*, p. 183).

Next, Spencer suggests that it might be more judicious to say that, when founding a political community, participants place their rights in a fiduciary trust administered by government. Spencer then rhetorically asks, "A government, then, is a kind of agent employed by members of a community to take care of, and administer for their benefit, something given into its charge?" (*Social Statics*, p. 183). When his adversary agrees, Spencer delivers his knockout blow:

> "And the things committed to its charge still belong to the original owners? The title of the people to the rights they have placed in trust continues valid; the people may demand from this agent the full benefit accruing from these rights and may, if they please, resume possession of them?"
>
> "Not so."
>
> "Not so! What, can they not reclaim their own?"
>
> "No. Having once consigned their rights to the keeping of a legislature, they must be content with such use of them as that legislature permits."
>
> And thus we arrive at the curious doctrine above referred to, that the members of a community, having entrusted an estate (their rights) to the care of a steward (their government), thereby lose all proprietorship in such estate and can have no benefit from it, except what their steward pleases to vouchsafe! (*Social Statics*, p. 184)

Having debunked and humbled his hypothetical opponent to his satisfaction, Spencer proceeds to defend the "right to ignore the state" in the brief and provocative chapter by the same name. The chapter opens as follows:

> As a corollary to the proposition that all institutions must be subordinated to the law of equal freedom, we cannot choose but admit the right of the citizen to adopt a condition of voluntary outlawry. If every man has freedom to do all that he wills, provided he infringes not the equal freedom of any other man, then he is free to drop connection with the state – to relinquish its protection and to refuse paying toward its support. It is self-evident that in so behaving he in no way trenches upon the liberty of others, for his position is a passive one, and while passive he cannot become an aggressor. It is equally self-evident that he cannot be compelled to continue one of a political corporation without a breach of the moral law, seeing that citizenship involves payment of taxes; and the taking away of a man's property against his will is an infringement of his rights (p. 121). Government being simply an agent employed in common by a number of individuals to secure to them certain advantages, the very nature of the connection implies that it is for each to say whether he will employ such an agent or not. If any one of them determines to ignore this mutual-safety confederation, nothing can be said except that he loses all claim to its good offices and exposes himself to the danger of maltreatment – a thing he is quite at liberty to do if he likes. He cannot be coerced into political combination without a breach of the law of equal freedom; he can withdraw from it without committing any such breach, and he has therefore a right so to withdraw. (*Social Statics*, p. 185)[3]

This passage, of course, is extraordinary for the way it foreshadows Nozick's theory of the minimal state. Nozick, appropriately, acknowledges Spencer's influence.[4]

The "right to ignore the state" is a perplexing right because Spencer is never clear whether this right is a "right properly so-called" or merely a "political right." The passage cited above implies that this right is a "corollary" of the principle of equal freedom. In other words, "the right to ignore the state" is a "right properly so-called" and not an inferior "political right." This inter-

[3] See also the chapter "The Limit of State Duty," pp. 246–7.

[4] Nozick refers to Spencer in *Anarchy, State and Utopia* (New York: Basic Books, 1974) in two endnotes in his chapter, "Demoktesis." While discussing "ancorpy," Nozick acknowledges Spencer's "right to ignore the state." By "ancorpy," Nozick means "isolated nonstockheld individuals" living independently in the midst of more-than-minimal states. See especially Nozick, *Anarchy, State and Utopia*, pp. 289–90. Nozick, however, does not defend the right of individuals to opt out of the minimal state's protection as Spencer does. He only defends this right with respect to more-than-minimals. Minimal states, by contrast, can force independents to join provided they receive compensation which, in effect, amounts to discounted protection. Whereas for Spencer, individuals can relinquish their citizenship and take their chances to defend their rights as best they can alone, for Nozick, nobody goes unprotected.

pretation is supported by the closing paragraphs of the chapter, where Spencer says that the "practicability" of this right "varies directly as social morality." While it would produce "anarchy" in a "thoroughly vicious" society, it would become "innocuous and inevitable" in a "completely virtuous" one (*Social Statics*, p. 193).[5] In other words, the "right to ignore the state" is an attribute of moral perfection. Yet, with moral progress, as the state begins withering away, this right becomes ironically superfluous.

Usually, though, Spencer infers that the "right to ignore the state" is but a "political right." For example, the chapter entitled "The Right to Ignore the State" appears in Part III of *Social Statics*. Part III analyzes various "political rights" as well as the limits of state responsibility. In short, it focuses on interim political arrangements for liberal utilitarian societies still in the thick of social transformation.

Spencer's "right to ignore the state" is puzzling in other respects. Except for the original 1851 edition of *Social Statics*, Spencer never discusses this right systematically again. The abridged and revised 1892 *Social Statics* drops the original's chapter on the "right to ignore the state" altogether. Spencer, nevertheless, may be thinking of this right in *The Principles of Sociology* when he claims that, in highly advanced industrial societies, people shall not only carry out private transactions voluntarily but shall also "voluntarily cooperate to form and support a governmental agency" (vol. II, p. 612).

By 1894, when Spencer wrote his *An Autobiography*, he explicitly repudiated the "right to ignore the state." In a hypothetical review of *Social Statics* included in *An Autobiography* and meant to illustrate how his views had changed since the publication of *Social Statics*, he says that the "right to ignore the state" is the "strangest and most indefensible doctrine in the book." And of the implication, which he formerly endorsed, that this right entitles one to ignore the state so long as one also forsakes all advantages of state protection, he now observes:

But how can he surrender them [the advantages of state protection]? In whatever way he maintains himself, he must make use of sundry appliances which are indirectly due to governmental organization; and he cannot avoid benefiting by the social order which government maintains. Even if

[5] Spencer goes on to say that the "right to ignore the state" originates with our moral sense just like the principle of equal freedom.

> he lives on a moor and makes shoes, he cannot sell his goods or buy the things he wants, without using the road to the neighboring town, and profiting by the paving and perhaps the lighting when he gets there. And though he may say he does not want police-guardianship, yet, in keeping down footpads and burglars, the police necessarily protect him whether he asks them or not. Surely it is manifest – as indeed Mr. Spencer himself elsewhere implies – that the citizen is so entangled in the organization of his society, that he can neither escape the evils nor relinquish the benefits which come to him from it. (*An Autobiography*, vol. I, p. 362)

So now the "right to ignore the state" allows for freeriders, undermining our obligations to society which derive from the benefits of living in society. It harms others and, therefore, violates the principle of equal freedom. It is no genuine moral right at all but, instead, undermines basic moral rights.

Spencer discusses suffrage rights at length in *Social Statics*, *The Principles of Ethics* and in some intervening essays. However, insofar as *Social Statics* and the later *The Principles of Ethics* represent the chronological and theoretical spectrum along which his views on suffrage rights moved, we shall focus mostly on them.

Spencer's defense of universal suffrage in *Social Statics* occurs in the chapter, "The Constitution of the State," which immediately follows "The Right to Ignore the State." Spencer opens "The Constitution of the State" boldly though not without ambiguity. Few deductions from the "law of equal freedom," he affirms, are more evident than the conclusion that "all members of a community have like claims to political power." This conclusion follows because if each "has freedom to do all that he wills, provided he infringes not the equal freedom of any other man, then each is free to exercise the same authority in legislation as his fellows; and no individual or class can exercise greater authority than the rest without violating the law" (*Social Statics*, p. 194). Equal legislative participation, insofar as it is a deduction from equal freedom, is effectively, therefore, a "right properly so-called."

However, Spencer continues:

> Evidently, therefore, a purely democratic government is the only one which is morally admissible – is the only one that is not intrinsically criminal. As lately shown, no government can have any ethical authority. The highest form it can assume is that in which the moral law remains passive with regard to it – tolerates it – no longer protests against it. The first condition of that form is that citizenship shall be voluntary; the second, that it shall confer equal privileges. (*Social Statics*, p. 195)

In other words, universal suffrage ("equal privileges" of participation) is one of two conditions for making government as morally unobjectionable as possible. Together with the "right to ignore the state," the right to vote insures that government, a necessary evil even at its libertarian best, transgresses the principle of equal freedom minimally. Therefore, the right to vote is necessarily a "political right." It cannot be a "right properly so-called." And like all political rights, it would wither into irrelevance as the last vestiges of government wither away as liberal societies reach liberal utilitarian maturity. Hence, no less than with "the right to ignore the state," Spencer's theory of "political rights" is ambiguous. Sometimes suffrage rights are genuine moral rights and sometimes they are merely a species of evanescent political rights.

The remainder of "The Constitution of the State" is principally devoted to justifying universal suffrage. For instance, Spencer claims that "the interest of the whole society can be secured only by giving power into the hands of the whole people," that granting the masses voting rights would not result in legislation inevitably "twisted to serve the ends of labor regardless of the claims of property," that the lower classes are no less moral than the upper and middle classes and would therefore vote just as responsibly, that they are not politically more ignorant than other voters, and that the "failure of past efforts made by society to preserve the erect attitude of democracy by no means shows that such an attitude is not the proper one" (*Social Statics*, pp. 197–214). Yet Spencer also concedes that universal suffrage might legitimately generate legislation overriding the property of the "rich hundreds" if the "poor thousands" benefited. Hence, a mere "political right" can sometimes trump the "properly-so called" right of property (p. 198)!

Spencer concludes "The Constitution of the State" reassuringly. Skeptics of universal suffrage need not worry because, he says, moral refinement will prevent democracies from passing legislation violating, rather than upholding, "men's rights" (*Social Statics*, p. 218). Moreover, we will know that their moral sensibilities have become sufficiently refined as soon as the masses begin peacefully agitating for universal suffrage. Such agitation is symptomatic of their readiness to handle democracy responsibly, of their recognition that the whole point of democracy is the protection of basic rights. Furthermore, each episode of peaceful agitation is a "kind of apprenticeship to the liberties obtained by [universal suffrage]. The power to get freedom becomes the measure of the power to use it" (p. 222).

Spencer's defense of universal suffrage in *Social Statics* clearly reveals that he does not generally consider the right to vote a genuine moral right. The former is merely a political device for protecting the latter. This evaluative distinction between mere "political rights," like the right to vote, and "rights properly so-called" becomes sharper in Spencer's later writings helping to account for his declining enthusiasm for democracy.

We next encounter Spencer's treatment of democracy and suffrage in the 1857 "Representative Government – What is it Good For?," an essay that begins listing the flaws of representative government. Spencer now claims, firstly, that voters seldom possess the "will" to elect honest and diligent representatives. Secondly, even if they possess the requisite will, their "ability" to follow its dictates is doubtful.[6] Lastly, representative democracy is "complex and cumbrous" and is "manifestly inferior to monarchial government" in terms of administrative efficiency (*Essays*, vol. III, p. 309). Still, democratic representation is the lesser evil: "Abundant evidence shows that the maintenance of equitable relations among its subjects, which forms the essential business of a ruling power, is surest when the ruling power is of popular origin" (vol. III, p. 317).

Spencer treats universal suffrage again in his 1860 "Parliamentary Reform," an essay mainly aimed at discouraging legislation beyond that required for protecting basic rights. Spencer recommends: (1) making taxation direct in order to make voters feel immediately the added cost of each new piece of legislation and (2) spreading "sounder views" among the working class. For Spencer, "sounder views" result from the "knowledge of Social Science" giving us a "true theory of government – a true conception of what legislation is for, and what are its proper limits."[7]

"Parliamentary Reform" betrays Spencer's deepening misgivings about universal suffrage inasmuch as it discloses his growing tendency to view universal suffrage as a usually efficacious, though *not* foolproof, means for promoting equal freedom and moral rights. As Spencer declares, "The greatest attainable amount of individual liberty being the true end; and the diffusion of political power being

[6] Herbert Spencer, "Representative Government – What is it Good For?," *Essays*, vol. III, pp. 292–4.

[7] Herbert Spencer, "Parliamentary Reform," *Essays*, vol. III, p. 378.

regarded mainly as a means to this end; the real question when considering further extension of the franchise is – whether the average freedom of action of citizens will be increased? – whether men will be severally freer than before to pursue the objects of life in their own way?" (*Essays*, vol. I, p. 382).[8]

By the time he wrote *The Principles of Ethics*, Spencer's souring enthusiasm for universal suffrage gives way to antipathy. In the chapter, "Political Rights – So-Called," he again observes that the right to vote has been the most effective tool for protecting fundamental rights:

> The confusion between means and ends has in this case been almost inevitable . . . And as experience has shown that a wider distribution of political power is followed by decrease of these trespasses, maintenance of a popular form of government has come to be identified with the maintenance of rights, and the power of giving a vote, being instrumental to maintenance of rights, has come to be regarded as itself a right. (*The Principles of Ethics*, vol. II, pp. 195–6)

However, he concludes that political rights no longer secure basic rights:

> Hence voting being simply a method of creating an appliance for the preservation of rights, the question is whether universal possession of votes conduces to creation of the best appliance for preservation of rights. We have seen above that it does not effectively secure this end; and we shall hereafter see that under existing conditions it is not likely to secure it. (vol. II, pp. 198–9)

Spencer's analysis of the relationship between political and basic moral rights in *The Principles of Ethics* removes an ambiguity which plagues his earlier works, particularly *Social Statics*. Remember that in the latter, universal suffrage is sometimes a "right properly so-called" and sometimes a "political right." By "Political Rights – So-Called" of *The Principles of Ethics*, this ambiguity vanishes. Spencer now disparages universal suffrage as merely a means, as one appliance among others (and not even the best at that), for defending

[8] Twenty-two years later, in *The Study of Sociology*, Spencer remains skeptical about universal suffrage: "This worship of the *appliances* of liberty in place of liberty itself, needs continually exposing. There is no intrinsic virtue in votes. The possession of representatives is not itself of benefit. These are but *means* to an end; and the end is the maintenance of those conditions under which each citizen may carry on his life without further hindrances from other citizens than are involved by their claims" (p. 252, my italics).

genuine rights. Indeed, by the end of the chapter, Spencer condemns universal suffrage as a peril to equal freedom and basic rights.

Spencer concludes "Political Rights – So-Called" by observing that the concept of a right is a "composite" and that the unwary may err in mistaking the presence of both elements of the composite when only one is present. He continues:

> As repeatedly shown, the positive element in the conception is liberty, while the negative element is the limitation implied by other's equal liberties. But the two rarely coexist at all. There may be liberty exercised without any restraint; resulting in perpetual aggressions and universal warfare. Conversely, there may be an equality in restraints which are carried so far as practically to destroy liberty . . . Now the confusion of thought above pointed out, which leads to this classing of so-called political rights with rights properly so-called, arises in part from thinking of the secondary trait, equality, while not thinking of the primary trait, liberty. (*The Principles of Ethics*, vol. II, p. 198)

In other words, overemphasizing the importance of equality when theorizing about rights leads to confusing merely "political" with genuine rights. Presumably, an overexaggerated concern for equality causes people to believe that greater equality necessarily expands freedom and that therefore whatever promotes the redistribution of wealth (as universal suffrage tends to do) also promotes freedom.

Two chapters later, in "The Constitution of the State," Spencer is more explicit. The right to vote no longer follows deductively from the principle of equal freedom: "It appears undeniable that if, in pursuance of the law of equal freedom, men are to have equal rights secured to them, they ought to have equal powers in appointing the agency which secures such rights." He then adds that "this is not a legitimate corollary" (*The Principles of Ethics*, vol. II, pp. 211–12). Universal suffrage is not a universal right.

As an alternative to universal suffrage, Spencer advocates limited suffrage based on "interests." He says:

> It is not true, then, that the possession of political power by all ensures justice to all. Contrariwise, experience makes obvious that which should have been obvious without experience, that with a universal distribution of votes the larger class will inevitably profit at the expense of the smaller class. Those higher earnings which more efficient actions bring to the superior, will not be all allowed to remain with them, but part will be drafted off in some indirect way to eke out the lower earnings of the less diligent or the less capable; and in so far as this is done, the law of equal freedom must be broken. Evidently the constitution of the state appropriate

to that industrial type of society in which equity is fully realized, must be one in which there is not a representation of individuals but a representation of interests. (*The Principles of Ethics*, vol. II, p. 213)

Spencer has now emphatically repudiated his earlier views by affirming that universal suffrage generates class-biased legislation violating equal freedom by violating property rights and thereby penalizing the upper and middle classes. On this score, in any case, Wiltshire and others correctly accuse Spencer of drifting towards political conservatism.[9]

Spencer was never shy about retreating into ambiguity when his views risked embroiling him in unpleasant, emotionally draining, public controversies. Thus, he concludes his discussion of suffrage in *The Principles of Ethics* insisting that it remains an "unanswerable question" whether or not universal suffrage will ultimately result in legislation penalizing the propertied classes. Because industrial societies, structured around "cooperative organization" mitigating class distinctions "may" yet arise, universal suffrage "may" yet be defensible. Nevertheless, such a possibility remains distant: "But the truth we have to recognize is that with such humanity as now exists, and must for a long time exist, the possession of what are called equal political rights will not ensure the maintenance of equal rights properly so-called."[10] We have returned to a familiar irony. As with the "right to ignore the state," universal suffrage will be warranted only after it has become irrelevant.

Spencer's treatment of women's suffrage displays the same conservative shift away from universal suffrage and the same growing eagerness to distinguish suffrage rights from genuine moral rights. For instance, in his 1892 abridged and revised edition of *Social Statics*, Spencer drops a crucial section from the chapter, "The Rights of Women," where he argues that although the "giving of political power to women may disagree with our notions of propriety, we must conclude that, being required by that first prerequisite to greatest happiness – the law of equal freedom – such a concession is unquestionably right and good" (*Social Statics*, p. 152).[11]

[9] See Wiltshire, *The Social and Political Thought of Herbert Spencer*, pp. 110–19.

[10] Spencer, *The Principles of Ethics*, vol. II, pp. 213–14.

[11] He also omits other sections from the original chapter, such as where he contends that English law and custom partially enslave women to men both publicly and in their private lives. In new prefaces to the unabridged 1865 American and the 1877 English and 1878 American editions of *Social Statics*, Spencer stresses that his views on the status of women have changed since the original 1851 edition. For these various editions, see Spencer, *Social*

Moreover, in *The Principles of Ethics*, he argues that insofar as women do not share with men some of the responsibilities of citizenship, such as military service, they do not deserve voting rights. He allows, however, that women may be granted such rights should "permanent peace" ever make military service unnecessary (vol. II, p. 183).[12] Once again, we see that universal suffrage will be legitimate as it becomes irrelevant. This follows because "permanent peace" implies international harmony which, in turn, implies internal harmony.

Spencer's waning commitment to female suffrage is equally apparent in his correspondence with Mill. In August 1867, Mill wrote to Spencer requesting that he join the Women's Suffrage Society, an organization dedicated to promoting female suffrage. Spencer declined on the grounds that his views had changed since he wrote *Social Statics*:

> The modification goes as far as this, that while I should advocate the extension of suffrage to women as an ultimate measure, I do not approve of it as an immediate measure, or even as a measure to be shortly taken. I hold, as I doubt not you also hold, that political liberties or powers, like that of voting, are simply a *means* to an end . . . The unhindered exercise of faculties by each, limited only by the claims of others, is that which the right of voting serves to obtain and maintain. This is the real liberty in comparison with which the right of voting is but a *nominal* liberty. (my italics)[13]

Earlier the same year, Spencer declined Mill's request on behalf of his stepdaughter, Helen Taylor, to include "The Rights of Women" from *Social Statics* in a collection of essays she was publishing. And in 1869, Spencer wrote Mill thanking him for the complimentary copy of *The Subjection of Women* and complaining that women exercise too much veiled influence over men which helps counterbalance their subjection to men. He suggests that an essay entitled *The Supremacy of Women* might usefully be written to expose their hidden influence

Statics (New York: D. Appleton and Co., 1865); Spencer, *Social Statics* (London: Williams and Norgate, 1877) and Spencer, *Social Statics* (New York: D. Appleton and Co., 1878). See also Spencer, *Social Statics*, abridged and revised together with *The Man vs. the State* (London: Williams and Norgate, 1892).

[12] Spencer adds, curiously, that his opposition to female suffrage does not affect women's claims to "equal shares in local governments and administrations."

[13] Spencer to J. S. Mill, August 9, 1867 in Duncan (ed.), *The Life and Letters of Herbert Spencer*, p. 138. For Mill's initial letter to Spencer, see Mill to Herbert Spencer, August 2, 1867 in F. E. Mineka and D. N. Lindley (eds.), *Collected Works* (1972), vol. XVI, pp. 1299–1300.

over men. Mill replied pointedly that "two contradictory tyrannies do not make liberty."[14]

Premature universal suffrage, then, threatened to undermine liberal utilitarian ideals with socialistic excesses. In *An Autobiography*, Spencer lamented: "Unhappily this prophecy [of growing state interference] has been fulfilled, – fulfilled, too, much sooner than I expected. Another extension of the franchise since made, so great as entirely to destroy the balance of powers between classes, and so made as to dissociate the giving of votes from the bearing of burdens, will inevitably be followed by a still more rapid growth of socialistic legislation" (vol. II, pp. 55–6).[15]

Spencer's steady retreat from universal suffrage was a product of the changing political climate of late Victorian England.[16] However rooted in this changing climate, his deepening political conservatism exposed more clearly a crucial distinction in his thinking about rights. His growing conservatism highlighted in bold the difference between mere political rights and fundamental moral rights.

Of course, Spencer was not the only utilitarian of his time to make this conceptual distinction. Joseph Priestley had something like it in mind in distinguishing between "political liberty" and "civil liberty" in his *Essay on the First Principles of Government.* Whereas, for Priestley, political liberty "consists in the power, which members of the State

[14] For Spencer's early commitment to women's suffrage as a full moral right, see "The Rights of Women" in Spencer, *Social Statics*, p. 152. Also note that "The Rights of Women" falls under Part II of *Social Statics* which is devoted to analyzing full moral rights. For additional evidence of his waning enthusiasm for women's suffrage, see "The Rights of Women" in *The Principles of Ethics*, vol. II. For Spencer's 1869 letter to Mill, see Spencer to J. S. Mill, June 9, 1869 in Duncan (ed.), *The Life and Letters of Herbert Spencer*, p. 139. For Mill's response, see Mill to Herbert Spencer, June 14 1869 in F. E. Mineka and D. N. Lindley (eds.), *Collected Works*, (1972), vol. XVII, pp. 1614–15. See also T. S. Gray, "Herbert Spencer on Women: A Study in Personal and Political Disillusionment," *International Journal of Women's Studies*, 7 (1984).

[15] See also Spencer's February 17, 1859 letter to Mill thanking him for sending him a copy of his just published *On Liberty*. After first warmly praising Mill's essay, Spencer continues "Unfortunately, the notion of liberty has been so much mixed up with that of organic reforms, that, with the mass of men, it has come to be synonymous with democratic government; and many of those who think themselves its warmest advocates are above all others inclined to increase the tyranny of the State over individuals. Indeed, the strong tendency there is on the part of the working classes to Over-legislate has given me the only qualms I have had of late years respecting the effects of increased popular power." See Spencer to J. S. Mill, February 17, 1859 in Duncan (ed.), *The Life and Letters of Herbert Spencer*, p. 93.

[16] According to David Thomson in *England in the Nineteenth Century* (Middlesex: Penguin Books, 1985), pp. 133–4, "Social betterment made further extension of the franchise possible and more probable and extensions of the franchise led to fresh programmes of social improvement."

reserve to themselves, of holding public offices, or, at least, of having votes in the nomination of those who fill them," civil liberty is "that power over their own actions, which the members of the State reserve to themselves, and which their officers must not infringe."[17] And in his *Considerations on Representative Government*, Mill offered a similar distinction in defending plural voting which gave educated voters more influence by allocating more votes to each of them until the masses became sufficiently educated. For Mill, voting was not a basic moral right but a mechanism for protecting rights. As long as large numbers of voters were insufficiently educated, they risked misusing this mechanism, causing basic rights to be protected ineffectively. The right to vote was a tool requiring operating skill and was thus subject to weighted licensure.[18]

More recently, Isaiah Berlin has carefully worked this distinction in "Two Concepts of Liberty." Drawing on Benjamin Constant in particular, Berlin holds that democratic self-government is not the same thing as personal liberty and, therefore, is related to it contingently:

> Freedom in this [negative] sense is not, at any rate *logically*, connected with democracy or self-government. Self-government may, on the whole, provide a better guarantee of the preservation of civil liberties than other regimes, and has been defended as such by libertarians. But there is no *necessary* connexion between individual liberty and democratic rule. The answer to the question "Who governs me?" is *logically* distinct from the question "How far does government interfere with me?" (*Four Essays on Liberty*, pp. 129–30; my italics)[19]

Fred Rosen, by contrast and following Bentham, rejects Berlin's effort to define freedom in such a way as to expel democratic self-determination from its meaning. For Rosen, freedom and democracy are analytically interwoven: "If I wish to be free from interference, I would want to be able to ask the question, 'By whom am I ruled?' because if those who rule are corrupt or oppressive, I want to be able to remove them from office." Moreover and more importantly, in

[17] Joseph Priestley, *Essay on the First Principles of Government* (London: J. Dodsley, 1768), pp. 12–13.

[18] Mill, *Considerations on Representative Government*. See especially chapter 8, "Of the Extension of the Suffrage."

[19] See also J. L. Mackie who remarks, "The specifically political liberties may not be thus vital to many people, but they are important, far more widely, in an indirect way, as providing means for the defense of more central freedoms." J. L. Mackie, "Can There Be a Right-Based Moral Theory?" *Midwest Studies in Philosophy*, 3 (1978), 356.

Rosen's view, Berlin "has not appreciated the philosophical connection between liberty and forms of government because he has divorced his argument from the main traditional approaches to democracy through rights theory and utilitarianism."[20]

Spencer certainly cannot be accused of divorcing his "argument" from "traditional approaches to democracy through rights theory and utilitarianism." Yet, Spencer's theory of democracy, in all its vicissitudes, looks back to Priestley and Mill, and ahead to Berlin, and not back to Bentham and ahead to Rosen. Like the former group of theorists, Spencer sees no analytic connection between universal suffrage and safeguarding freedom and moral rights. Like the former group, he detects no necessary connection between the question, "Who governs me?" and the question, "How far does government interfere with me?" Both questions are as conceptually distinct for him as they are for Priestley, Mill and Berlin. Both questions were merely contingently related in Spencer's view. Both questions appealed to separate normative dimensions that differed in their sanctity. In other words, for Spencer, "rights properly so-called" were stringent while "political rights" were not. "Rights properly so-called" pertained to the question "How far does government interfere with me?" whereas "political rights" pertained to the question "Who governs me?" The juridical mechanisms of "Who governs me?" were merely instrumental and, therefore, less sacred than the juridical mechanisms of "How far does government interfere with me?" And Spencer, lest we forget, was a utilitarian!

THE MORAL FORCE OF RIGHTS AND THE DEMANDS OF UTILITY

"Political rights" and "rights properly so-called" were conceptual cousins, albeit distant ones. They were related insofar as both types of rights were indirect strategies for maximizing utility. However, though members of the same extended conceptual family, the differences between them overshadowed whatever attributes they shared. Though both were conditions for realizing happiness, both differed in terms of their stringency. "Political rights" were much more moderated and less precious and consequently readily discardable. Hence, the differences between political and moral rights were

[20] F. Rosen, "Thinking About Liberty," Inaugural Lecture, University College London, November 29, 1990, p. 12.

effectively differences of kind thus threatening the logical coherence of Spencer's liberal utilitarianism.

While we may feel that there is something logically Sisyphean about trying to marry stringent moral rights with the principle of utility, there is certainly nothing absurd in trying to marry "political rights" with utility. Being defeasible, "political rights" invariably bow to the demands of utility in Spencer's moral theory whenever both values conflict. On this dimension, his utilitarianism is unremarkable. Indeed, how else shall we make sense out of his willingness to abandon suffrage rights? How else shall we fully make sense out of his deepening political conservatism? Once he began to doubt the utilitarian efficacy of universal suffrage, once he became convinced that it was a source of the legislative excesses of the "new Toryism," he discarded it in practice if not in principle. But such pedestrian theoretical vicissitudes are of limited interest. Spencer's Sisyphean endeavor to wed strong moral rights and utility is surely more intriguing. Let us focus on this logically troubled marriage.

In "Supply Without Burthen or Escheat Vice Taxation," his celebrated unmasking of the folly of natural rights doctrine, Bentham says, "I know of no natural rights except what are created by general utility: and even in that sense it were much better the words were never heard of."[21] In other words, considerations of utility trump the force of natural rights in the final analysis. Though one might insist on referring to basic rights as natural rights, one must nevertheless concede that such rights are ultimately defeasible. Indefeasible natural rights, assuming that they exist, would be incompatible with utility. Therefore, we would do better to abandon the idea of natural rights altogether.

Now, variations of this criticism have repeatedly arisen in response to recurrent attempts to salvage utilitarianism by fortifying it with liberal principles in order to make it more ethically appealing. For its critics, liberal utilitarianism founders as an "intrinsically unstable compromise" which "tries to occupy a non-existent middle ground."[22] For these critics, liberal utilitarianism is a fruitless struggle to reconcile incompatible normative principles, namely stringent rights and utility.

Mill, as just suggested, initiated this ostensibly foolhardy enter-

[21] Jeremy Bentham, "Supply Without Burthen or Escheat Vice Taxation" [1843] in Jeremy Waldron (ed.) *Nonsense Upon Stilts* (London: Methuen, 1987), p. 72.

[22] Samuel Scheffler (ed.), *Consequentialism and Its Critics* (Oxford University Press, 1988), p. 8.

prise of liberal utilitarian reform. More than any of Bentham's followers, he endeavored to make utilitarianism more ethically attractive by inoculating it with powerful juridical constraints on the pursuit of utility. These constraints make Mill an indirect, liberal utilitarian of the first order.

The logical perils of efforts like Mill's to improve Benthamism by liberalizing it did not go unnoticed by nineteenth-century opponents of utilitarianism. In response to Paley's theological utilitarianism, but as if anticipating Mill's utilitarianism, William Whewell observed in his 1852 *Lectures on the History of Moral Philosophy in England* that utilitarianism cannot accommodate meaningful moral rules without risking inconsistency. In order to be consistent, utilitarianism cannot permit moral rules "any greater rigour" than the principle of utility allows.[23]

Some years later, both Fitzjames Stephen and F. H. Bradley accused Mill of inconsistent and absurd reasoning for insisting that moral rules, such as those embodying rights, be honored even if doing so plainly generated disutility. As Bradley saw it, Mill's utilitarianism requires that I abide by the rules of my moral "Nautical Almanack" even when I know that more utility could be produced by violating them. But, on the other hand, consistent utilitarianism also requires that I disregard what my Almanack commends:

> And the consequence is, that the Almanack and its moral rules are no authority. It is right to act according to them. It is right to act diametrically against them. In short they are not laws at all; they are only rules, and rules, as we know, admit of and imply exceptions. As Mr. Stephen has said, 'A given road may be the direct way from one place to another, but that fact is no reason for following the road when you are offered a short cut. It may be a good rule not to seek for more than 5 per cent. in investments, but if it so happens that you can invest at 10 per cent. with *perfect safety*, would not a man who refused to do so be a fool?' (my italics)[24]

More recently, Alan Ryan and John Charvet have pressed similar criticisms against Mill. Despite being favorably disposed to Mill, Ryan nonetheless echoes Mill's earlier critics accusing Mill of

[23] William Whewell, *Lectures on the History of Moral Philosophy in England* [1852] (Cambridge: Deighton Bell, 1862), pp. 173–4. For Mill's response to Whewell, see J. S. Mill, "Whewell on Moral Philosophy" [1852] in Robson (ed.), *Collected Works*, (1969), vol. x.

[24] F. H. Bradley, *Ethical Studies*, [1876] (New York: G. E. Stechert and Co., 1927), p. 102. See note 9, page 4 for Stephen's original quote.

disguising "from himself the conflict between utility and justice" and for failing to show "how a distributive ideal can be subsumed under an aggregative one."[25] Charvet likewise observes:

If we mean by the principle of justice, the basic rule requiring that persons be given an equal value, then we are involved in the absurdity of on the one hand affirming a principle of equal value which commits us to valuing individuals in themselves, and on the other hand claiming that the value of this principle lies in its relation to another principle which holds that pleasure alone is the good. Justice, as a binding rule involving the principle of equal value, cannot coherently be said to be utilitarianly good.[26]

So, for Ryan and Charvet, Millian utilitarians must choose. They must choose between stringent rules of justice and maximizing good. Whereas choosing the latter leads us back to traditional Benthamism, choosing the former, in Bernard Williams' words, leads utilitarianism to retire to the "totally transcendental standpoint from which all it demands is that the world should be ordered for the best." And when this happens, "utilitarianism has disappeared" and the "residual position is not worth calling utilitarianism."[27]

Even John Gray, who once so vehemently defended Mill's liberal utilitarianism (as we saw in chapter 4), has since recanted, condemning Mill for foolishly trying to align a maximizing theory of good with a robust theory of right. In a recently co-authored essay, Gray repudiates what he so persuasively argued in *Mill on Liberty: A Defence* now averring:

No utilitarian theory, however, not even the complex, pluralistic, and hierarchical indirect utilitarianism attributed to Mill by Gray, can from its aggregative maximizing premises derive a distributive principle such as Mill's Principle of Liberty. Such principles act as constraints on the promotion of happiness even as Mill conceives it. The traditional view appears, then, to be vindicated: in attempting to derive from the Principle of Utility a principle that constrains the pursuit of general welfare (by reference to the value of liberty) Mill is engaged in a strictly impossible enterprise.[28]

[25] Ryan, *The Philosophy of John Stuart Mill*, pp. 223 and 228.

[26] Charvet, *A Critique of Freedom and Equality*, pp. 94–5.

[27] Bernard Williams, "A Critique of Utilitarianism" in J. C. C. Smart and Bernard Williams (eds.), *Utilitarianism: For and Against* (Cambridge University Press, 1973), pp. 134–5.

[28] John Gray and G. W. Smith, "Introduction" in John Gray and G. W. Smith (eds.), *J. S. Mill on Liberty in Focus* (London: Routledge, 1991), p. 12. See also Gray's "Liberalism and the Choice of Liberties," where Gray admits changing his assessment of Millian utilitarianism because "liberal justice cannot be derived from within a wholly consequentialist morality." John Gray, *Liberalisms: Essays in Political Philosophy* (London: Routledge, 1989), p. 153. Given

In sum, as far as Gray is now concerned, liberal utilitarianism necessarily fails succumbing under the weight of its own impossible logic. Insofar as Mill insists on remaining a genuine utilitarian, he must opt for maximizing utility, no matter how marginal or trivial, over respecting moral rights whenever the former conflicts with the latter. Gray concludes that underneath its glossy liberal veneer, Mill's utilitarianism remains but a "form of sophisticated act-utilitarianism" and for a "sophisticated act-utilitarian, however, there can be no question of adherence to exceptionless principles such as Mill's Principle of Liberty."[29]

David Lyons, however, has deployed these kinds of criticisms of Millian utilitarianism in the most compelling fashion. According to Lyons, in "Utility and Rights," all versions of liberal utilitarianism must forsake either their liberalism or their utilitarianism. If rights are granted *independent* "moral force" of their own, then they either trump utilitarian considerations or they conflict with them. In the former case, utilitarianism vanishes. In the latter case, it succumbs to inconsistency. So if liberal utilitarianism is to remain genuinely utilitarian, then utilitarian considerations must always trump juridical constraints on the pursuit of utility whenever such constraints interfere, no matter how insignificantly, with maximizing utility. According to the Lyons' well-known example of Mary's ownership rights over her driveway, utilitarians, especially liberal ones, must tolerate violations of these rights even for the sake of insignificant additions to overall utility. For instance, if I am *certain* that blocking Mary's driveway for a few hours late at night when she is sleeping will convenience me while I visit a friend recuperating in a nearby hospital, then I ought to do it. In short, I ought to violate her driveway rights even when slight increases in marginal utility result. And, as Lyons is quick to remind us, this would strip Mary's property rights in her driveway of all independent "moral force." It would render these rights empty. But if I ought to respect her property rights by not parking in her driveway, then I am no longer much of a utilitarian for I have failed to act in a way that the principle of utility prescribes. I have denied the principle of utility independent "moral force" rendering it an empty principle.

that Gray has abandoned his earlier defense of Mill's liberal utilitarianism, one might wonder why I make so much of it in chapter 4. My answer is that I continue to find Gray's earlier interpretation sufficiently compelling.

29 Gray, "Mill's and Other Liberalisms," p. 223.

According to Lyons, we must choose between our liberalism or our utilitarianism. We can allow either one or the other independent "moral force" but not both. There can only be one *ultimate* criterion of right conduct, not two. Either we respect Mary's driveway rights or we violate them by blocking her driveway. Either we respect Mary's integrity or we use her in the name of slight marginal utility.

Many liberal utilitarians have not found Lyons' criticisms compelling.[30] Michael Freeden, though arguably not a liberal utilitarian, has suggested that it is "equally plausible to define human welfare not only in terms of pleasure widely understood but in terms of the wholesome exercise of human faculties. Welfare can quite readily encompass expressiveness and autonomy as well as enjoyment and health" (my italics).[31] According to Freeden, when we supplement our revised definition of good by incorporating a "communitarian viewpoint" rather than an "aggregative one," then "modified constrained consequentialism" makes logical sense. "Modified constrained consequentialism," in other words, preserves individual integrity and respect for strong rights all-the-while remaining undeniably consequentialist. In Freeden's words: "Another way of looking at the problem is to limit the divergence between goal-based and right-based principles by suggesting that one kind of goal-based theory will *include* as a central goal the protection of those attributes that right-based theories deem precious" (*Rights*, p. 98). Hence, contrary to Lyons, there is more than one way to approach the question of whether or not to block Mary's driveway so that choosing either utilitarianism or rights are not our only options. Liberal utilitarianism may not be such a misbegotten enterprise after all. Or rather *liberal consequentialism*, as distinctively different from *liberal utilitarianism*, may not be so misbegotten.

Freeden has not been alone in advancing this kind of liberal utilitarian response to Lyons' challenge. In *The Moral Foundations of Rights*, L. W. Sumner argues that Lyons' criticisms of liberal utilitarianism hold only for utilitarian infallible observers, of which none actually exist. Whereas it would be irrational for an infallible

[30] See Chapman and Pennock (eds.), *Ethics, Economics and the Law*, Nomos 24, for replies to Lyons by Flathman, Gewirth, Greenawalt and Hare. See also Brandt, "Utilitarianism and Moral Rights."

[31] Michael Freeden, *Rights* (Minneapolis: University of Minnesota Press, 1991), p. 87.

utilitarian (like Stephen and Bradley's investor who "can invest at 10 per cent. with perfect safety") to respect rights when doing so would unquestionably jeopardize maximizing utility, it would not be irrational for a fallible utilitarian, given the limited information available to him or her, to respect them. As Sumner puts it, the very same action may be "both the right one to have chosen and the wrong one to have done."[32] Respecting Mary's driveway rights may be both the right choice but the wrong action. In order to choose rightly given our fallibility, we need, according to Sumner, a reliable "theory of moral decision-making." And the best "theory of moral decision-making" is an indirect consequentialist strategy which takes rights seriously. The best consequentialist strategy, in other words, is one that places firm juridical constraints on its own pursuit:

> Thus you are likely to do better if you adopt a constrained strategy, one of whose constraints is an inhibition against violating the morally justified rights of others. This inhibition need not, and doubtless should not, be indefeasible. Thus your decision-making policy need not, and doubtless should not, entirely exclude direct appeals to your basic goal. But your internalized constraint will raise a threshold against such appeals – the "moral presumption" of which Lyons speaks – so that you will not violate rights to realize merely marginal and speculative gains. (*The Moral Foundations of Rights*, p. 196)

The best consequentialist strategy, therefore, turns out to be one that privileges rights given our imperfect intelligence, given the fact that we are such "crooked [intellectual] timber." Since a "constrained strategy accords independent deliberative weight to rights, it *seems* to acknowledge their moral force" (p. 196, my italics).[33]

Nonetheless, for Sumner, since there will undoubtedly be exceptional cases in which the utilitarian cost of sticking to basic rights will be high, an indirect strategy would tolerate overriding rights on these occasions. That is, *some* overriding will *probably* work out for the consequentialist best.[34] But this need not necessarily be the case. Treating rights as indefeasible constraints with absolute moral force

[32] Sumner, *The Moral Foundations of Rights*, p. 179.

[33] See also p. 197, where Sumner continues that a constrained consequentialist policy requires no more than that "you treat the existence of rights as independent reasons for action." If Sumner means "as if they were" by "as," then the independent moral force of rights is merely chimerical; a utilitarian noble lie the likes of which Sidgwick found so worrisome.

[34] Sumner does not offer a criterion for determining when overriding becomes permissible, and I am not sure that he can without injecting his moral theory with arbitrariness.

of their own might conceivably turn out to be our optimal decision-making strategy. Hence, as Sumner concedes *and as Spencer would concur*, "absolute rights are not an impossible output for a consequentialist methodology" (*The Moral Foundations of Rights*, p. 212).[35]

Nevertheless, absolute rights might eventually be an "impossible output" for Spencer's mature political theory insofar as human history engenders observer infallibility as it achieves perfection. As noted previously, future utilitarians might, ironically, find indefeasible rights redundant. Future utilitarians might not need to "pre-commit" themselves to juridical constraints in order to successfully maximize utility. If they could always be, in fact, successful act utilitarians, they therefore ought to behave as act utilitarians. For them, nobody's driveway rights would be sacrosanct.[36]

In this chapter, as well as the two previous ones, I have endeavored to demonstrate how Spencer understood moral rights as both natural and as instrumental decision procedures.[37] For Spencer, "rights properly so-called," in contrast to mere "political rights," are normative devices which must be taken seriously but not with such blind seriousness that their consequentialist justification vanishes. Basic rights promote happiness over the long run but not always in every case (though nearly in all cases as liberal societies approach perfection). Moreover, especially after *Social Statics*, moral rights are not to be taken with that kind of intuitive certainty which forgets that they are, after all, practices which have emerged over time. They are artifacts which we have learned to cherish. They are not

[35] We should not confuse absolute rights, which Sumner seems to think will be rare at best, with natural rights, which he holds won't be so rare. However, his notion of natural rights is peculiar: "A natural right (in this sense) is a right the criterion for possession of which is a natural property" (*The Moral Foundations of Rights*, p. 205).

[36] We might recall our earlier observation that basic rights would, on Spencer's reasoning, loose their relevance as liberal societies matured.

[37] These three chapters also put me at odds with Miller's view of Spencer more than chapter 2 suggests. While chapter 2 concurs with Miller that desert plays an important role in Spencer's moral theory, chapters 3 and 4 reveal that rights and utility play an important, if not more important, role. Thus Miller's three paradigms of justice (rights, desert and need), epitomized by Hume, Spencer and Kropotkin respectively, may be inadequate. Miller's characterization of Spencer as epitomizing justice as desert should be modified as follows: insofar as the principles of equal freedom and desert are synonymous as shown earlier, rights are specifications of desert as well as of equal freedom. Hence, if equal freedom is the form which desert takes in sociality, then rights are constitutive of this form. Rights are not opposed to desert.

written indelibly into our hearts awaiting disclosure under the light of reason although reason establishes and refines them. In short, basic rights are fashioned by us even if an increasingly *stringent* array of them just happens to maximize happiness best.

Spencerian moral rights, from *Social Statics* to *The Principles of Ethics*, are stringent. They mimic traditional natural rights. They are silhouettes of them, thus making Spencer's liberal utilitarianism uniquely engaging. And when we keep in mind Spencer's theory of the evolution of moral self-restraint in his later works, his liberal utilitarianism becomes even more engaging. That is, the practice of respect for rights amounts to the practice of moral self-restraint. Hence, the practice of this latter virtue is no less than the practice of indirect utility. The richness of Spencer's liberal utilitarianism is therefore formidable.

Herbert Spencer is not readily associated with utilitarianism. This is most unfortunate because it is profoundly inaccurate and because Spencer's liberal utilitarianism is enterprising. But to suggest that it is enterprising is not to declare that Spencer successfully accommodates stringent moral rights with utility. Being so stringent, Spencerian moral rights seem to possess independent "moral force" which David Lyons would say makes them incompatible with utility. As we have seen, this is because independent "moral force" seems to introduce something else besides utility, like respect for persons as ends, as an ultimate criterion of right action. But even if we grant formal *logical* incompatibility here, it is nonetheless conceivable that the *practical* price for fallible observers such as ourselves, in terms of lost long-term utility, might be nonexistent. The cost of sticking to stringent moral rights might be the kind of *contingent* bargain that few utilitarians (following Sumner's example) dare not ignore.

In any case, why should we admit to anything but meager conceptual incompatibility? If we take Spencer as never relenting in claiming that moral rights maximize general happiness understood as *each and everyone's* optimal happiness (a variety of consequentialist good favored by Michael Freeden), then it seems that we can have our "moral force" cake of respect for persons and eat our consequentialism too. It seems that we can have both especially when we keep in mind Spencer's contention that each person's happiness is solely a function of his or her own *activity*. Hence, even the integrity-destroying specter of everyone mindlessly attaching themselves to experience machines yields but hollow consternation. And it seems that liberal opponents of utilitarianism like Alan Gewirth might welcome this kind of utilitarianism as being sufficiently liberal as well as utilitarian.[38]

[38] See especially Alan Gewirth, "Can Utilitarianism Justify Any Moral Rights?" in Chapman and Pennock (eds.), *Ethics, Economics and the Law*, Nomos 24. For Gewirth, rights secure "conditions" or "components of welfare" which are "necessary" for "successful action" of "each" and "all." Thus, though they proscribe welfare pooling, they are nevertheless instrumental and consequentialist.

CHAPTER 6

Spencer's ethical reasoning

In the "Preface" to the "Data of Ethics" in *The Principles of Ethics*, Spencer laments the sorry quandary into which he felt nineteenth-century moral philosophy had fallen:

> I am the more anxious to indicate in outline, if I cannot complete, this final work, because the establishment of rules of right conduct on a scientific basis is a pressing need. Now that moral injunctions are losing the authority given by their supposed sacred origin, the secularization of morals is becoming imperative . . . Thus between these extreme opponents [the critics and defenders of theological ethics] there is a certain community. The one holds that the gap left by disappearance of the code of supernatural ethics, need not be filled by a code of natural ethics; and the other holds that it cannot be so filled. Both contemplate a vacuum, which the one wishes and the other fears. As the change which promises or threatens to bring about this state, desired or dreaded, is rapidly progressing, those who believe that the vacuum can be filled, and that it must be filled, are called on to do something in pursuance of their belief. (*The Principles of Ethics*, vol. I, p. 32)

Foremost among these "rules of right conduct" that Spencer so anxiously sought to establish scientifically was, of course, the principle of equal freedom. Scarcely less important, for Spencer, was the scientific establishment of basic moral rights.

This chapter examines the methodological strategies Spencer deploys to justify his principles of "right conduct." Consequently, this chapter is more metaethical than previous ones. And inasmuch as Spencer was a utilitarian, our analysis of how he justifies his fundamental principles of obligation will invariably return us to his hedonistic theory of good. Thus, we shall also examine Spencer's theory of good including his justification of good.

Treating this latter issue entails braving the question of whether Spencer was a crude ethical naturalist as many of his interpretative accusers have charged, particularly G. E. Moore. Ever since the quick work which Moore made of Spencer in chapter 2 of *Principia Ethica*, Spencer's moral theory never recaptured its former stature among serious philosophers. According to Moore, Spencer committed a particular glaring version of the naturalistic fallacy. But although Moore's Spencer may have served Moore well in developing his larger metaethical claims, his Spencer is a caricature.

Moore wasn't alone among Spencer's philosophical contemporaries in finding serious fault with Spencer on this score. Henry Sidgwick, several years prior to Moore's celebrated appropriation of Spencer, likewise reproached Spencer for succumbing to the reassuring temptations of ethical naturalism. But Sidgwick's dissatisfaction with Spencer's moral reasoning is better informed and his rendering of the wayward nature of Spencer's thinking is therefore more effective. We shall not ignore Sidgwick's treatment of Spencer either.

In sum, this chapter testifies to the particular ignominy that has befallen Spencer at least since *Principia Ethica*. But it also endeavors to ameliorate this ignominy in order to rehabilitate Spencer further as an instructive, if not entirely successful, proponent of liberal utilitarianism.

THE GOOD

I shall confine my assessment of Spencer's theory of good to the early portions of *Social Statics* and to Parts II and IV of *The Principles of Ethics*. As with much else in Spencer's moral and political theory, these texts chronologically and thematically frame Spencer's extended excursions into metaethical theorizing.

In the "Second Preface" to the 1877 edition of *Social Statics*, Spencer observes that the "scientific system of ethics" set forth in Parts I and II of the 1851 edition need refining. Yet, like his earlier edition, his 1877 edition still fails to discuss good systematically. Plainly, though, good is happiness, for "greatest happiness is the creative purpose" of humankind, and it and "morality are the face and obverse of the same fact" (*Social Statics*, p. 61). Unfortunately, Spencer does not say clearly whether good should be operationalized as "greatest [individual] happiness" or as "greatest happiness" for the greatest number. Though he occasionally deploys the expression "the greatest happiness of the greatest number," he often does so by placing it in quotations and when criticizing Bentham. Thus, we should not rashly conclude that he was unequivocally a universal hedonist. The following passage is especially instructive:

So that in directing us to this "greatest happiness to the greatest number," as the object toward which we should steer, our [Benthamite] pilot "keeps the word of promise to our ear and breaks it to our hope." What he shows us through his telescope is a *fata morgana*, and not the promised land. (*Social Statics*, p. 9)

Social Statics, then, offers no systematic account of good in either its original or its later editions. Spencer never expressly *defines* good nor does he attribute goodness to anything unreservedly. And certainly, he never defines good as, or attributes goodness to, anything like evolution or survival of the fittest. Yet, as we have seen, by good Spencer means primarily happiness.

By the time of his revealing 1863 letter to Mill, discussed in chapter 4, Spencer explicitly identifies himself as a utilitarian, albeit not as a Benthamite utilitarian. While not the "proximate end," Spencer insists, we should recall, that happiness is the "ultimate end" of human action.

With the publication of *The Principles of Ethics* years later, Spencer's treatment of good became considerably more textured. In a chapter entitled "Good and Bad Conduct" in volume 1, Spencer says flatly that "the good is universally the pleasurable" (vol. 1, p. 66). At first glance, this assertion seems unproblematic. Compared with *Social Statics*, Spencer now seems clear about the meaning of good. However, the full context of this claim is more nuanced:

And here we are brought round to those primary meanings of the words good and bad, which we passed over when considering their secondary meanings. For on remembering that we call good and bad the things which immediately produce agreeable and disagreeable sensations, and also the sensations themselves – a good wine, a good appetite, a bad smell, a bad headache – we see that by referring directly to pleasures and pains, these meanings harmonize with those which indirectly refer to pleasures and pains. If we call good the enjoyable state itself, as a good laugh – if we call good the proximate cause of an enjoyable state, as good music – if we call good any agent which conduces immediately or remotely to an enjoyable state, as a good shop, a good teacher – if we call good considered intrinsically, each act so adjusted to its end as to further self-preservation and that surplus of enjoyment which makes self-preservation desirable – if we call good every kind of conduct which aids the lives of others, and do this under the belief that life brings more happiness than misery; then it becomes undeniable that, taking into account immediate and remote effects on all persons, the good is universally the pleasurable. (*The Principles of Ethics*, vol. 1, pp. 65–6)

Good has myriad nuances. First, it is the experience of pleasure. Second, it is the *means* to this experience. And, third, "considered intrinsically," good is also "each act so adjusted to its end as to further self-preservation and that surplus of enjoyment which makes self-preservation desirable." In effect, this third species of good constitutes a crucial sense in which good is a *means* to pleasurableness. Recall that the principle of desert (results adjusted to actions) and the principle of equal freedom are identical. Both principles embody a single underlying principle of justice. Hence, insofar as the means to pleasure are good and insofar as the interchangeable principles of desert and equal freedom are crucial in generating pleasure, then both principles are vital goods. Hence, justice is a crucial good, for the principles of desert and equal freedom constitute justice.

Good as "each act so adjusted to its end as to further self-preservation and that surplus enjoyment" entails deeper implications. The adjustment of acts to ends is instrumentally good not simply because "surplus enjoyment" is generated but *also* because "self-preservation" is more effectively secured. Hence, self-preservation, as distinct from pleasurableness, is equally good. Elsewhere in *The Principles of Ethics*, Spencer makes the same distinction between self-preservation and pleasure when he contrasts long-term "prolongation of life" with "amount of life" and "length of life" with "breadth of life." Whereas "prolongation of life" and "length of life" are equivalent to self-preservation, "amount of life" and "breadth of life" are roughly equivalent to the quality of life, ergo, happiness (vol. 1, pp. 48–9).

Other difficulties afflict Spencer's theory of good. Spencer writes: "Thus far we have considered only those adjustments of acts to ends which have for their final purpose complete individual life. Now we have to consider those adjustments which have for their final purpose the life of the species" (*The Principles of Ethics*, vol. 1, p. 49). Thus, we can safely assume that preservation of the human species, and not simply individual self-preservation, is good as well.

Spencer underscores the same point in other ways. Acts are good if they promote the "greatest totality of life in self, in offspring and in fellow men" (*The Principles of Ethics*, vol. I, p. 61). Hence, inasmuch as goodness characterizes acts that promote this "greatest totality," this "greatest totality" is necessarily good. By "greatest totality of life in self, in offspring and in fellow men," Spencer seems to mean greatest "length" plus greatest "breadth" of life for all members of society. He seems to mean, in other words, all persons enjoying long and maximally pleasant lives.

Volume II of *The Principles of Ethics* says relatively little about good that Spencer hasn't already said in volume I. However, in Part II ("Justice"), Spencer embellishes his theory of good unpropitiously. On the one hand, and in keeping with volume I, Spencer says that "though not the immediate end, the greatest sum of happiness is the remote end" and that the "sphere within which each may pursue happiness has a limit, on the other side of which lie the similarly limited spheres of action of his neighbors" (vol. II, p. 62). On the other hand, he also says, "It was there shown [in volume I] that the conduct which ethics treats of is not separable from conduct at large; that the highest conduct is that which conduces to the greatest length, breadth, and completeness of life; and that, by implication, there is a conduct proper to each species of animal, which is the relatively good conduct – a conduct which stands toward that species as the conduct we morally approve stands toward the human species" (vol. II, p. 19). So it seems that "greatest length, breadth and completeness" of life is equally an axiological value applicable to the behavior of animals.

Spencer provides several amusing illustrations of how scientific ethics includes "animal ethics":

> Egoistic acts, as well as altruistic acts, in animals are classed as good or bad. A squirrel which lays up a store of food for the winter is thought of as doing that which a squirrel ought to do; and, contrariwise, one which idly makes not provision and dies of starvation, is thought of as properly paying the penalty of improvidence. A dog which surrenders its bone to another without a struggle, and runs away, we call a coward – a word of reprobation. (*The Principles of Ethics*, vol. II, p. 20)

Notwithstanding the naturalistic implications of "animal ethics" and ambiguities in Spencer's theorizing about good in *The Principles of Ethics*, we can nevertheless piece together an overall picture of Spencer's theory of good. First, at the end of the interpretative day, Spencer holds that good should be maximized. Second, happiness generously understood is good for Spencer if anything is. This is unquestionably true of *Social Statics* if less so of *The Principles of Ethics*. Third, Spencer never explicitly *defines* good one way or another. Hence, he never commits the definist version of the naturalistic fallacy. Whatever else may be said of Spencer's theory of good, it does not exhibit this metaethical transgression both because good, though essentially hedonistic, was nuanced and because reproaching Spencer for committing the definist fallacy is anachronistic. Such reproach is best confined to analytical philosophizing of our era and not extended backwards into analytic philosophy's nineteenth-century prehistory.

These conclusions leave much unresolved. Perhaps Spencer's utilitarianism was nevertheless not fully utilitarian given the nuances of his theory of good. Perhaps because his treatment of sympathy had "nothing moral in it" in Mill's sense (as we saw in chapter 2), Spencer was simply an egoistic hedonist. If he was, shall we conclude that his egoistic hedonism was merely prudential (about motivation) or genuinely ethical (about justification)? It seems that Spencer was in good company here. For instance, Leslie Stephen once observed that Bentham was never clear as to "whether human action is or is not necessarily 'selfish'."[1] Elie Halévy is less hesitant. For Halévy, Bentham's utilitarianism, as well as that of James Mill, was fundamentally egoistical and prudential.[2] John Plamenatz also interprets the utilitarianism of Bentham and James Mill as being essentially a form of prudential egoism.[3] Ross Harrison, by contrast, holds more typically that Bentham combines a prudential theory of motivation with a universalistic theory of justification.[4] And many have criticized J. S. Mill for trying to reconcile prudential egoism, egoistic ethical hedonism and universal hedonism by attempting to derive the second from the first and then the third from the second in his famous proof of utility.[5] Finally, we have Sidgwick's reluctant conclusion that the latter two kinds of hedonism are self-evident and fundamental and yet dishearteningly irreconcilable.[6]

Spencer's utilitarianism plainly suffers from kindred strains. On the one hand, Spencer seems little more than some sort of egoist as

1 Leslie Stephen, *The English Utilitarians* [1900], 3 vols. (New York: P. Smith, 1950), vol. I, p. 313.
2 Halévy, *The Growth of Philosophic Radicalism*, pp. 66–8 and 474–8.
3 John Plamenatz, "Preface" to Halévy, *The Growth of Philosophical Radicalism*, p. xi.
4 Harrison, *Bentham*, Chapter 5.
5 See, for instance, C. D. Broad, *Five Types of Ethical Theory* (London: Routledge and Kegan Paul, 1930), pp. 183–4.
6 Sidgwick, *The Methods of Ethics*, pp. 496–509.

our analysis of his psychology of egoism, altruism and sympathy demonstrated in chapter 2. As we saw earlier, the happiness of others was no more than a means to, or an extension of, one's own happiness. If Spencer's utilitarianism is indeed based on either prudential egoism or egoistic ethical hedonism, there would be "nothing moral in it" in Mill's sense. On the other hand, Spencer often embraces universal hedonism. We saw above that, in *Social Statics*, he arguably accepts the principle of "the greatest happiness of the greatest number" as our ultimate criterion of right action. And as we also saw, Spencer frequently refers to the "greatest sum of happiness" as the end and "purpose" of life in both *Social Statics* and *The Principles of Ethics.*

Spencer's moral theory exhibits a third variety of hedonism as well. Perhaps it is more accurate to say that this variety is itself a species of universal hedonism. Moreover, this variety seems most in keeping with much of what Spencer says about the ultimate consummation of equal freedom. Near the end of *Social Statics*, Spencer describes the realization of equal freedom as "a progress toward that constitution of man and society required for the complete manifestation of everyone's individuality. To be that which he naturally is – to do just what he would spontaneously do – is essential to the full happiness of *each*, and therefore to the greatest happiness of *all*" (p. 389; my italics). Clearly, Spencer envisions a future in which *each and all* achieve maximum happiness. The happiness and integrity of some will never be sacrificed on the altar of pooled utility because maximizing aggregate utility will fortuitously coincide with maximizing every individual's utility.

In "Natural Rights: Bentham and John Stuart Mill," H. L. A. Hart addresses the issue of multiple criteria in Mill's justification of moral rights. Hart is not so much disturbed by the tension between egoistic ethical hedonism and universal hedonism in Mill as he is by the conflict between our two varieties of universal hedonism. On the one hand, Hart suggests that Mill justifies moral rights on the grounds that they promote the most essential interests of *all* individuals. On the other hand, according to Hart, Mill also justifies legal enforcement of moral rights by appealing to general utility. In Hart's words, "He is therefore committed to a criterion for the identification of moral rights which has two components: essential individual good and the general utility of legal or social enforcement. If his theory is to avoid contradiction, it must be shown not merely that these two halves of the criterion may coincide but (exceptions for particular cases apart) that they cannot diverge."[7]

Hart goes on to say that Mill could demonstrate this convergence by defining the non-aggregative sum of individual utilities by the term "general utility." According to Hart, this demonstration would be vacuous since definition is not demonstration. Alternatively, Hart says, Mill could demonstrate this convergence if he held that general utility was distinct and aggregative and if he could show that aggregate utility happens to be maximized by maximizing all individual utilities. Mill, that is, would either have to prove this fortunate coincidence empirically or have to assume it.

These complaints against Mill are applicable to Spencer. At least, they are applicable to Spencer insofar as he was a universal hedonist in both the senses described above.

What kind of hedonist was Spencer? In answering this question, we must keep in mind what John Plamenatz has said of Bentham and James Mill despite the prominence of egoism in their respective theories of good: "But for all this, they do not cease to be utilitarians."[8] Likewise, despite the egoism in Spencer's theory, he does not cease to be a utilitarian either. More generally, and in keeping with our earlier comments about whether Spencer committed the definist fallacy, we ought to avoid reading back into earlier utilitarians distinctions which we now take for granted in modern utilitarian theory.

We have come full circle, returning to claims in the final parts of the previous chapter. There, we saw that liberal consequentialism was a version of consequentialism and that Spencer's moral and political theory, like J. S. Mill's, is best understood as an example of the former. Liberal consequentialism, and Spencer's utilitarian brand of liberal consequentialism in particular, were shown to derive their liberal credentials from the seriousness of their juridical concerns. But, as was alluded to at the close of chapter 5, liberal consequentialism also derives its liberal credentials from its *distributive* conception of hedonistic good, namely greatest happiness understood as *each and everyone's* greatest happiness. This method of operationalizing good aspires to preserve everyone's integrity. Accordingly, individuality is not devalued; nobody is intentionally sacrificed as a means for maximizing

[7] Hart, "Natural Rights: Bentham and John Stuart Mill," p. 96.

[8] John Plamenatz, *English Utilitarians* (Oxford University Press, 1966), p. 8.

aggregate utility. I hope my analysis of Spencer's theory of good in this chapter successfully underscores the salience of this kind of good-operationalizing strategy for Spencer. To the extent that Spencer was a universal hedonist of the third variety, we certainly have all the more reason to regard him as an advocate of a thoroughly liberal form of utilitarianism.[9]

SPENCER'S ETHICAL NATURALISM ACCORDING TO MOORE

Spencer's theory of good, as we have now seen, was mostly hedonistic as well as consequentialist. But then why did G. E. Moore use Spencer as his primary example of "naturalistic ethics" in his chapter by the same name in *Principia Ethica*? Why was Moore convinced that Spencer was such a fitting example of this particularly glaring version of the naturalistic fallacy?

Moore's reproof of Spencer's theory of good was, however, misguided. Moore sometimes seems to acknowledge as much; he more than once admitted that he was ambivalent about how to categorize Spencer's ethical naturalism. Though Alan R. White, one of Moore's more sympathetic interpreters, has denied that "the perpetrators of the naturalistic fallacy were men of straw set up by Moore," our examination of Moore on Spencer suggests otherwise.[10]

[9] Charvet would claim that this variety of universal hedonism amounts to an "equal right to happiness, which includes an equal right to the means of happiness." For Charvet, Benthamism cannot possibly accommodate such implications because, according to Benthamism, "no one has any claim other than to have his units of pleasure and pain counted in the calculation of the total." See Charvet, *A Critique of Freedom and Equality*, p. 93. Charvet also faults Mill's utilitarianism on the same grounds, particularly when, near the end of *Utilitarianism*, Mill says that "Bentham's dictum 'everybody to count for one, nobody for more than one'" entails the "equal claim of everybody to happiness" as well as the "equal claim to all the means of happiness." Mill's elaboration of this dictum also includes his long footnote on Spencer mentioned previously. There, Mill says that, for Spencer, the principle of utility presupposes the anterior principle that "everybody has an equal right to happiness." Of course, Bentham's alleged dictum has never been found in any of Bentham's published or unpublished writings or in his correspondence. And if this dictum can't be attributed to Bentham, then Charvet's criticisms of utilitarianism may be a historical red herring. However, see Jeremy Bentham [1817], "Plan of Parliamentary Reform" in John Bowring (ed.), *The Works of Jeremy Bentham* [1838–43], 11 vols. (New York: Russell and Russell, 1962), vol. III, p. 459, where Bentham asks rhetorically: "The happiness and unhappiness of any one member of the community – high or low, rich or poor – what greater or less part is it of the universal happiness and unhappiness, than that of any other?"

[10] Alan R. White, *G. E. Moore* (Oxford: Basil Blackwell, 1958), p. 126. Regarding Moore's claims that Mill, Spencer and Sidgwick committed different versions of the naturalistic fallacy, White adds, "There is some justification of accusing [Moore] of unwittingly flogging a dead horse, but at least there was once life in it."

One can't help wondering whether Moore deliberately made Spencer into an Aunt Sally for the sake of better illustrating the argument of his chapter, "Naturalistic Ethics."[11]

For Moore, at least in *Principia Ethica*, the naturalistic fallacy is equivalent to the definist fallacy. To attempt to define good is to commit the fallacy. More specifically, committing the fallacy amounts to an unwarranted bid to define good by equating it with some other natural or non-natural object or phenomenon. Committing the fallacy entails confusing goodness *per se* with natural or non-natural objects or phenomena as opposed to recognizing that good is an independent, non-natural property which may or may not be ascribable to, or attach itself to, the objects or phenomena in question.[12] Moreover, committing the fallacy as Spencer supposedly did entails treating good *as if* its meaning was complex by identifying good with some other bona fide complex phenomenon, namely human evolution. Spencer, as far as Moore was concerned, transformed the course that social evolution has thus far followed into one that ought to be followed: "These doctrines [like Spencer's] are those which maintain that the course of 'evolution,' while it shews us the direction in which we are developing, thereby and for that reason shews us the direction in which we ought to develop."[13]

Moore also says, without specifically referring to Spencer though he is probably thinking of him, that ethical naturalism equates good with "natural" in the sense of an "arbitrary minimum of what is

[11] Moore's interpretation of Spencer may be the most philosophically sophisticated example of the bad name that Spencer has acquired as an unrepentant social Darwinist. A much less philosophically sophisticated but equally influential example is Richard Hofstadter's *Social Darwinism in American Thought* (Boston: Beacon Press, 1955), chapter 2. For a recent example that continues to perpetuate, unfairly, Spencer's bad name, see Jagdish Hattiangadi, "Philosophy of Biology in the Nineteenth Century" in C. L. Ten (ed.), *The Nineteenth Century, Routledge History of Philosophy* (London: Routledge, 1994), vol. VII, pp. 288–9. According to Hattiangadi, Spencer was one of Darwin's "most ardent admirers" and "proposed a doctrine called Social Darwinism" whose "popularity with some despicable political movements in the twentieth century (e.g. with the National Socialists, or Nazis) has left many intellectuals with a horror of social theoretical biologists."

[12] As critics of Moore have noted, there is no necessary connection between indefinability and the four following possibilities for committing the fallacy: (1) confusing a natural with another natural property; (2) confusing a non-natural with another non-natural property; (3) confusing a natural with a non-natural property; and (4) confusing a non-natural with a natural property. In other words, rejection of Moore's claim that good is indefinable is compatible with acceptance of the possibility of committing the naturalistic fallacy in either of its four versions above. One may hold that good is definable and then simply proceed to misdefine it by the wrong property.

[13] Moore, *Principia Ethica*, p. 46.

necessary for life" (*Principia Ethica*, p. 44). Hence, if Moore is also attributing this view to Spencer, then he is imputing a much starker rendering of good to Spencer. Spencer's good becomes not simply the path that human evolution happens to be taking, thus far a path of enlightened progress, but brute survival. Mere survival is good and those who manage to survive do what they ought to be doing. Moore neglects to add that good *qua* mere survival is meaningless, in any case, unless we know *how much* survival makes for good survival.

We have now arrived, via Moore's appropriation of Spencer, at the standard criticism of evolutionary ethics where "survival of the fittest" means survival of the best. A. G. N. Flew puts this criticism as well as anyone:

> For that theory provides no independent criterion of fitness. It is, as has very frequently but too often ineffectively been pointed out, a theory of the survival of the fittest only and precisely in so far as actual or possible survival is to be construed as the sufficient condition of fitness to survive. If some further and independent criterion were to be introduced then the deductive argument would no longer be valid: natural selection is necessarily selection only for exactly what at precisely the time in question it in fact takes to survive, and where anything else seems to be being picked it is because that something else then happens to be linked contingently with what at that time happens to be required for survival. The Darwinian guarantee that it is always the fittest who have survived, the fittest who do survive, and the fittest who will survive is by itself neither an assurance that any particular thing which has survived so far will continue to do so, nor an undertaking that everything which is most worth while must survive. If anyone were to complain, using this present Darwinian criterion of fitness, that some particular social arrangement encourages the multiplication of the unfit and the extermination of the fit, then his complaint would be plainly self-contradictory.[14]

Moore, to his credit, is not always comfortable about imputing such a barren and vulgar form of ethical naturalism to Spencer. He acknowledges that Spencer's ethical theory is not always easy to interpret. He admits that Spencer sometimes identifies good with pleasure and then wonders how this rendering of good fits with good as evolution. Perhaps, says Moore, Spencer was a "naturalistic Hedonist." Perhaps Spencer meant no more than "that a tendency to increase quantity of life is merely a criterion" of good conduct (*Principia Ethica*, p. 46). That is, Spencer's view "may also be held

[14] A. G. N. Flew, *Evolutionary Ethics* (London: Macmillan and Co., 1967), p. 14.

without fallacy" to the extent that Spencer meant that "the more evolved, though not itself the better, is a *criterion*, because a concomitant, of the better" (p. 55). Evolution and good may not be identical after all. They may be contingently connected, thereby allowing the former to serve as a "presumption" for the existence of the latter. Being a "presumption" for good, makes evolution a "criterion" for good. Hence, Moore concedes that it might have been better to treat Spencer in *Principia Ethica*'s chapter 3 on hedonism.[15]

Moore's notion of criterion is ambiguous. He seems to be suggesting that developed Western societies have evolved thus far as they ought to have evolved. Historical trends, fortunately, have been the normatively correct trends, though there is no guarantee that they will continue as the best ones. Hence, human evolution is not necessarily good though, contingently speaking, it has happily turned out to be good. And, hence, we must not resign ourselves willy-nilly to any and all evolutionary developments. What we ought to do remains irrevocably and logically distinct from what we have done so far.

Nevertheless, in suggesting that evolution might legitimately serve as a "criterion" or a "presumption," Moore seems to hold that human evolutionary trends are nonetheless normatively serviceable. Insofar as past trends *happened*, by and large, to be those that ought to have happened, then they might serve as normative clues, or signposts, for evaluating human behavior. In other words, the history of where we have come from might be helpful in guiding us to where we ought to be going.

Interpreted in this way, Moore's revised assessment of Spencer ironically anticipates the nearly identical interpretative moves that defenders of Mill have deployed against Moore's claim that Mill also committed a version of the naturalistic fallacy. D. P. Dryer, for instance, has argued convincingly that Mill never posits a logical relationship between "desire" and "desirable" in his controversial proof of utility in *Utilitarianism.* Rather, for Mill according to Dryer, what people happen to desire serves simply as "evidence" for what is desirable. It simply indicates what is probably desirable. Because people do, as a matter of fact, desire happiness most of all, one

[15] In *The Elements of Ethics*, Moore provides nearly the same disclaimer verbatim. See G. E. Moore, *The Elements of Ethics* (ed.), Tom Regan (Philadelphia: Temple University Press, 1991), pp. 35–6.

should not conclude that happiness is *necessarily* desirable. One is only entitled to conclude that happiness is our best candidate. The link between "desire" and "desirable" is merely contingent and probable rather than logical and necessary. In short, on this interpretation of Mill's proof, people's desires are simply a "criterion" of desirable just as evolution seems to be for Spencer.[16]

Moore's irresolution about Spencer betrays his uncertainty regarding how far Spencer actually goes in embracing ethical naturalism. Moore's Spencer was a straw man and indeed Moore half-heartedly admits as much, as the above analysis of Moore's conception of "criterion" demonstrates. Moore's ambivalence towards Spencer's theory of good also underscores my earlier conclusion that Spencer never defined good. Unlike Moore, Spencer was never preoccupied with larger metaethical issues of definition including definitional pronouncements about good.

Moore's muddled reading of Spencer may stem, in part, from the fact that Moore takes "quantity of life" as the key to understanding what Spencer means by good. Inasmuch as by "quantity of life" Spencer means length of life, we should not be surprised by Moore's belief that Spencer defined good as survival.

Furthermore, Moore's confused reading of Spencer is exacerbated by his evident unfamiliarity with much of Spencer's writings. Indeed, his criticisms seem to be drawn primarily from "The Data of Ethics" in *The Principles of Ethics*. When Moore says that "Mr. Spencer does not, after all, tell us clearly what he takes to be the relation of Pleasure and Evolution in ethical theory," we must conclude that Moore has given short shrift to the full body of Spencer's work (*Principia Ethica*, p. 51). The previous discussion of Spencer's moral psychology demonstrates that Spencer devoted considerable attention to this very relationship.

Spencer's 1893 essay, "Evolutionary Ethics," furnishes additional powerful reasons for insisting that Spencer was not an ethical naturalist in the vulgar Darwinist sense according to which all that evolves and survives is good. *The Man Versus the State*, however

[16] See D. P. Dryer, "Mill's Utilitarianism" in Robson, (ed.), *Collected Works* (1969), vol. x, pp. lxiii–lxxxv. Sidgwick has likewise been defended as offering an "evidentiary view of desire" with regard to establishing the identity of good. See Thomas Christiano, "Sidgwick on Desire, Pleasure and the Good" in Bart Schultz (ed.), *Essays on Henry Sidgwick* (Cambridge University Press, 1992), pp. 274–6.

steeped in Darwinist polemic, should not be fetishized as typifying Spencer's mature evolutionary moral theory.[17]

"Evolutionary Ethics" was first published by the *Athenaeum* as a response to T. H. Huxley's "Evolution and Ethics," delivered at Oxford in the spring of 1893 as that year's Romanes Lecture. In his lecture, Huxley attacked Spencer as Moore later attacked him, although not with the same analytic rigor. Huxley labeled Spencer's "ethics of evolution" a "fallacy" because it rested upon the ambiguity of the phrase "survival of the fittest." Survival of the fittest wrongly assumes that because, "on the whole, animals and plants have advanced in perfection of organization by means of the struggle for existence and the consequent 'survival of the fittest,' therefore men in society, men as ethical beings, must look to the same process to help them towards perfection." But, Huxley warns, fittest has a "connotation of best; and about best there hangs a moral flavor." By contrast, "what we call goodness or virtue – involves a course of conduct which, in all respects, is opposed to that which leads to success in the cosmic struggle for existence. In place of ruthless self-assertion it demands self-restraint . . . It repudiates the gladiatorial theory of existence."[18]

In private correspondence of March 1894, Huxley again denies that evolutionary theory can serve as a normative principle. We must not confuse evolution as an account of morality with evolution as morality:

There are two very different questions which people fail to discriminate. One is whether evolution accounts for morality, the other whether the principle of evolution in general can be adopted as an ethical principle.

[17] See, once more, note 7 in chapter 3 for the political motives that prompted Spencer to write *The Man Versus the State*.

[18] T. H. Huxley, "Evolution and Ethics" in T. H. Huxley, *Evolution and Ethics and Other Essays* [1893] (New York: D. Appleton and Co., 1929), pp. 80 and 82. In "T. H. Huxley's 'Evolution and Ethics': The Politics of Evolution and the Evolution of Politics," *Victorian Studies*, 20 (1977), Michael Helfand argues that Huxley was not interested in affirming the independence of ethics like Moore was. Rather, he was more interested in "warning" the middle and upper classes of the need to abandon strict *laissez-faire* lest the lower classes become overly despondent and revolutionary. Few of Huxley's philosophical contemporaries, including Spencer and Leslie Stephen, seem to have been aware of any such hidden agenda. For Stephen's response, see Leslie Stephen, "Ethics and the Struggle For Existence," *The Contemporary Review*, 64 (1893), 157-70. Stephen mostly agrees with Huxley's claim that ethical behavior requires opposing the struggle for existence though he thinks that Huxley has overstated the gap between ethics and other evolutionary phenomena.

The first, of course, I advocate, and have constantly insisted upon. The second I deny, and reject all so-called evolutional ethics based upon it.[19]

Spencer, greatly distressed by Huxley's misconstrual of his moral theory, responded vigorously in "Evolutionary Ethics." Emphatically agreeing with Huxley that the survival of the fittest does not always produce the survival of the best, Spencer insists that he has never held any other view, referring to his earlier essay, "Mr. Martineau on Evolution," as proof. Following this earlier essay, he reemphasizes that the fittest "throughout a wide range of cases – perhaps the widest range – are not the 'best.'"[20] Furthermore, he continues:

We agree that the survival of the fittest is often not survival of the best. We agree in denouncing the brutal form of struggle for existence. We agree that the ethical process is part of the process of evolution. We agree that the struggle for life needs to be qualified when the gregarious state is entered, and that among gregarious creatures lower than man a rudiment of the ethical check is visible. We agree that among men the *ethical check*, becoming more and more preemptory, has to be enforced by the society in its corporate capacity, the State. (*Essays*, vol. I, p. 128; my italics)[21]

[19] Leonard Huxley, *The Life and Letters of Thomas Henry Huxley*, 2 vols. (New York: D. Appleton and Co., 1901), vol. II, p. 382. Huxley was considerably influenced by Hume and Adam Smith. According to James Paradis, Huxley "incorporated Hume and Darwin in the argument that moral behavior was based on the intuitive responses of an evolved psychological faculty . . . As Darwin had done in *The Descent of Man*, Huxley cited Smith's *Theory of Moral Sentiments*, which made the innate human sympathy borrowed from Hume the coin of the ethical realm." James Paradis, "*Evolution and Ethics* in Its Victorian Context," James Paradis and George C. Williams (eds.), *Evolution and Ethics* (Princeton University Press, 1989), p. 14. Huxley's rejection of evolutionary theory as a normative principle is surely derived from Hume's insistence that conclusions about what ought to be cannot be deduced from premises about what factually is. Huxley also published a study of Hume. See T. H. Huxley, "Hume," *Collected Essays* [1893], 9 vols. (London: Macmillan and Co., 1894), vol VI.

[20] Herbert Spencer, "Evolutionary Ethics," *Various Fragments* [1897] (New York: D. Appleton and Co., 1898), p. 125.

[21] See also Spencer, "M. De Laveleye's Error," *Various Fragments*, p. 116, where Spencer rebuts the latter's accusation that by survival of the fittest, he countenances violent elimination of inferior and weaker humans by stronger ones. Spencer replies that M. De Laveleye "ignores the fact that [*Social Statics*] as a whole is an elaborate statement of the conditions under which, and limits within which, the natural processes of elimination of the unfit should be allowed to operate." And see Spencer to T. H. Huxley, February 6, 1888, *The Huxley Collection*, Imperial College of Science and Technology. Writing in response to Huxley's "The Struggle For Existence in Human Society," Spencer says, "I have nothing to object, and everything to agree to." Nonetheless, Spencer continues, "But while I am at one with you in this preliminary argument, I dissent from the conclusion drawn and from the corollaries." Since Spencer proceeds to differ with Huxley regarding state relief for the poor, increased educational opportunities for the poor, state regulation of alcohol sales and improvement of the status of women, Spencer disagrees with Huxley as to what policy measures constitute limitations on the struggle for existence. Spencer and Huxley, that is,

For Spencer, the survival of the best, as opposed to the survival of the fittest, necessitates that humans learn to "check" their behavior morally. Principally, basic moral rights must be respected if human evolution is to be good rather than merely successful. Evolutionary ethics refuses to make the struggle for survival into a normative principle:

> It [evolutionary ethics] is represented as nothing but an assertion of the claims of the individual to what benefits he can gain in the struggle for existence; whereas it is in far larger measure a specification of the *equitable limits* to his activities, and of the *restraints* which must be imposed on him . . . So far from being, as some have alleged, an advocacy of the claims of the strong against the weak, it is much more an insistence that the weak shall be guarded against the strong, so that they may suffer no greater evils than their relative weakness itself involves. And no one has more vehemently condemned that "miserable *laissez-faire* which calmly looks on while men ruin themselves in trying to enforce by law their equitable claims." (*Essays*, vol. 1, pp. 125–6; first two sets of italics mine)[22]

Furthermore, evolutionary ethics is no cause for fatalism or moral resignation. As Spencer scornfully says, "It is supposed that societies, too, passively evolve apart from any conscious agency; and the inference is that, according to the evolutionary doctrine, it is needless for individuals to have any care about progress, since progress will take care of itself. Hence, the assertion that 'evolution erected into the paramount law of man's moral and social life becomes a paralyzing and immoral fatalism.'" On the contrary, such a supposition is an "error."[23]

In sum, the principle of equal freedom and its corollaries tame remorseless struggle in the name of the good. Though born of the social evolutionary process itself, they gradually discipline it. Social evolution favors cultures that develop primitive sentiments of equal freedom and basic rights. Once sufficiently widespread, these primitive sentiments grow, via the mechanism of the inheritance of acquired characteristics, into moral habits. Eventually, members of these lucky cultures discover that these moral habits promote

agree that all which evolves is not ethically best but they disagree about what sort of juridical "checks" are needed to tame sufficiently the human evolutionary process.

22 One might think that Spencer is being inconsistent given that he holds, as we saw in chapter 2, that the value of restraint is secondary to the value of freedom. But recall that restraint is necessary given sociality. As Spencer says here, restraint is necessary so that the weak "may suffer no greater evils than their relative weakness itself involves." Given sociality, restraint is necessary if everyone, including the weak, is to reap what he or she deserves.

23 Herbert Spencer, "Social Evolution and Social Duty," *Various Fragments*, p. 131.

happiness as well as survival. Living well, and not just living, becomes the end of human activity. Humans begin to choose maximizing happiness for its own sake. Certain moral habits become refined into stringent decision procedures because everyone's living well favors such indirect strategies. In short, justice eventually "checks" the struggle for existence in the name of maximizing the good.[24] Spencer, then, was closer to Huxley than Huxley realized.[25] He was no more a fatalist than Huxley.

Surely, anxieties about "immoral fatalism" stimulated Moore's interest in exposing the purported fallacies of Spencer's moral theory especially if we accept Tom Regan's claim that Moore was passionately committed to defending the "autonomy of ethics" and, hence, the "autonomy of individuals." According to Regan:

> But at another level it is the autonomy of individuals that is lost or diminished if one or another naturalistic definition of Good is accepted . . . There would be no room – there *could* be no room – for individual judgment about *what sorts of things ought to exist for their own sakes*. That would be settled: All and only those things that are more evolved would fall into this category. The meanings of words would take over the work of the value judgments of individuals, and the determination of what things actually are good would be the business of those most qualified to decide what things actually are more evolved. In this case biologists [like Spencer presumably] would become our authorities.[26]

However not even biologists would have much to say if crude evolutionary ethics were true. Insofar as "whatever is more evolved" effectively amounts to "whatever survives," then fatalism would be so thoroughgoing as to exclude even biologists from making authoritative moral judgements.

[24] L. T. Hobhouse followed Spencer in claiming that progress depended upon moral self-consciousness subduing the struggle for existence. "Orthogenic evolution" was "a series of advances in the development of mind involving a parallel curtailment of the sphere of natural selection." L. T. Hobhouse, *Development and Purpose*, [1913] (London: Macmillan and Co., 1927), p. xxiii. See also L. T. Hobhouse, *Social Evolution and Political Theory* (New York: Kennikat Press, 1911), pp. 8–9, where Hobhouse says: "The fact that a thing is evolving is no proof that it is good, the fact that society has evolved is no proof that it has progressed. The point is important because under the influence of biological conceptions the two ideas are often confused, and the fact that human beings have evolved under certain conditions is treated as evidence of the value of those conditions, or perhaps as proving the futility of ethical ideas which run counter to evolutionary processes."

[25] In *The Ant and the Peacock* (Cambridge University Press, 1991), p. 375, Helena Cronin suggests that Huxley was closer to Spencer than either of them realized. She adds that although, "Spencer saw morality as a natural outcome of evolution, he also, as a Lamarckian, saw human striving as an essential contribution to that process."

[26] Tom Regan, *Bloomsbury's Prophet* (Philadelphia: Temple University Press, 1986), p. 202.

Spencer's commitment to the autonomy of ethics further reveals how misguided Moore's interpretation of Spencer's moral theory was. Though sometimes not easy to characterize, Spencer's theory of good was not an exercise in vulgar "naturalistic ethics." It did not exemplify the biological version of the naturalistic fallacy. This is not to deny that Spencer may have committed some other version of the naturalistic fallacy. Rather, it is to deny that he committed it in the particular way that Moore claims.[27]

THE METHODS OF JURIDICAL REASONING

We have seen that Spencer was essentially a universal hedonist and that Moore's unflattering appropriation of Spencer as part of his defense of the autonomy of ethics was misguided. Hence, we may conclude that, axiologically speaking, Spencer's moral theory is not quite so unappealing and, perhaps, deserves better from posterity. But such an assessment leaves untouched the cogency of the ways in which Spencer derives his intermediate principles of obligation. Such an assessment neglects Spencer's methods of juridical reasoning.

By methods of juridical reasoning, I mean the methods by which Spencer establishes his principles of justice or his decision procedures. Since liberal utilitarianism can consist in alternative justice strategies, what reasons make one strategy superior? Why opt for one decision procedure strategy more than another and why opt for Spencer's strategy specifically? Spencer deploys three different modes of reasoning, the third of which arguably functions as a Moorean "criterion," in answering such concerns.

The first method of reasoning is best described as a rational-

[27] Spencer's later fears that human evolution had entered a long, dark night of moral decline further belies the attempts of those who would force him, like a round peg, into the square hole of vulgar ethical naturalism. These doubts reinforce my position that Spencer did not think that the actual course of human evolution was necessarily the best course. And they also underscore Moore's misreading of Spencer on another account where Moore suggests that Spencer failed to appreciate that evolution could degenerate into a "converse process" of "Involution." Moore, *Principia Ethica*, p. 57. T. S. Gray contends that although in his "individualist doctrines" Spencer insisted on separating facts from values, in his "organicist doctrines" he "closed the gap" between them, often conflating them. By deploying a more "instrumentalist or functional" moral criterion in these latter doctrines rather than a "deontological" one, by making good prior to right, Spencer allegedly confused description and evaluation. Gray's assessment is specious. Consequentialist practical reasoning does not, of itself, entail confusing fact with value. Moore, after all, was a consequentialist. For Gray's position, see Gray, *The Political Philosophy of Herbert Spencer*, pp. 32–7.

deductive method. Spencer employs this method extensively in *Social Statics*. Near the outset of *Social Statics*, he rhetorically asks whether or not a "strictly scientific morality" can be discovered that can provide us with a "definite answer when we ask, 'Is this act good?' " Can we formulate a systematic moral theory that "can give us an axiom from which we may develop successive propositions until we have with mathematical certainty solved all our difficulties?" (p. 4). Rejecting "greatest happiness" as being too vacuous to be an effective candidate for such an axiom, Spencer adds that, after all, "greatest happiness" is our ultimate end, our "problem to be solved." We need, by contrast, a more substantive axiom to which we can appeal for normative guidance. We need a decision procedure.

Not surprisingly, according to Spencer, the principle of equal freedom proves to be just the axiom that we require and basic moral rights are its "successive propositions." Both this axiom and its derivative propositions are pivotal "*conditions* by conforming to which this greatest happiness may be attained" (*Social Statics*, p. 61).

This method of reasoning also purports to be logical: "For the most conspicuous trait of the chapter [chapter 4 of *Social Statics*] quoted from is the endeavor to establish by *reason* a definite and absolute principle of restraint. And the aim of the work as a whole is to deduce by reason, from this fundamental principle reached by reason, a set of derivative restraints" (p. 82). Given the important empirical fact that humans live socially, and given that they value happiness above all else, reason commends the principle of equal freedom as our fundamental axiom of obligation. If we wish to maximize happiness, then logical considerations supposedly dictate that we embrace equal freedom as our principal decision procedure. But this kind of reasoning is hypothetical in the Kantian sense. It concerns means rather than ends. In A. N. Prior's words, it "instruct[s] us how to best achieve some end which we desire ('If you want X, you ought to do Y')."[28]

So Spencer's corollaries of the principle of equal freedom are contingently, or conditionally, necessary. They are not really logically necessary as chapter 3 suggests Spencer thought they were. They are necessary in terms of what one must do to achieve a given end such as maximizing some global value, like happiness. We may choose to

[28] A. N. Prior, *Logic and the Basis of Ethics* (Oxford University Press, 1965), p. 37.

act otherwise and thereby fail to do what it necessarily takes to promote happiness. But if we do, we have failed not as good logicians but rather as prudent strategists.

The Principles of Ethics also makes use of the rational-deductive method of juridical reasoning but in a way that Spencer thinks highlights important methodological differences between his liberal utilitarianism and Benthamism. In that revealing letter to Mill professing his utilitarian loyalties (discussed in chapter 4), Spencer says that the task of moral science is "to deduce, from the laws of life and the conditions of existence, what kinds of action necessarily tend to produce happiness, and what kinds to produce unhappiness." He then adds that by deduction he means scientific deduction, in the sense that scientific generalizations explain causal relations between natural phenomena. Just as the science of astronomy generates "deductions showing why the celestial bodies *necessarily* occupy certain places at certain times," so scientific utilitarianism ought to exhibit similar explanatory power and rigor:

> Doubtless if utilitarians are asked whether it can be by mere chance that this kind of action works evil and that works good, they will answer no; they will admit that such sequences are parts of a necessary order among phenomena. But though this truth is beyond question; and though if there are causal relations between acts and their results, rules of conduct can become scientific only when they are deduced from these causal relations; there continues to be entire satisfaction with that form of utilitarianism in which these causal relations are practically ignored. (*The Principles of Ethics*, vol. I, p. 91)

Thus, what most distinguishes Benthamism from his own version of utilitarianism, as far as Spencer is concerned, is the purported scientific methodology of the latter. Where Benthamites, in Spencer's view, are satisfied with *inductive* generalizations from experience in establishing their moral rules, he is not. Such generalizations leave utilitarianism unfinished. Such generalizations are the stuff of "empirical utilitarianism" which Spencer says is but a "transitional form to be passed through on the way to rational utilitarianism" (*The Principles of Ethics*, vol. I, p. 90).[29] "Rational utilitarianism," by contrast, is more theoretical, packing more

[29] On the same page Spencer says, "But acceptance of these generalizations and the inferences from them, does not amount to recognition of causation in the full sense of the word. So long as only *some* relation between cause and effect in conduct is recognized, and not *the* relation, a completely scientific form of knowledge has not been reached."

explanatory punch missing from "empirical utilitarianism." Hence, as far as Spencer is concerned, "rational utilitarianism" also predicts better than its less sophisticated predecessor. It more successfully predicts which *categories* of actions, which fundamental obligations, will tend to maximize general happiness.[30] Moreover, it concludes that respect for basic rights will *always* maximize happiness over the long run. Where "empirical utilitarians" purportedly rely upon crude guesswork, "rational utilitarians" deploy scientific thinking in their quest to discover the single best overall strategy for maximizing happiness.

In sum, "rational utilitarianism" purportedly supersedes "empirical utilitarianism" in rigor and completeness. Arguably no less empirical than "empirical utilitarianism," it surpasses the latter by building its normative recommendations on hard predictive generalizations.

Spencer's second method of juridical reasoning is best categorized as a psychological-descriptive method. In *Social Statics*, this method is the method of his theory of the moral sense which he also calls the "method of nature" (p. 19). In chapter 2, we saw that for Spencer in *Social Statics* the moral sense is a faculty that gradually becomes more sensitive with social progress. Moreover, as we also saw, it is a "feeling" that "tends to generate convictions that things are good or bad, according as they bring it pleasure or pain" (p. 25). In short, the moral sense is partially an evaluative emotion that is fused with our feelings of pleasure or pain. Experiences of pleasure and pain carry, in piggy-back fashion, our feelings of positive and negative evaluation.

In time, our moral sensibilities develop analytic power. Spencer describes how our "moral sense" evolves by comparing its development to that of our "geometric sense." According to Spencer, humans possess a geometric sense that allows us to assess intuitively linear relations. As our mental skills improve, we learn to refine these rough intuitions about linear relations by analytically "comparing notes." We soon discover the truth of basic geometric axioms such as "Things which are equal to the same thing are equal to one another." We next learn to make "successive deductions" in order to

[30] See also Spencer, *The Principles of Ethics*, vol. 1, p. 90, where Spencer says: "The implication is simply that we are to ascertain by induction that such and such mischiefs or benefits *do* go along with such and such acts; and are then to infer that the like relations will hold in the future."

solve even the most complicated geometric problems. Similarly, our moral sense intuits fundamental moral axioms (the principle of equal freedom, for instance) "from which reason may develop a systematic morality" (pp. 28–9).[31]

Spencer's early descriptive moral psychology is meant to do more than provide us with an *account* of how our most important normative skills develop, more than merely *describe* how we have formulated our particular principles of obligations by analytically honing our moral intuitions. By converging with the first method of reasoning, insofar as the second method purports to describe how this first method develops, the second method reinforces our faith in the first method's results, namely the decision procedures that it generates.

The Principles of Ethics, as we saw in chapter 2 refines Spencer's account of the development of our moral sentiments. According to this improved account, pleasure-producing activities have tended to enhance human survival. That is, "those races of beings only can have survived in which, on the average, agreeable or desired feelings went along with activities conducive to the maintenance of life . . . and there must ever have been, other things equal, the most numerous and long-continued survivals among races in which these adjustments of feelings to actions were best" (vol. I, p. 115).

Moreover, as the survival value of pleasant activities becomes understood, pleasure begins to be pursued self-consciously. Whenever "sentiency makes its appearance as an accompaniment, its forms must be such that in the one case the produced feeling is of a kind that will be sought – pleasure, and in the other case is of a kind that will be shunned – pain" (*The Principles of Ethics*, vol. I, p. 115). And because pleasure becomes increasingly valued for its own sake, the pursuit of pleasure gradually becomes purposive and scientific. Vague intuitions about how best to promote pleasure give way to cognitive sentiments that, in turn, mature into stringent decision procedures:

> Though the moral sentiments generated in civilized men by daily conduct with social conditions and gradual adaptation to them, are indispensable as incentives and deterrents; and though the intuitions corresponding to these sentiments, have, in virtue of their origin, a general authority to be reverently recognized; yet the sympathies and antipathies hence originating, together with the intellectual expressions of them, are, in their

[31] See also pp. 85–94 where Spencer discusses the growing respect for basic rights in terms of the analytic refinement of our moral ideas.

primitive forms, necessarily vague. To make guidance by them adequate to all requirements, their dictates have to be interpreted and made definite by science, to which end there must be analysis of those conditions to complete living which they respond to, and from converse with which they have arisen. And such analysis necessitates the recognition of happiness for each and all, as the end to be achieved by fulfillment of these conditions. (*The Principles of Ethics*, vol. 1, p. 204)

Social evolution favors, but does not justify, the pursuit of pleasure. Once pleasure begins to be pursued for its own sake, its pursuit starts becoming scientifically strategized. Intuitionism evolves into "empirical" utilitarianism which, in turn, evolves into "rational" utilitarianism following the descriptive outline of the development of ethics in *Social Statics*. But given the more sophisticated, evolutionary account of the development of justice in *The Principles of Ethics*, we are even more warranted in accepting the principles of justice resulting from the now scientifically fortified, rational-deductive method as true. Moral psychology, in Spencer's mind, again reinforces utilitarian strategizing by explaining, but now with much greater scientific sophistication, how such strategizing has developed. Understanding how, evolutionarily speaking, we have gotten the decision procedures we have gotten, justifies them however we may continue to refine them or take them more stringently. But, of course, a psychological account of one version of instrumental justice is not any more a justification of it than a descriptive or explanatory account of one version of the good is a justification of this version as correct. Here, if anywhere, Spencer's moral reasoning succumbs to the temptations of ethical naturalism.

Spencer deploys a third method of juridical reasoning, best described as sociological and anthropological. This method consists of providing diverse sociological and historical examples of our slowly growing respect for the principle of equal freedom and its derivative corollaries. For example, in *Social Statics*, Spencer observes, "It is by their greater harmony with [equal freedom] that the laws, opinions, and usages of a civilized society are chiefly distinguished from those of a barbarous one" (p. 85). Spencer then lists several historical and sociological examples which purportedly support this conclusion.

Like *Social Statics*, *The Principles of Ethics* deploys this third method liberally. Spencer seems to feel that by offering example after sociological example of the direction which human morality is ostensibly taking, we are further warranted in taking the findings of "rational" utilitarianism seriously. Here, sociology and anthropology indeed provide *evidence*, in the Moorean sense of "criterion," of the morally right.

Although Spencer's three methods of moral reasoning are mutually reinforcing, they are not equally important. The rational-deductive method is primary. Even after Spencer begins retheorizing it after *Social Statics*, it remains his method of juridical reasoning of choice.

But how shall we understand the deductive nature of this first method in detail especially given its importance? Shall we take Spencer at his word, even in later works, and concede that this method is, after all, genuinely deductive or are our earlier doubts concerning its deductive nature justified? Deductive moral reasoning has held considerable appeal in English moral theorizing, going back at least to Thomas Reid in the eighteenth century. So Spencer inherited a respected English philosophical tradition, but it would have been better for him to have done without it.

In *Men Versus the State*, Michael Taylor maintains that Spencer "reworked" nineteenth-century utilitarianism and that the core of this reworking consisted in his effort to replace "empirical" Benthamite utilitarianism with "rational" or "deductive" utilitarianism.[32] Although Taylor correctly characterizes Spencer's *intentions*, he seems to take Spencer's rational "reworking" of utilitarianism as a genuine methodological departure.

Furthermore, Taylor is correct in underscoring Spencer's belief that "rational" utilitarianism was a vast methodological improvement over "empirical" utilitarianism in the way that Newtonian physics was an decisive improvement over previous astronomical theories.[33] Whereas "empirical" utilitarianism errs for Taylor's Spencer by relying on *contingent* generalizations from experience for generating fundamental rules of obligation, "rational" utilitarianism correctly deduces them as *necessary* conditions to happiness. Finally, Taylor is correct in suggesting that Spencer regarded "rational" utilitarianism as a methodological bulwark against the dangers of Benthamite welfarism. Insofar as "rational" utilitarianism generates

[32] For Taylor's analysis of Spencer's "reworked" utilitarianism, see chapter 6, "The Reworking of Utilitarianism" Spencer, *Men Versus the State*.

[33] Bentham, likewise, saw himself as a Newton of social and moral science. But he was not enough of a Newton for Spencer.

indefeasible rights, then governments are sharply *constrained* in what they may justly do to their citizens in the name of utility. Rights serve as powerful side-constraints on the pursuit of general happiness.

Perceiving the importance of Spencer's distinction between "rational" and "empirical" utilitarianism, Taylor also appreciates how misunderstanding this distinction has caused Spencer to be misclassified. For instance, John Gray, according to Taylor, wrongly claims that *both* Mill and Spencer were "rational" utilitarians whereas, in truth, only Spencer was. Mill, by contrast, was a traditional "empirical" utilitarian whose theory of justice was grounded in induction, observation and experience. But Taylor mistakenly accepts Spencer's own conviction that "rational" and "empirical" utilitarianism were in fact so *methodologically* different. Contrary to Spencer's claims, and Taylor's understanding of them, the rational-deductive method of juridical reasoning was neither uniquely rational nor uniquely deductive. Hence, the differences between Spencer and his nineteenth-century utilitarian predecessors (especially Mill) are less than they seem; certainly they were less than they seemed to Spencer.[34] Taylor, in other words, buys into Spencer's endeavor to distinguish sharply between "rational" and "empirical" utilitarianism and thus buys into Spencer's own confusion. He misunderstands Spencer in the very way that Spencer misunderstood himself.

The discussion of the rational-deductive method earlier in this section and of the relationship between the principle of equal freedom and moral rights in chapter 3 suggest that Spencer's "rational" utilitarianism was less than methodologically unique. As we are beginning to see, it was really a disguised version of "empirical" utilitarianism. Even Spencer sometimes concedes that "rational" utilitarianism was essentially methodologically "empirical."

In his 1860 *Education*, Spencer insists that "Proper conduct in life is much better guaranteed when the good and evil consequences of actions are rationally understood, than when they are merely

[34] These differences were also exaggerated by Spencer's contemporaries. Supporters and adversaries frequently pointed out that Spencer was fond of reasoning downwards from a priori axioms. For instance, see Francis Galton's remark that Spencer "loved to dogmatise from a priori axioms." Francis Galton, "Reminiscences of HS," *The Herbert Spencer Papers*, MS. 791/355/8i. Spencer, by the way, defiantly proclaimed his ignorance of formal logic.

believed on authority."[35] In other words, acting morally requires clearly understanding the contingent connection between our actions and their consequences. Such understanding is rational but only in the sense of being empirically more scientific and in better predicting what actions will cause what effects. By implication, then, rational utilitarianism is simply a more scientific empirical utilitarianism.[36]

Rational utilitarianism, moreover, recommends liberal politics because liberal politics cause citizens to experience the connection between their actions and the consequences of their actions more vividly. Liberal politics are therefore a better education in rational utilitarianism. They teach us to see, more effectively than other political alternatives, what kinds of actions produce what kind of results. When we suffer the painful consequences of our own mistakes unshielded by government paternalism, we purportedly quickly learn not to make them again. Like the small child who burns his or her fingers upon touching a candle's flame, we quickly learn how best to minimize pain and, ultimately, how best to maximize happiness. What Spencer says of the child's moral education is no less true of the adult's:

> Bear constantly in mind the truth that the aim of your discipline should be to produce a *self-governing* being; not to produce a being to be *governed by others*. Were your children fated pass their lives as slaves, you could not too much accustom them to slavery during their childhood; but as they are by-and-by to be free men, with no one to control their daily conduct, you cannot too much accustom them to self-control while they are still under your eye. This it is which makes the system of discipline by natural consequences, so especially appropriate to the social state which we in England have now reached. (*Education*, pp. 220–1)

In "Morals and Moral Sentiments," Spencer again defends rational utilitarianism as improved empirical utilitarianism. He contends that "there exists a primary basis of morals independent of, and in a sense antecedent to, that which is furnished by experiences of utility; and consequently, independent of, and, in a sense antecedent to, those moral sentiments which I conceive to be generated by such

[35] Herbert Spencer, *Education* (New York: D. Appleton and Co., 1924), pp. 189–90.

[36] See also pp. 77–8 where Spencer links science, causal necessity and rationality together: "On the other hand, the relations which science presents are casual [*sic*] relations; and, when properly taught, are understood as such. Instead of being practically accidental, they are necessary; and as such, give exercise to the reasoning faculties. While language familiarizes with non-rational relations, science familiarizes with rational relations."

experiences" (*Essays*, vol. 1, p. 334). But, contrary to the way that he says others have misunderstood him, particularly Richard Hutton in an essay entitled "A Questionable Parentage for Morals," Spencer claims that our a priori intuitions of right and wrong are *not*, "when scientifically analysed," simply "our ancestors' *best observations and most useful empirical rules*" (*Essays*, vol. 1, p. 338).[37] Rather, our intuitions stem from our ancestors' subconscious experiences of utility, from their subconscious experiences of acts and their consequences:

> The experiences of utility I refer to are those which become registered, not as distinctly recognized connexions between certain kinds of acts and certain kinds of remote results, but those which become registered in the shape of associations between groups of feelings that have often recurred together, though the relation between them has not been consciously generalized – associations the origin of which may be as little perceived as is the origin of the pleasure given by the sounds of a rookery; but which, nevertheless, have arisen in the course of daily converse with things, and serve as incentives or deterrents. (*Essays*, vol. 1, p. 338)

Moreover, our intuitions become part of our physiology, part of our nervous system, and are passed on to subsequent generations. With each generation, they grow stronger until they become consciously generalized as rational principles (or decision procedures) of behavior especially once we begin valuing happiness for its own sake. That is, we begin appreciating why certain classes of action invariably promote, and why certain classes of actions invariably undermine, utility. And once these truths become "distinctly recognized" and refined, we may conclude that our utilitarian theory has matured, has become sufficiently scientific and rational.

What differentiates mature, scientific utilitarianism from its predecessors is not so much logical methodology but rather utilitarian *self-awareness*. What makes "rational utilitarianism" rational is what makes some instrumental strategies more rational than others, namely the self-conscious rigor with which it formulates strategies for success.[38]

[37] Hutton's "A Questionable Parentage of Morals" appeared in *Macmillan's Magazine* in July, 1869 whereas Spencer's reply, "Morals and Moral Sentiments," first appeared in *The Fortnightly Review* in April, 1871. Hutton, in turn, replied to Spencer that same year with "Mr. Herbert Spencer on Moral Intuitions and Moral Sentiments" in *The Contemporary Review*. There, Hutton argued that utilitarian reasoning is always empirical.

[38] See also Spencer, *The Study of Sociology*, pp. 279–80 where Spencer says that "empirical" utilitarianism is "unconsciously made" and rests on the "accumulated results of past human experience" whereas "rational" utilitarianism is "determined by intellect."

The Man Versus the State engenders much the same interpretative assessment. "Rational utilitarianism," in contrast to older versions, "implies guidance by the general conclusions which analysis of *experience* yields" (my italics). It does not rely on "facts on the surface" but on "fundamental facts" of human experience, namely that life is maintained by certain activities and that sociality requires that these activities be mutually limited. Moreover, in comparison with its predecessors, "rational utilitarianism" does not ignore the "distant effects" of its strategies on the "lives of men at large" (pp. 162–5). "Rational utilitarianism," in short, is more precise, more attentive to crucial facts and more sensitive to long-term results. Still, it is wholly empirical.

Jonathan Riley has suggested that Spencer's utilitarianism is not wholly empirical, that it is indeed rational. In Riley's view, while Mill holds that our basic moral principles are contingent generalizations from experience, Spencer contends that they are necessary truths that "are known intuitively to us *prior* to our experience: we simply cannot conceive certain things other than as we do because of those *a priori* truths."[39] These moral truths are innate genetic inheritances and reflect the working out of a grand evolutionary purpose. The principle of equal freedom and moral rights are self-evident, moral sense intuitions implanted by evolution as it unwinds towards its culmination. Mill, by contrast, "refuses to assert that progress is predetermined by some mysterious mechanism (divine or otherwise) that feeds successful *group* norms and beliefs back into the innate mental capacities of subsequent generations of *individuals*." He would probably "dismiss any such mechanism as a 'rationalist fiction'" ("Individuality, Custom and Progress," p. 238). In sum, according to Riley, Spencer is a rationalist idealist for whom human evolution consists in the gradual recognition of the moral truths necessary to realizing our purpose, namely greatest happiness. Hence, Spencer's liberal utilitarianism is also teleological. Reason is the fulfillment of divine purpose.

Riley's Spencer is, at best, the Spencer of *Social Statics*, for after *Social Statics* Spencer repudiates his belief in divine purpose. Thus, Spencer's utilitarianism is not teleological after *Social Statics*. In any case, even in *Social Statics*, reason's role is more seeming than substantive. There, reason purportedly refines our moral sense

[39] Jonathan Riley, "Individuality, Custom and Progress," *Utilitas*, 3 (1991), 238.

intuitions which are intuitions precisely because the moral strategies they commend are necessary to maximizing happiness. Thus, reason simply causes us to recognize cognitively what we already intuitively know through *experience*. But how? Is cognitive recognition syllogistic? Spencer never defends the sanctity of the principle of equal freedom and moral rights syllogistically in *Social Statics*. Rather, he continually insists that, as they progress, societies will increasingly appreciate the strategic value of liberal principles. Given that such appreciation is never syllogistic, it is presumably experientially grounded. Thus, even in *Social Statics*, rational utilitarianism is, at bottom, empirical. The rational refinement of our moral intuitions can only be a matter of testing them systematically through experience. Otherwise, our moral intuitions remain only intuitions and *Social Statics* would be little more than disguised intuitionism.

In a "Note to Chapter IV," appended to the 1877 edition of *Social Statics* in response to criticisms by Henry Sidgwick in *The Methods of Ethics*, Spencer remarks that the aim of *Social Statics* was to "establish by reason" an "absolute principle of restraint" and to "deduce by reason" from this principle a "set of derivative restraints" (p. 82). But Spencer next adds:

> The entire motive of the work [*Social Statics*] is that of establishing judgments rationally formed in place of unenlightened moral intuitions and vague estimations of results. For guidance by mere unaided sentiment it would substitute guidance by a definitely formulated fundamental principle to which that sentiment emphatically responds; and for guidance by the *unscientific non-quantitative* reasoning of mere empirical utilitarianism it would substitute guidance by *scientific or quantitative* reasoning – reasoning pervaded by that cardinal idea of *equalness*, which alone makes possible exact conclusions. (pp. 82–3; my italics)

"Rational" utilitarianism is "scientific" rather than intuitive. It is "quantitative" because its calculations are scientifically made.[40] Its reasoning is "pervaded" by the "idea of equalness" because

[40] Claude Bernard's 1865 account in H. C. Greene (trans.), *An Introduction to the Study of Experimental Medicine* (New York: Dover Publications, 1957), p. 27, of the experimental method, aptly characterizes Spencer's mature method of moral reasoning even though Spencer continued to call his method "rational." According to Bernard: "The metaphysician, the scholastic, and the experimenter all work with an *a priori* idea. The difference is that the scholastic imposes this idea as the absolute truth which he has found, and from which he then deduces consequences by logic alone. The more modest experimenter, on the other hand, states an idea as a question, as an interpretative, more or less probable anticipation of nature, from which he deduces consequences which, moment to moment, he confronts with reality by means of experiment."

happiness is measured in equal units. In other words, "rational" utilitarianism is more sophisticated than "empirical" utilitarianism because its strategic calculations are more precise and nuanced. But it remains empirical nonetheless. Thus, Spencer's 1877 reinterpretation of *Social Statics* is fully in keeping with his reformed conception of "rational" utilitarianism in *The Principles of Ethics.* By the 1870s, Spencer began to retheorize "rational" utilitarianism as a scientifically more rigorous version of "empirical" Benthamite utilitarianism. His drift towards political conservatism beginning about this time, moreover, is surely linked to this empirical retheorizing of his liberal utilitarianism. As his liberal utilitarianism became more manifestly empirical, it simultaneously became less vehemently liberal though Spencer continued to hold that indefeasible, liberal utilitarian principles would ultimately prevail.

I must continue to insist, then, that Spencer's liberal utilitarianism, at least in its maturer manifestation, was just as empirical, just as a posteriori as Mill's. For Spencer, evolution simply makes us better strategists because it makes us better social scientists.

Now, one might argue that I have stretched the meaning of empirical unduly. But one ought not to be misled by Spencer's conviction that a fixed set of moral rights just happens to emerge from the evolutionary process. There is no logical connection between strong moral rights and a priori reasoning. A posteriori reasoning can just as plausibly generate stringent, or even indefeasible, moral principles. To recall Sumner from the last chapter (p. 136), "absolute rights are not an impossible output for a consequentialist [empirical] methodology."

In sum, the differences between "rational utilitarianism" and "empirical utilitarianism" are methodologically far less than Spencer believed. Hence, Spencer's use of the terms "rational" and "empirical" is misleading. By calling his own utilitarianism "rational," he obscures the fact that his utilitarianism is closer to Benthamism than he realizes. Like the latter, it begins with facts about human behavior and then endeavors to derive utility-maximizing strategies accordingly. Unlike the latter, it builds upon what Mill calls the "unanalysed experience of the human race."[41] But unlike Benthamism, though, Spencer's utilitarian strategy features stringent moral rights as secondary decision procedures.

[41] Mill, "Bentham," p. 90.

Ironically, and despite Spencer's characterization of it, Benthamism was likewise suffused with similar rationalistic pretensions according to some interpreters. For instance, according to Elie Halévy, "By the beginning of 1832, Bentham and James Mill had organized constitutional law as a sum of corollaries of the principle of greatest happiness and of the principle of universal egoism, and it was Macaulay, a Whig, and a disciple of Bacon and Locke, a partisan of the principle of utility, but at the same time an upholder of the experimental method, who denounced their claim to solve political problems deductively."[42] Ross Harrison shares Halévy's assessment that Benthamism appears to be more a priori than it actually is:

> Bentham's use of the term "axioms" and his apparent unwavering confidence in the principle that all men pursue their own interests might lead one to think that his psychology must be purely *a priori*; that is, that it is a deductive or demonstrative science similar to geometry based on unquestionable first assumptions about how people are or behave, similar to classical economic theory. With the hindsight of J. S. Mill this would be natural, since the "geometric" method was exactly how he described the method of his father's work in political theory, and James Mill's *Essay on Government* looks to be a highly Benthamite production, starting with a factual principle about what people do do (pursue their own interest) and with an evaluative principle about what they ought to do (act in a way which results in the greatest happiness) and showing deductively that the only form of government which jointly satisfies these two principles is democracy . . . However, the assumption that Bentham's psychology is purely *a priori* is not correct. (*Bentham*, pp. 140–1)[43]

Like Bentham on some interpretations, then, Spencer saw himself as doing moral science that placed a premium on rational analysis. And like Bentham on some interpretations of him, Spencer seemed convinced, especially in his earlier writings, that rational analysis entailed logical deduction primarily. Both Bentham (on one view of

[42] Halévy, *The Growth of Philosophic Radicalism*, p. 494.

[43] For an example of Mill's interpretative "hindsight" depicting Bentham's utilitarianism as being overly rationalistic, see Mill's second corrective footnote about Spencer's utilitarianism in Mill, *Utilitarianism*, p. 65. Mill says, "Bentham, certainly, to whom in the *Social Statics* Mr Spencer particularly referred, is, least of all writers, chargeable with unwillingness to deduce the effect of actions on happiness from the laws of human nature and the universal conditions of human life. The common charge [presumably Mill's view] against him is of relying too exclusively upon such deductions, and declining altogether to be bound by the generalisations from specific experience which Mr Spencer thinks that utilitarians generally confine themselves to."

him) and Spencer saw themselves as improving utilitarian moral theory by rationalizing it though Spencer regarded his improvements as repairing the inadequate and partial improvements of Benthamism. That is why he continued to regard the latter as, regrettably, still too empirical. But, in the end, the juridical rules of both Bentham's and Spencer's versions of utilitarianism were not determinations of "logical necessity." At best, these rules were a "natural necessity, in that they follow from a characterization of human nature and purposes."[44] Perhaps, no version of utilitarianism can ever escape the purgatory of empiricism.

Even if all versions of utilitarianism are fated to empiricism, the substantive differences between varieties of utilitarianism can nonetheless be considerable. To claim that both Bentham and Spencer were empirical utilitarians is not to deny their differences. Utilitarianisms can be more or less liberal by being committed to substantively *different* decision procedures. Utilitarianisms can also be more or less liberal by being more or less committed to *stringent* decision procedures. Here, Bentham and Spencer surely part company. Here, if anywhere, Spencer's utilitarianism deviates from, if not improves upon, that of Bentham.

We can also appreciate the wholly empirical nature of Spencer's liberal utilitarianism by once more comparing Spencer and D. G. Ritchie. In chapter 3 we saw how similar Spencer and Ritchie's theories of natural rights were despite appearances to the contrary. For both, rights were natural merely insofar as they were essential conditions of human flourishing and well-being. For both, remember, humans have gradually been recognizing, through *experience*, the instrumental indispensability of rights.

Ritchie, like Spencer, likewise saw himself as nonetheless advocating a form of rational utilitarianism. According to Ritchie, "rational selection" supersedes "natural selection" with the rise of utilitarian practical reasoning:

> The ideas of 'natural selection' will apply perfectly to human evolution, if we remember that the variations on which natural selection works in human phenomena arise, not merely (1) 'spontaneously' or 'accidentally' . . . but (2) by imitation – which is at least a half-conscious process – and (3) by deliberate effort, as the result of reflection, with a view to obtain certain ends. Where such reflection has really anticipated what is

[44] Kelly, *Utilitarianism and Distributive Justice*, pp. 208–9.

advantageous, natural selection seems to be superseded in successful artificial or rational selection.[45]

Particular moralities, in other words, arise fortuitously by taking root in early societies that happen to survive in intersocietal struggle. These moralities, in turn, make survivors more internally harmonious, further strengthening them in their struggle with their rivals. Their success encourages rivals to mimic their moral codes. Mimicry, a kind of "half-conscious" utilitarian practical reasoning, spreads these codes, making them ubiquitous, intuitive and seemingly unconnected with considerations of their usefulness.

Eventually, fully conscious utilitarian practical reasoning replaces moral intuitionism as well-being becomes deliberately and scientifically pursued for its own sake irrespective of the intersocietal, competitive advantages that utilitarian morality bestows. Hence, full-blown, scientific utilitarianism emerges from its intuitionist adolescence completely transcending, at last, the haphazard sluggishness and cruelty of "natural selection" as an engine of moral progress. Utilitarian "rational selection" accelerates the realization of general well-being, eliminating the unnecessary suffering generated by the unwitting, natural development of intuitionist utilitarianism. "When reflection appears, however, a higher form of morality becomes possible; the useful . . . The utilitarian reformer reflects for his society, and anticipates and obviates the cruel process of natural selection by the more peaceful methods of legislative change. The theory of natural selection thus gives a new meaning to Utilitarianism."[46] Natural selection has "vindicated all that has proved most permanently valuable in Utilitarianism."[47]

45 D. G. Ritchie, "What Are Economic Laws?", *Darwin and Hegel* (London: Swann Sonnenschein and Co., 1893), p. 170.

46 D. G. Ritchie, "Evolution and Democracy" in S. Coit (ed.), *Ethical Democracy: Essays in Dynamics* (London: G. Richards, 1900), pp. 105–6.

47 Ritchie, *Darwin and Hegel*, p. 62. Ritchie continues: "Natural selection (as I have tried to show more fully elsewhere) is a perfectly adequate cause to account for the rise of morality – in that same sense of 'cause' in which we use the term in scientific explanations of natural phenomena . . . Morality, to begin with, means those feelings and acts and habits which are advantageous to the welfare of the community. Morality comes to mean the conscious and deliberate adoption of those feelings and acts and habits which are advantageous to the welfare of the community; and reflection makes it possible to alter the conception of what the community is, whose welfare is to be considered" (pp. 62–3). Utilitarianism, for its part, rids social evolutionary theory of its fatalism by infusing it with a standard of right and, thus, with the spirit of reform. See Ritchie, "Evolution and Democracy," p. 15. For an informative discussion of the relationship between "rational" and "natural" selection in Ritchie's moral theory, see Den Otter, *British Idealism and Social Explanation*, pp. 104–9.

Despite being self-styled "rational" utilitarians, Ritchie and Spencer disagreed sharply regarding the mechanisms of moral development. Spencer, as we have seen, was a Lamarckian for whom our moral sentiments were strengthened through exercise and biologically transmittable. Utilitarian practical reasoning was therefore biologically tethered. Ritchie, by contrast, rejected Lamarckianism as scientifically specious. According to Ritchie, utilitarian morality has been developing via the mechanism of "objectified mind" which includes language and custom as well as the other "definite institutions" of civilization.[48] "Objectified mind" channels and refines our utility-generating moral principles as natural selection gradually succumbs to "rational" selection in human normative development.

Nevertheless, Ritchie grants that it may matter little, practically speaking, whether we accept "objectified mind" or use-inheritance as the vehicle of moral advance. Ritchie concedes: "Whether our ideals of goodness are due entirely to natural selection (of individuals and societies and usages) or partly to natural selection and partly to use-inheritance may be an interesting historical problem: but it has no direct bearing on the problem of what meaning there is in calling anything 'good' at all."[49]

Both Ritchie and Spencer, then, were evolutionary utilitarians. As we saw in chapter 3 (pp. 72–4, 78–9 and 80–1), both championed strong rights though not natural rights; at least not natural rights on any traditional understanding. Both were, therefore, liberal utilitarians though Ritchie advocated a much more socialist, indirect utilitarian strategy that included empowering welfare rights. Ritchie, after all, was a new liberal who looked back as much to T. H. Green as to J. S. Mill. But he was utilitarian whereas Green was not. Hence, Ritchie was what we might call a new liberal utilitarian where Spencer was simply a liberal utilitarian.[50]

48 D. G. Ritchie, "Has the Hereditability or Non-Hereditability of Acquired Characteristics Any Direct Bearing on Ethical Theory?", *Proceedings of the Aristotelian Society*, 3 (1895–6), p. 145.

49 Ibid., p. 147.

50 As Ritchie says in *Natural Rights*, p. 274, probably thinking of Spencer compared to himself: "How far this end [happiness] can be attained by leaving people alone, and how far it can be attained by interference – on this the great practical differences of opinion would begin. Where some [such as himself] would lay more stress on the need of directly removing obstacles to physical health, to intelligence and moral development, others [such as Spencer] would lay more stress on the need for 'freedom,' – on the need of letting people learn even by mistakes and failures, in order that their ultimate progress may be more secure."

But more importantly, for our purposes here, both Ritchie and Spencer were fundamentally empirical utilitarians although Spencer's empirical utilitarianism was harder to see. Ritchie, like Spencer, regarded his brand of liberal utilitarianism as rational utilitarianism but he clearly did not mean that it was rational in the deductive, logical sense. He merely meant that as utilitarian practical reasoning matured, it became more scientific and sophisticated. And, in the end, this is all that Spencer really meant as well. Comparing Ritchie to Spencer helps us to appreciate the truth of this verdict better.

SPENCER AND SIDGWICK

The two previous sections of this chapter have addressed Spencer's theory of good and the methodological status of his theory of right. As we have seen, his theory of good was largely hedonistic and utilitarian and, consequently, Spencer did not commit the naturalistic fallacy in the way Moore claims. Spencer's reasoning about good was not just another unvarnished exercise in evolutionary ethics. And as we have seen, his theory of right deployed a complex methodology that averred to be mostly rational yet proved to be essentially empirical. Though my interpretation may not be the received view of Spencer's method of reasoning about right, at least one other interpreter embraced something like it in Spencer's lifetime. Henry Sidgwick understood Spencer's ethics similarly, though Sidgwick found Spencer unimpressive.[51]

Ethical naturalism was very much in the formative metaethical air in England after 1850. Hence, its opponents, like Sidgwick, were bound to adumbrate the naturalistic fallacy as systematically later

[51] For Sidgwick's general estimation of Spencer, see A. Sidgwick and E. Sidgwick, *Henry Sidgwick, A Memoir* (London: Macmillan, 1906), pp. 277, 344 and 347. See especially Sidgwick's 1873 letter to H. G. Dakyns (p. 277), where Sidgwick says: "I am now working at a review of Herbert Spencer, which, I think, adds to my general despair. I find myself compelled to form the lowest opinion of a great deal of the results, and yet I have an immense admiration for his knowledge, his tenacious hold of very abstract and original ideas throughout a bold and complicated construction, his power of Combination and Induction. But the grotesque and chaotic confusion of his metaphysics!" Sidgwick's review (of *The Principles of Psychology*) appeared in *The Academy*, 4 (1973) as "Philosophy and Physical Science." Spencer likewise held Sidgwick in low regard. See, for instance, his 1878 letter, Spencer to W. Williams, *The Herbert Spencer Papers*, A.L. 112, where Spencer dismisses *The Methods of Ethics* commenting "I do not regard it as worth the paper it is printed upon."

worked out by Moore. Indeed, A. N. Prior suggests that Moore was probably "inspired" by Sidgwick's work on the problems of ethical naturalism (*Logic and the Basis of Ethics*, pp. 104–7). Prior believes that Moore was primarily influenced by Sidgwick's criticisms of Bentham in *The Methods of Ethics*. However, Moore was probably influenced more by Sidgwick's extensive criticisms of Spencer in his 1880 "Mr. Spencer's Ethical System," in his 1903 *Lectures on the Ethics of T. H. Green, Mr. Herbert Spencer, and J. Martineau* and in his *The Methods of Ethics*.[52]

In the first pages of *The Methods of Ethics*, Sidgwick sharply distinguishes ethics and politics from science. The former concern what "ought to be" and, therefore, are not sciences. Each of the former, properly speaking, is a "study." Whereas sciences such as psychology and sociology *explain* human conduct, ethics and politics do nothing of the kind. Explanation is "essentially different from an attempt to determine" which among "varieties of conduct is *right*" (pp. 1–2). Hence, theories which explain our behavior tell us nothing about what our behavior should be.

Not surprisingly, then, in *Lectures on the Ethics of T. H. Green, Mr. Herbert Spencer, and J. Martineau*, Sidgwick deprecates the kind of ethical reasoning that Moore accuses Spencer of using:

> I will only now observe that according to me an ethical end cannot be proved by biology. If biology presents me with a generalisation from lower forms of life to the effect that 'all actions are adjusted to preservation,' I answer that that proves nothing as to the total and complete end; and that mere preservation of life is palpably not adequate to this. To live well, as Aristotle says, we must live somehow; but that does not make life identical with living well.[53]

But, Sidgwick adds, this kind of spurious reasoning cannot be attributed to Spencer. Spencer, he says, is not interested in establishing normative ends via biology. Nor, according to Sidgwick, does Spencer mean preservation, adaptation or survival by good. By

[52] Schneewind notes that Moore heard Sidgwick lecture while a Cambridge undergraduate but found him boring. *Sidgwick's Ethics and Victorian Moral Philosophy* (Oxford University Press, 1977). Paul Farber concurs with Schneewind claiming that Moore heard "most of the telling arguments against evolutionary ethics" from Sidgwick while an undergraduate. The undergraduate lectures that Moore heard were Sidgwick's posthumously published *Lectures on the Ethics of T. H. Green, Mr. Herbert Spencer and J. Martineau*. See Paul Farber, *The Temptations of Evolutionary Ethics* (Berkeley: University of California Press, 1994), p. 111.

[53] Henry Sidgwick, *Lectures on the Ethics of T. H. Green, Mr. Herbert Spencer and J. Martineau* (London: Macmillan and Co., 1902), p. 144.

good, he means "pleasurable." In effect, then, Sidgwick is suggesting that the version of ethical naturalism that Moore later attributed to Spencer is incorrect. However, in Sidgwick's view, Spencer sometimes tends to assume that human adaptation coincides with, or invariably accompanies, increasing pleasure. For Sidgwick, this assumption is based on nothing more than "faith" (pp. 143–56).[54]

In *Philosophy and Its Scope and Relations*, Sidgwick repeats his view that Spencer never confuses good with evolutionary phenomena. Spencer never treats the "ultimate end of right conduct" scientifically. However, as far as Sidgwick is concerned, Spencer nevertheless fails to avoid related metaethical errors.[55] The mistaken kinds of ethical reasoning that Sidgwick accuses Spencer of deploying are, in effect, the psychological-descriptive and sociological methods discussed earlier. Sidgwick has both methods in mind when he remarks:

> Such an investigation is obviously a legitimate branch of Sociology or Psychology; and Chapters VII and VIII of Mr. Spencer's *Data of Ethics*, which treat of the 'Psychological View' and 'Sociological View,' seem to be largely concerned with speculations of this kind . . . What I wish to point out is that this species of inquiry, however successfully conducted, has not necessarily any tendency to 'establish' the authority of the morality of which it explains the existence; indeed, it has more often, I think, an effect of the opposite kind. A scientific explanation of current morality which shall also be an 'establishment' of it, must do more than exhibit the causes of existing ethical beliefs; it must show that these causes have operated in such a way as to make these beliefs true. (p. 137)[56]

[54] See also Henry Sidgwick, "Mr. Spencer's Ethical System," *Mind*, 5 (1880), 217-22. For those like Leslie Stephen who, by contrast, supposedly equate good with survival, see Sidgwick, *The Method of Ethics*, pp. 395–7 and 471.

[55] Henry Sidgwick, *Philosophy and Its Scope and Relations* (London: Macmillan and Co., 1902), pp. 23–4.

[56] See, too, Henry Sidgwick, "Symposium – Is the Distinction Between 'Is' and 'Ought' Ultimate and Irreducible?", *Proceedings, Aristotelian Society*, 2 (1892–4), 89–90. Sidgwick is probably thinking of Spencer's two methods when he observes: "I have not taken into account of the notions of life and development, and their place in psychology and sociology, that possessing these notions, science in this department does not merely ascertain resemblances and general laws of co-existence and change, but in so doing brings out the notion of an end to which psychical and social changes are related as means, and in relation to which alone they are really intelligible; and that this end supplies the requisite reduction of 'what ought to be' to what is. For in this end – variously conceived as vital or social 'health' or 'equilibrium' or 'life measured in breadth as well as length,' – we have (it is thought) a criterion of truth and error in moral judgments." See also Henry Sidgwick, "The Theory of Evolution in Its Application to Practice," *Mind*, 1 (1876), 54; Henry Sidgwick, "The Relation of Ethics to Sociology," *Miscellaneous Essays and Addresses* (London: Macmillan, 1904) p. 261 and Sidgwick, "Mr. Spencer's Ethical System," 217.

Sidgwick's remarks are not wholly inappropriate. Spencer does appear, as suggested earlier, to hold that by knowing how conduct and moral principles have evolved, we can better "establish" how we ought to act in terms of what basic principles of obligation we ought to embrace. That is, Spencer *sometimes* seems to believe that his second method of reasoning in particular was a genuine method.

Sidgwick's differences with Spencer went beyond criticizing Spencer's misuse of psychology and sociology. Sidgwick also had little use for Spencer's distinction between "absolute" and "relative" ethics which differentiated between ideal normative rules applicable to ideal liberal societies and those applicable to societies still evolving. To begin with, Sidgwick accused Spencer of disingenuously shifting his assessment of "relative" ethics. Although, in *Social Statics*, according to Sidgwick, Spencer adamantly maintained that the only genuine moral principles for us here and now were also those appropriate for perfect humans, he later abandoned this view without acknowledging having done so. Whereas in *Social Statics*, Spencer held that genuine ethics treats the "straight" man, and never the "crooked" man, and that any ethical system modified to deal with human imperfections was "useless" and "cannot be devised" in any case, he later embraced ethics of the "crooked" man as legitimate. In *The Principles of Ethics* in particular, Sidgwick pointed out, Spencer repeatedly invoked the interim usefulness of "relative" ethics for societies of the still "crooked."[57]

Spencer's revised assessment of "relative" ethics, however, may be less disingenuous as well as less of a shift than Sidgwick thinks. The very fact that in *Social Statics* Spencer mentions "relative" ethics contrasting it with "absolute" ethics and the very fact that he ascribes value to "so-called political rights" tacitly amounts to theorizing for "crooked" men.

But more significantly, as far as Sidgwick was concerned, Spencer's notion of "absolute" ethics was not "of much avail in solving the practical problems of actual humanity."[58] In other

[57] Sidgwick, *The Methods of Ethics*, pp. 18–19 and Sidgwick, "Mr. Spencer's Ethical System," 223. However, see "Absolute Political Ethics," *Essays*, vol. III, pp. 222 and 228, where Spencer concedes that absolute ethics is an unreachable ideal. Also note that the adjective "political" in the title implies that absolute ethics concerns humans who are sufficiently imperfect that they still must practice politics.

[58] Sidgwick, *Lectures on the Ethics of T. H. Green, Mr. Herbert Spencer and J. Martineau*, p. 206.

words, what would promote happiness in a perfect utilitarian society is unlikely to promote happiness here and now. Hence, the normative stipulations of "absolute" ethics are irrelevant for solving our present practical dilemmas. A perfect society would be so differently "situated" (to borrow from Charles Taylor) that its moral rules would be inapplicable to us. Moreover, Sidgwick contends that Spencer's utopia where all would be "pleasure unalloyed by pain anywhere," and where each person would harmoniously fulfill his or her ends in conjunction with others doing likewise, would be completely unlike anything we have experienced and therefore unlike anything we could possibly know. And being so alien to us, being such an "illimitable cloudland," we could not possibly specify the moral rules that would hold for it. Being so differently "situated," its moral rules would be not only irrelevant; they would be unavailable (*Lectures on the Ethics of T. H. Green, Mr. Herbert Spencer and J. Martineau*, p. 206). [59]

Spencer's responses to Sidgwick's criticisms, particularly in his "Replies to Criticisms," are unsatisfying. Spencer misunderstands Sidgwick's complaint that the distinction between "absolute" and "relative" ethics is incoherent. Instead of counterattacking, Spencer merely restates his initial views on "absolute" and "relative" ethics claiming that insofar as human behavior is evolving, pleasure-producing actions are also evolving. Because such actions will ultimately congeal into fixed ideal types, then we must endeavor to formulate ideal moral rules sanctifying these ideal types. And insofar as we need to formulate ideal principles of justice, then we also need to transcend somehow our "empirical" utilitarian habit of unscientifically estimating our moral principles from current pleasure-producing kinds of behavior.[60]

[59] See also Sidgwick, *The Methods of Ethics*, p. 470 where Sidgwick says that "it still seems to me quite impossible to forecast the natures and relations of the persons composing such a community, with sufficient clearness and certainty to enable us to define even in outline their moral code." Sidgwick's criticisms of Spencer parallel his criticisms of T. H. Green. Not only does Sidgwick regard Green's notion of good as excessively vague, but he also reproves Green's moral theory for being incapable of generating "practical guidance." See Sidgwick, *Lectures on the Ethics of T. H. Green, Mr. Herbert Spencer, and J. Martineau*, pp. 73–4. See also Malcolm Guthrie, *On Mr. Spencer's Data of Ethics* (London: The Modern Press, 1884), p. 72, for a similar criticism of Spencer's conception of absolute ethics. Guthrie's criticism, however, is less nuanced than Sidgwick's.

[60] As far as Spencer was concerned, Sidgwick's utilitarianism was a variety of direct utilitarianism and was therefore inferior. See, in particular, *The Principles of Ethics*, vol. I, p. 188. Sidgwick believed that Spencer never understood his criticisms of absolute and relative ethics and, consequently, felt compelled to belabor the same points each time he

Sidgwick's two criticisms of "absolute" ethics (impossibility and non-applicability) are plainly rooted in the basic features of his utilitarian methodology. For Sidgwick, insofar as there is no unchanging and irreducible human nature, there is no such thing as humankind in the abstract. Hence, there is no serviceable, unvarying moral psychology and, hence, no derivative ideal moral code. There can be no ethics *de novo*, no "absolute" ethics in effect. All that we have are common-sense, culturally specific utilitarian moralities which good utilitarians can try to refine by making them more systematic, coherent and precise.[61]

Sidgwick's rejection of ideal ethics in general, and "absolute" ethics in particular, also accounts for his dissatisfaction with "deductive ethics." In a chapter from *The Methods of Ethics* by the same name, in which he is undoubtedly thinking of Spencer, Sidgwick observes, "We seem then, forced to conclude that there is no scientific short-cut to the ascertainment of the right means to the individual's happiness: every attempt to find a 'high priori road' to this goal brings us back inevitably to the empirical method" (p. 195).

In Sidgwick's estimate, then, "absolute" ethics was a conceptual nonstarter for several interwoven reasons. Inasmuch as human nature and society are variable, moral theorizing must always fall short of conclusive results, must always lead to frustration in the quest after absolute, deductive ethics. "Rational" ethics is simply methodological fool's gold. And since "rational" ethics is so futile and illusory, then all forms of utilitarianism, including Spencer's, are arguably empirical in the end. Once the doubtful "value of Absolute Ethics" is exposed, then "it is made clear that Mr. Spencer . . . does not really offer us any other general system than Empirical Utilitarianism."[62]

replied to Spencer. Sidgwick first criticized Spencer in the 2nd edition of *The Methods of Ethics*, again in "Mr. Spencer's Ethics" and finally in *Lectures on the Ethics of T. H. Green, Mr. Herbert Spencer and J. Martineau.* Spencer, in turn, replied to Sidgwick's first set of criticisms in "The Data of Ethics," *The Principles of Ethics.* He replied to Sidgwick's later set of criticisms in "Replies to Criticisms" which first appeared in *Mind* in January, 1881 and republished as "Appendix E," *The Principles of Ethics*, vol. II.

[61] My remarks here owe much to Schneewind's *Sidgwick's Ethics and Victorian Moral Philosophy*, pp. 338–9 and to Stefan Collini, "The Ordinary Experience of Civilized Life: Sidgwick and the Method of Reflective Analysis" in S. Collini, D. Winch and J. W. Burrow (eds.), *That Noble Science of Politics* (Cambridge University Press, 1983), pp. 291–3.

[62] Sidgwick, *Lectures on the Ethics of T. H. Green, Mr. Herbert Spencer and J. Martineau*, p. 219. In saying that "empirical" ethics is all that there is, Sidgwick is also saying that relative ethics is all that there is.

Once again, we see that Taylor is *half* correct. He is certainly correct in describing Sidgwick as an "empirical" utilitarian and Spencer as a *self-proclaimed* "rational" utilitarian. However, despite Spencer's proclamations and methodological aspirations, Spencer was what Sidgwick said he was: just another empirical utilitarian. Sidgwick has come as close as anyone has to getting Spencer *fully* right.

This chapter has built on themes developed in previous chapters. But whereas previous chapters addressed the liberal nature of Spencer's utilitarianism, this chapter has endeavored to describe and assess the methods of reasoning which Spencer deployed in constructing his liberal utilitarian theory.

We have seen that even though Spencer never defined good nor offered a systematic theory of good, his notion of good was nevertheless essentially hedonistic and universalistic. We have also identified his three methods of utilitarian strategic reasoning of which the second and third (or psychological-descriptive and sociological) were shown to be palpably the least tenable. That is, even when well-armed with the latest psychological and sociological discoveries, liberal utilitarians are still faced with the daunting task of formulating credible decision procedures. Liberal utilitarians still must decide, on the basis of additional empirical considerations, what patterns of strong obligations will work out for the utilitarian best. And, of course, this says nothing about justifying the utilitarian best in the first place.

By contrast, Spencer's rational-deductive method of juridical reasoning might seem more promising. Given sociality and assuming a hedonistic and universalistic theory of good, the principle of equal freedom seems to be an attractive decision procedure with which to begin. It is surely as strong a candidate as any other. Perhaps any form of universal hedonism dedicated to maximizing *everyone's* happiness entails necessarily this much in the way of the right. And it might even prove to be the case that maximizing everyone's happiness rests, of necessity, upon a system of stringent rights. But, as we have seen, such necessity is contingent and not logical. At the end of the methodological day, "empirical" utilitarianism seems to be the only kind of utilitarianism.

"Rational" utilitarianism, then, is quixotic in both the best and worst senses. It is heroic in the very best spirit of modernity. It aspires to a "view from nowhere." It is a pretense to methodological rigor, a quest for *unsituated* formal theorizing. All too often, though, heroism is born in futility. Sisyphus was a hero too. And so, all attempts to do *unsituated* moral reasoning are bound to be a little disappointing. Spencer's moral reasoning was no exception.

CHAPTER 7

Land nationalization and property

Land nationalization and property ownership were contentious issues in nineteenth-century English politics. Both issues, especially the former, embroiled Spencer in prolonged controversy causing him to recant his early support of sweeping land nationalization.

My final chapter begins by discussing Spencer's proposals for nationalizing land ownership. I shall first address Spencer's early theory of land nationalization in *Social Statics* and then the modifications which he made to this theory in his later writings. These modifications led critics like Henry George to accuse Spencer of disingenuously repudiating one of the most important implications of his theory of justice. Both Spencer's modifications and George's accusations should help us appreciate further the fundamentally empirical nature of Spencer's liberal utilitarianism. Spencer's declining enthusiasm for land nationalization, and his waning conviction that land nationalization followed as a corollary of the principle of equal freedom, reveal particularly well how his "rational" utilitarianism was simply "empirical" utilitarianism. Land nationalization became a corollary of the principle of equal freedom in name only once Spencer began recalculating its utility.

The second section of this chapter analyzes Spencer's rights of private property, exchange and contract. These rights stand or fall with Spencer's land reform proposals. In his earlier works, Spencer justified inequalities in wealth *only* insofar as they were grounded in equal access to land. The silhouette of new liberal equal opportunity is clearly evident in Spencer's theory of land nationalization. But this silhouette faded as he began concluding that land nationalization was a sub-optimal utilitarian strategy. Spencer's growing conservatism was the growing conservatism of an "empirical" utilitarian. It was not the conservatism of a "rational" utilitarianism simply repairing previous deductive mistakes.

LAND NATIONALIZATION

The right to equal use of the earth was no ordinary moral right for Spencer. To deprive others of this right, according to *Social Statics*, is to commit a "crime inferior only in wickedness to the crime of taking away their lives or personal liberties" (p. 113). Hence, violating this cardinal right is a particularly flagrant violation of the principle of equal freedom:

Given a race of beings having like claims to pursue the objects of their desires; given a world adapted to the gratification of those desires – a world into which such beings are similarly born – and it unavoidably follows that they have equal rights to the use of this world. For if each of them "has freedom to do all that he wills, provided he infringes not the equal freedom of any other," then each of them is free to use the earth for the satisfaction of his wants, provided he allows all others the same liberty. And conversely, it is manifest that no one, or part of them, may use the earth in such a way as to prevent the rest from similarly using it; seeing that to do this is to assume greater freedom than the rest, and consequently to break the law. (*Social Statics*, p. 103)

Equal use, moreover, proscribes private ownership, since private ownership of land would result in the entire earth's surface being privately appropriated. This, in turn, would generate the following unacceptable consequences:

Supposing the entire habitable globe to be so enclosed it follows that if the landowners have a valid right to its surface, all who are not landowners have no right at all to its surface. They are trespassers. Save by permission of the lords of the soil, they can have no room for the soles of their feet. Nay, should others think fit to deny them a resting place, these landless men might equitably be expelled from the earth altogether. If, then, the assumption that land can be held as property involves that the whole globe may become the private domain of a part of its inhabitants; and if, by consequence, the rest of its inhabitants can then exercise their faculties – can then exist even – only by the consent of landowners, it is manifest that exclusive possession of the soil necessitates an infringement of the law of equal freedom. (*Social Statics*, p. 104)[1]

[1] Spencer also claims that, even if private ownership of land is legitimate in principle, present property titles are illegitimate because they are based on centuries of violence and fraud. Spencer's theory of land ownership resembles J. A. Hobson's. According to Hobson in *The Crisis of Liberalism* [1909] (New York: Barnes and Noble, 1974), pp. 97-8, land reform was the first principle of the New Liberal Charter: "It is, I think, plain that in the front of this charter of individual liberty comes the right of every man to an equal share with every other in the use of the land and of other natural resources of his native country. This right, if it has been

Following Locke, Spencer asserts that the earth was originally given to all humans as "God's bequest." But, unlike in Locke, Spencer claims that God gave this bequest to humans as common property (p. 107). And as all humans *jointly* own this original bequest, nobody can justifiably turn portions of this common bequest into private property simply by mixing in his or her labor: "You may plow and harrow, and sow and reap; you may turn over the soil as often as you like; but all your manipulations will fail to make that soil yours, which was not yours to begin with" (p. 107).[2] The matter is little different, as far as Spencer is concerned, from the case of your renovating an abandoned house whose owner suddenly reappears. The improvements, representing the added value created through mixing your labor with the unimproved structure, do not make the improved structure yours.

Although, as with the abandoned house example, improvements to land do not create private ownership of it, they nevertheless create ownership in the improvements. In other words, one owns whatever value one adds to land through labor. And should society ever reclaim what is rightfully its own by nationalizing land holdings, it must compensate current landowners for the entire value of all the improvements that have ever been made.

Nationalization, however according to Spencer, would not entail the socialism of "Messrs. Fourier, Owen, Louis Blanc, and Co." as land reform would not involve major changes in existing tenure arrangements. Rents, instead of going to individual landlords, would

alienated or compromised, must be restored. That the bulk of the land of any nation should continue to be the property of a few thousand persons who are thereby legally empowered to determine to what use it shall be put, or whether large numbers of their fellow-citizens shall be free to work and live in the village or the countryside where they were born and bred, is a manifest infringement of this doctrine of equality. The legal status of a landless man in England to-day lacks the elements of personal liberty: upon enclosed land (virtually all the land); he may not trespass so as to obey the primeval law bidding him earn his bread in the sweat of his face; upon the public thoroughfares he may not rest, and moving on continually he becomes a rogue and vagabond. In order to live at all in his native land he must succeed in making a bargain with some owner, who has a 'right' to refuse him this right to live." Like Spencer, Hobson recommends that "by means of public ownership, or by taxation, the annual values of land, as distinct from its improvements, shall become a public income to be expended for the equal advantage of all members of the community" (p. 98).

[2] See also p. 115, where Spencer continues: "It may be quite true that the labor a man expends in catching or gathering gives him a better right to the thing caught or gathered than any *one* other man; but the question at issue is whether by labor so expended he has made his right to the thing caught or gathered greater than the pre-existing rights of *all* other men put together. And unless he can prove that he has done this, his title to possession cannot be admitted as a matter of right, but can be conceded only on the ground of convenience."

simply go to the state. "Stewards would be public officials instead of private ones, and tenancy the only land tenure" (p. 111). Justice would be achieved because:

> Under it all men would be equally landlords; all men would be alike free to become tenants. A, B, C, and the rest might compete for a vacant farm as now, and one of them might take that farm, without in any way violating the principles of pure equity. All would be equally free to bid; all would be equally free to refrain. And when the farm had been let to A, B, or C, all parties would have done that which they willed – the one in choosing to pay a given sum to his fellow men for the use of certain lands – the others in refusing to pay that sum. Clearly, therefore, on such a system, the earth might be enclosed, occupied, and cultivated in entire subordination to the law of equal freedom. (*Social Statics*, p. 111)

Justice, in other words, is incompatible with private ownership of land though it is compatible with a system of individual leasing from the state. The latter insures that society's joint ownership of unimproved land is respected all the while enabling lessees to own privately whatever improvements they make.

Spencer notes that private property in land might seem compatible with justice if present holdings were equitably redistributed among *all* citizens. However, according to Spencer, two practical considerations contravene this alternative. First, "such a division is vetoed by the difficulty of fixing the values of respective tracts of land." Properly compensating existing land owners would therefore prove impossible. Second, and equally importantly, "what is to be done with those who come of age on the morrow? . . . And what will be the fate of those whose fathers sell their estates and squander the proceeds?" (*Social Statics*, p. 108).

Spencer concedes that land nationalization, however formulated, was practically vexing. "But," according to Spencer, "with this perplexity and our extrication from it, abstract morality has no concern." Having gotten themselves "into the dilemma by disobedience to the law, men must get out of it as well as they can" though "with as little injury to the landed class as may be" (p. 112). In any case, land owners have already "implicitly" acknowledged the rectitude of common land ownership by granting Parliament's right to seize private lands for public purposes provided that compensation is paid. Land nationalization merely extends Parliament's prerogative as fiduciary of society's common bequest.

We can now appreciate why, in *Social Statics*, Spencer holds that private tenancy under state ownership was consonant with the principle of equal freedom while private ownership was not. Private ownership is incompatible with equal freedom because it denies most citizens, present and future, equal access to the earth's surface. Equal access to the earth's surface is imperative because faculty exercise, and thus happiness, depend upon using land and its resources one way or another. By contrast, private tenancy under state ownership satisfies equal freedom because everyone is supposedly equally free to become a tenant insofar as everyone is free to bid for leases to land parcels. Everyone, therefore, supposedly has an equal chance to exercise his or her faculties by cultivating and otherwise utilizing land.[3]

The radicalism of Spencer's land reform proposals in *Social Statics* was not lost on his readers. Some viewed his proposals as consistent with sound liberal principles. Others, such as Thomas Hodgskin, viewed his proposals about land nationalization as a regrettable deviation from otherwise sound liberal radicalism. In an 1851 review of *Social Statics* for *The Economist*, Hodgskin mostly praised the book though he faulted Spencer's land reform theory on two accounts. First, in Hodgskin's view, Spencer confused the right to exercise faculties with the right to use the soil. The latter did not follow from the former and was illegitimate anyway. Moreover, the first right could be realized without land reforms provided that laborers received full value for their labor. Second, according to Hodgskin, Spencer failed to understand that all value, including that of land, derives from labor. Unowned land was valueless. Hence, leasing would violate the "right of property in labour and its products" because it would wrongly siphon away as rent a portion of the value created by the lessee.[4] Leasing from the state, in short, was exploitative.

Though opposed to Spencer's land reform proposals, Hodgskin was no friend of the landowning aristocracy. In *The Natural and Artificial Right of Property Contrasted*, he proposed that the amount of land an individual could own ought to decline to an "ever decreasing

[3] A. R. Wallace also defended land nationalization as an essential condition of "faculty exercise." See especially his chapter "Land Nationalization to Socialism and the Friends They Brought Me" in A. R. Wallace, *My Life*, 2 vols. (New York: Dodd, Mead and Co., 1905), vol. II. See also A. R. Wallace, "Herbert Spencer on the Land Question: A Criticism," *Studies Scientific and Social*, 2 vols. (London: Macmillan and Co., 1900), vol. II.

[4] Cited in Elie Halévy, *Thomas Hodgskin* (London: Benn, 1956), p. 143.

space." Since improved agricultural methods were enabling farmers to provide for themselves on smaller parcels of land, the amount of land any individual needed ought to shrink accordingly.[5]

The other larger similarities between Spencer in *Social Statics* and Hodgskin far outweigh their differences over land reform. Like the early Spencer, Hodgskin held that rights were natural in terms of being innate moral sentiments whose cognitive refinement was part of moral progress. And like the early Spencer, Hodgskin maintained that direct utilitarian legislation required impossibly complex calculations:

> Admitting therefore that the legislator ought to look at the general good, the impossibility that any individual can ascertain that which will promote it, leads directly to the conclusion that there ought to be no legislation. If the greatest happiness principle, be the only one that justifies law-making, and if that principle be suitable only to Omniscience – man, having no means of measuring it, there can be no justification of all Mr. Bentham's nicely adapted contrivances, which he calls civil and penal laws. (*The Natural and Artificial Right of Property Contrasted*, p. 22)[6]

Despite repeated attempts after *Social Statics* to clarify his position on land nationalization, controversy about it plagued Spencer for the remainder of his literary career, culminating in Henry George's vitriolic attack in 1893 entitled *A Perplexed Philosopher.* George accused

[5] Thomas Hodgskin, *The Natural and Artificial Right of Property Contrasted* [1832] (Clifton, N.J.: A. M. Kelley, 1973), especially "Letter the Fourth."

[6] Spencer and Hodgskin's affinities are unsurprising inasmuch as both worked for *The Economist* while Spencer was writing *Social Statics* between 1848 to 1850. Although Spencer once denied Hodgskin's influence on the development of his early thinking, he also admitted in his *An Autobiography*, vol. 1, p. 424, that "my later career was mainly determined by the conceptions which were initiated, and the friendships which were formed, between the times at which my connexion with *The Economist* began and ended." Elie Halévy makes a compelling circumstantial case for Hodgskin's influence on Spencer. As Halévy notes, Spencer and Hodgskin were in daily contact during Spencer's entire tenure at *The Economist* between 1848 through 1853. Halévy also claims that Spencer visited Hodgskin's home frequently and borrowed books from his library. See Halévy, *Thomas Hodgskin*, p. 142. Halévy himself corresponded with Spencer on at least one occasion while preparing his book about Hodgskin. After suggesting to Spencer that he must have known Hodgskin well, and after noting that Hodgskin reviewed *Social Statics* for *The Economist*, Halévy adds, "In fact his [Hodgskin's] ideas are so closely akin to yours (I mean of course his *social* ideas) that you will understand that it would be most important if you could let me know something about the particulars of his life, just to prevent his name from falling into oblivion." See Halévy to Herbert Spencer, May 28, 1902, *The Herbert Spencer Papers*, MS. 791/292i. See also Scott Gordon, "The London Economist and the High Tide of Laissez-Faire," *Journal of Political Economy*, 63 (1955), 475–6, for a discussion of Spencer's relationship to Hodgskin while both worked at *The Economist.*

Spencer of sheepishly repudiating, in his later writings, the position that he courageously adopted in *Social Statics*. While there is no need to retrace in detail Spencer's twists and turns as he gradually repudiated the land reform proposals of *Social Statics*, some of the particulars of Spencer's dogged retreat nevertheless deserve attention.[7] They support my contention that Spencer's liberal utilitarian methodology was essentially empirical.

Spencer next addressed the question of land nationalization in Part v of *The Principles of Sociology* originally issued as "Political Institutions" in 1882.[8] In Chapter 15, "Property," Spencer defends community land ownership much as he did in *Social Statics*, though more hesitantly. He now says ruefully that it "seems possible" that private property in land will one day disappear. "Perhaps the right of the Community to the land, thus tacitly asserted, will in time come to be overtly asserted; and acted upon after making full allowance for the accumulated value artificially given" (vol. II, p. 554).

On October 27, 1882, the conservative *St. James's Gazette* criticized Spencer's views on land nationalization in *The Principles of Sociology*. In January 1883, *The Edinburgh Review* reviewed Henry George's *Progress and Poverty*, comparing George's land reform measures to Spencer's. According to the reviewer, Spencer's proposals mirrored those of George and therefore warranted vigorous condemnation. Spencer replied in the *St. James's Gazette*, underscoring the tentative nature of his remarks in *The Principles of Sociology* by quoting from the chapter on property, italicizing those portions displaying his reservations about proceeding too hastily. Spencer warns that contemporary political and economic exigencies preclude a "purely ethical view of the matter."[9]

[7] At least one recent interpreter of Spencer argues that he did not substantially alter his views on land reform in his later writings. See Jeffrey Paul, "The Socialism of Herbert Spencer," *History of Political Thought*, 3 (1982).

[8] The 1877 English and 1878 American editions of *Social Statics* included Spencer's discussion of land nationalization in chapter 9, "The Right to Use of the Earth," unaltered from the original 1851 edition.

[9] For the complete text of Spencer's *St. James's Gazette* response, see Henry George, *A Perplexed Philosopher* (London: Kegan Paul, Trench, Trubner and Co., 1893), pp. 78–80. A few years later in a letter to Auberon Herbert, Spencer continues to waver and agonize. He admits that his views are "by no means settled" and, as in his response in the *St. James's Gazette*, he complains of his difficulty reconciling the "ethical view" of comprehensive land reform with the bureaucratic mechanisms that such reform would likely entail. Spencer to the Hon. Auberon Herbert, 13 October, 1883 in Duncan (ed.), *The Life and Letters of Herbert Spencer*, pp. 247-8.

In November 1889, land nationalization returned to haunt Spencer, plunging him into a fresh round of controversy and recrimination. On November 5, *The Times* published an account of a public debate where Spencer was invoked as advocating sweeping land nationalization. In a November 7 letter to *The Times*, Spencer replied, insisting that *Social Statics* defended "absolute political ethics, or that which ought to be, as distinguished from relative political ethics, or that which is at present the nearest practicable approach to it." Moreover, he warned, "with a humanity anything like what we know, the implied reorganization [of land] would be disastrous."[10]

Spencer's reply in *The Times* was followed by a series of letters to *The Times* both attacking and defending him. Even his close friend, T. H. Huxley, joined battle against him. Huxley criticized Spencer for simultaneously upholding the rectitude of land nationalization while disingenuously maintaining that the time was not ripe for instituting it. For Huxley, Spencer's hypocrisy about land reform was rooted in his bogus distinction between absolute and relative ethics. Huxley called Spencer's notion of absolute ethics and his method of a priori politics "stumbling-blocks." He asked rhetorically whether, according to absolute ethics, land bought several years ago "like a cabbage" truly belonged to its possessor or not?[11] Responding to Huxley in *The Times* on November 15 and 27, Spencer tried to clarify the distinction between absolute and relative ethics and complained about Huxley's inability to see it.[12]

By the time of "Justice," in *The Principles of Ethics*, Spencer abandoned advocating serious land reform. In the chapter "The Rights to the Uses of Natural Media," he begins as he began in *Social Statics*: "The Earth's surface cannot be denied to any one

[10] For a full text of Spencer's letter to *The Times*, see George, *A Perplexed Philosopher*, pp. 96–9.

[11] For Huxley's letter, see *A Perplexed Philosopher*, p. 119. Huxley's public exchange with Spencer on land reform caused an irreparable rift in their friendship. Walter Troughton's unpublished reminiscences of the years he spent as Spencer's personal secretary testify to the depth of this rift. According to Troughton: "When Huxley intervened in the Land Question controversy Mr Spencer felt it acutely. It was just like a stab in the back from a trusted friend, he used to say. I do not think anything in his later life upset him so much as this. The result was a definite cleavage, and although there was an epistolary reconciliation a year or so before Huxley's death in 1895, I should say that the wound never wholly healed, nor so far as I remember did they ever meet after the breach." See Walter Troughton, "Reminiscences of HS," *The Herbert Spencer Papers*, MS. 791/355/3, p. 31.

[12] For the complete text of the first of Spencer's two replies to Huxley, see George, *A Perplexed Philosopher*, pp. 120–3.

absolutely, without rendering life-sustaining activities impracticable. In the absence of standing-ground he can do nothing; and hence it *appears* to be a corollary from the law of equal freedom, interpreted with strictness, that the Earth's surface may not be appropriated absolutely by individuals, but may be occupied by them only in a manner as recognizes ultimate ownership by other men; that is – by society at large" (vol. II, p. 98; my italics).

Spencer then quickly retreats. First, he claims that public land ownership already exists, and has long existed, in Great Britain under the auspices of the Crown. According to Spencer, all land in England nominally belongs to the people because all land nominally belongs to the Crown. Parliamentary democracy has simply made common ownership more explicit. Second, should the state as fiduciary decide to manage the nation's land, it would have to pay existing landlords prohibitively high compensation. The state would have to compensate landlords for the added value stemming from centuries of "clearing, breaking-up, prolonged culture, fencing, draining, making roads, farm buildings, etc." (*The Principles of Ethics*, vol. II, p. 108).

The Principles of Ethics also contains an appendix on land reform where Spencer further repudiates it as practical folly. Because landlords have paid over 500,000,000 English pounds in poor law relief since 1600, this sum must be weighed against what landlords owe the community, namely land's natural value prior to improvement. And insofar as the latter is probably less than 500,000,000 English pounds, landlords have effectively purchased the land from the community. Hence, this sum supposedly paid by landlords must be returned to them, in addition to the artificial value created by improvements, should the community reassert ownership. According to Spencer, "a fuller consideration of the matter has led me to the conclusion that individual ownership, subject to State-suzerainty, should be maintained."[13]

Land is not the only natural resource discussed by Spencer in *The Principles of Ethics*. He also claims that the principle of equal freedom implies the "right of each citizen to unpolluted air" and therefore proscribes smoking in railway carriages and requires that "stenches" as well as "injurious fumes" and "smoke" from factories be regulated. Moreover, the principle of equal freedom also forbids disturb-

[13] Spencer, "Appendix B. The Land Question," *The Principles of Ethics*, vol. II, p. 460.

ing public noises "as in the case of street music and especially bad street music, or as in the case of loud noises proceeding from factories, or as in the case of church bells rung at early hours" and "as shown in the case of railway whistles at central stations, which are allowed superfluously to disturb tens of thousands of people all through the night and often to do serious injury to invalids."[14]

Spencer was preoccupied with noise pollution because he suffered from severe insomnia. In his reminiscences of Spencer, Walter Troughton describes Spencer's obsession with noise while recounting the difficulties he experienced, on one occasion, finding Spencer new lodgings. Troughton recalls "inquiring closely as to the proximity of poultry, dogs, church chimes, (against which as sleep disturbers he had an inveterate grudge) railways, and all other possible sources of nocturnal disturbance, all points of the utmost importance; gauging the salubrity of the air and the character and resources of the surrounding country from the point of view of pleasure, in addition to a variety of other things." Troughton adds, "Needless to say there were very few places where the desired conditions existed even approximately. Churches with their chimes were most frequently the obstacle."[15]

Spencer's waning enthusiasm for serious land reform, especially in *The Principles of Ethics*, greatly disappointed Henry George, who responded with *A Perplexed Philosopher* in 1893. Caustic and cynical, *A Perplexed Philosopher* castigated Spencer for repudiating his earlier views in order to curry favor with Britain's aristocracy. Spencer had succumbed to "intellectual prostitution" (p. 314). He deployed the distinction between absolute and relative ethics as a theoretical ruse for covering up his growing political conservatism. He demonstrated that he had become "as a philosopher ridiculous, as a man contemptible – a fawning Vicar of Bray, clothing in pompous phraseology and arrogant assumption logical confusions so absurd as to be comical."[16]

14 Spencer, *The Principles of Ethics*, vol. II, pp. 100–1. See also from Spencer to the Earl of Wemyss, June 1, 1892 in Duncan (ed.), *The Life and Letters of Herbert Spencer*, p. 314.

15 Troughton, "Reminiscences of HS," *The Herbert Spencer Papers*, MS. 791/355/3, pp. 16–17.

16 George originally viewed Spencer as a formidable ally in his crusade to abolish private property in land. Hence, George praised Spencer on several occasions in his 1880 *Progress and Poverty*. George's 1881 *The Land Question* also referred to Spencer approvingly sometimes condemning private property in land as a violation of equal freedom. See in particular Henry George, *The Land Question* (New York: Doubleday and Page, 1906), p. 109. George's relationship with Spencer soured when Spencer failed to acknowledge the receipt of a complimentary copy of *Progress and Poverty*. In 1882, George met Spencer during a visit to

George's criticisms of Spencer's theory for compensating landowners whose property had been nationalized are compelling. Not unlike Hodgskin, he questions Spencer's contention that the community owns all land in its primitive unimproved state only and that it is therefore entitled only to what this unimproved land is worth. Does Spencer mean, George wonders, that the community is merely entitled to "what value the land had before there were any people? and that they must pay the land-owners for the value of all the labor that has been expended on that land since Caesar landed?" (*A Perplexed Philosopher*, p. 217). George finds such reasoning absurd suggesting that land values partially derive from the presence of others, from the "social environment" (p. 218). In other words, according to George, presocial value is an incoherent concept.

George also criticizes Spencer's theory of compensation because it implicitly justifies theft. George denies that landlords are owed compensation simply because they or their forefathers purchased land in good faith, unaware that they were acting improperly in purchasing stolen property. Though they may have innocently purchased stolen property, their innocence does not justify ownership. In George's words, "innocence can only shield from the punishment due to conscious wrong; it cannot give right" (p. 264). Or, as Hillel Steiner has recently criticized Spencer but without referring to George, "Receiving stolen goods is, of course, not always a morally culpable offence. Nor, however, is it ordinarily regarded as creating rights on the part of the recipient."[17]

Henry Sidgwick likewise rejected Spencer's compensation theory as spurious. In Sidgwick's view, the 500,000,000 pounds purportedly paid out in poor law taxes should have no bearing on the amount of compensation owed landlords: "Suppose we were considering whether slavery should be abolished, we should not take into account money spent by slave-owners in keeping slaves alive whom

England. When George voiced sympathy for the Irish Land League, Spencer condemned it. Spencer also condemned George's Single Tax scheme. The 1884 publication of *The Man Versus the State* further alienated George. And when Spencer published "Justice" in 1891 and an abridged edition of *Social Statics* in 1892 which omitted the original version's chapter on land reform, George felt thoroughly betrayed. Hence, George turned on Spencer with caustic fulmination in his 1893 *A Perplexed Philosopher.*

[17] Hillel Steiner, "Land, Liberty and the Early Herbert Spencer," *History of Political Thought*, 3 (1983), 32. Steiner similarly criticizes Spencer's contention that landlords deserve compensation for improvements which they have made to their land. Steiner rhetorically asks, "If Red steals White's book and sells it to Blue, who then repairs its torn cover, does White owe Blue compensation upon reclaiming it?" (p. 532.)

they might have killed. If the poor were wronged by being kept out of the land, a pittance doled out under conditions of discredit seems inadequate to balance the past wrong, let alone the present."[18]

Other, more subtle difficulties afflict Spencer's theory of compensation. For instance, of the 500,000,000 English pounds in poor rates that landowners have supposedly paid the community over three centuries, only a fraction could possibly have been paid by mid-nineteenth-century English landowners to mid-nineteenth-century English poor. Therefore, it is unclear why the full sum is relevant in settling accounts between landowners and the community.[19] Why should a landowner whose property has been confiscated be entitled to compensation for the poor rates paid by previous owners? If a landowner's property had been legitimately inherited, then he or she might be entitled to greater compensation. Compensation might justifiably extend backwards through unbroken inheritance but no further. Spencer tacitly acknowledges as much in admitting that his theory of compensation assumes that all ancestors of present landowners were also landowners.[20] Nevertheless, Spencer seems to have believed that past poor rates were cumulative operating costs transferable to new owners with each sale and resale of a piece of land. Poor rates were simply liabilities turned over with each transfer whether by inheritance or sale.

In "Land, Liberty and the Early Herbert Spencer," Hillel Steiner says that by rejecting onetime land redistribution in favor of private tenancy under state ownership in *Social Statics*, because future generations would be cheated, Spencer implies that everyone reaching adulthood possesses a "veto" on all leases (p. 531). Steiner, who otherwise applauds Spencer's theory of land nationalization, claims that Spencer failed to see this salutary implication because he failed to appreciate fully the challenges of intergenerational justice. Although Steiner admits that such a veto would be exceedingly disruptive if frequently exercised, he insists that it would be employed sparingly. The disruptive efforts of its "widespread use would usually rebound to the disadvantage of its exerciser at least as

[18] Sidgwick, *Lectures on the Ethics of T. H. Green, Mr. Herbert Spencer and J. Martineau*, p. 288.

[19] As Sidgwick observes, socialists might argue that past poor rates were compensation paid to "past poor" and therefore had no place in settling accounts among present poor and present landlords. See ibid., p. 287. For another example of Sidgwick's dissatisfaction with Spencer's land-reform theory, see Sidgwick's review of Spencer's "Justice" in *Mind*, N.S., I (1892), 115–16.

[20] Spencer, "Appendix B. The Land Question," *The Principles of Ethics*, vol. II, p. 457.

much as to others." At the very least, others "would find it in their interest to offer him terms which would deprive him of any incentive to exercise it" (p. 531).[21]

Now, Steiner's interest in Spencer's early theory of land reform is not primarily as a historian of political thought. In an earlier essay entitled "Liberty and Equality," Steiner defends a theory of property and land ownership that closely resembles Spencer's in *Social Statics*. Written in the form of four parables, each improving upon the previous one in terms of articulating libertarian principles, Steiner's essay would gratify the ghost of Henry George. The last parable represents Steiner's full position and describes how ten persons, shipwrecked on an island without hope of rescue, ought to allocate and regulate the island's land. The parable closes with the following recommendation by one of the ten:

> I therefore recommend the following modification. The shareholders' body will *not* dissolve after making its set of allocations. Later arrivals, when and if there are any, will become shareholders as they reach the age of majority when they would normally assume the burdens and benefits of full legal responsibility. Since any prevailing set of allocations is contractually entitled to the respect of all – and only – those who were shareholders when that allocation was made, it follows that the only way in which the obligation to respect others' property can be said to be contractually incurred by more recent shareholders who were not parties to that earlier allocative decision, is if prevailing allocations are subject to their approval. Current shareholders would thus be well-advised, though by no means obliged, to take this consideration into account when making their decisions about who should get what and what should be done with it. The contracts into which the shareholding body enters would thereby assume the character of a lease for an unspecified term.[22]

Steiner defends this leasing scheme because it would limit "uncontracted enforceable restrictions on individual conduct" to two: restrictions stemming from violations of bodily integrity and restric-

[21] Steiner also regards Spencer as anti-utilitarian. He says that the veto in question, like any right for Spencer, is a "social decision rule conferring upon its owner an effective veto against some conceivable arrangement or practice which may well be of the utmost benefit to other persons. It is the affirmation of social decision rules of this kind that distinguishes a natural rights theory from a utilitarian one" (pp. 530–1). See also Steiner's contention that "In the final analysis, then ELP [equal freedom] is treated as a basic moral axiom which, as in Kant, can be founded neither on social utility nor general happiness nor the common good. Each individual's entitlement to equal liberty is of intrinsic and not instrumental, moral worth" (p. 524). As we have seen, while rights are absolute "decision rules" for Spencer and equal liberty is "intrinsic" for him, neither were anti-utilitarian.

[22] Hillel Steiner, "Liberty and Equality," *Political Studies* 29 (1981), 565.

tions stemming from violations of contract. According to Steiner, sound libertarianism seeks to minimize such restrictions. Unfortunately, according to Steiner, most libertarians, with the exception of George and Spencer, have tolerated a third kind of "uncontracted enforceable restriction," namely restrictions stemming from violations of private property in land. Even if our ten shipwrecked survivors contractually partitioned the island's surface among themselves, subsequent generations would have to respect these contracts. They would be compelled to respect contracts to which they had not been a party. Hence, generational newcomers must be allowed their veto. As Steiner concludes, "Each person's possession of a veto on the initial allocation of property eliminates the possibility of his being exploited, by minimizing the number of non-contractual enforceable obligations to which he is subject. Such an arrangement is, recognizably, a form of socialism" ("Liberty and Equality," p. 569).[23]

Steiner's refined version of Spencer's early land reform theory is overly sanguine. People surely lack the foresight that Steiner assumes. It would not take many shortsighted, or vindictive, people to cause confusion by exercising their vetoes. Steiner's libertarianism, in other words, is psychologically naive.

Spencer, of course, never anticipated Steiner's emendations and probably would not have welcomed them. Thus, many of the problems associated with Steiner's scheme do not apply to Spencer. That is not to say that Spencer's leasing alternative is not without other difficulties of its own. As Asirvatham, following W. F. Maitland, has pointed out, saying that everyone would be equally free to become tenants by having the opportunity to bid for leases stretches

[23] In "Mr. Herbert Spencer's Theory of Society," Part II, *Mind*, 8 (1883), 516–17, F. W. Maitland anticipates Steiner's reworking of Spencer in the name of intergenerational justice. In Maitland's view, the law of equal freedom does not privilege any particular generation. Equal freedom requires that land be redistributed on the "birth of every child." For a more recent and similar assessment regarding the demands of liberal intergenerational justice, see Ursula Vogel, "When the Earth Belonged to All: The Land Question in Eighteenth-century Justifications of Private Property," *Political Studies*, 36 (1988), 115. The logic of land reform holds for other scarce resources. Grant Allen, seldom shy in his flattering praise of Spencer, seems to have appreciated the pregnant implications of Spencer's logic. In an 1881 letter to Spencer, Allen says, "It seems to me that individualism, in order to be just, must strive hard for an equalization of original condition by the removal of all artificial advantages. The great reservoir of natural wealth that we turn up as land, (including mines etc.) ought, it seems to me, to be nationalized before we can say that the individual is allowed free play." See Allen to Herbert Spencer, August 15, 1881, *The Herbert Spencer Papers*, MS. 791/154.

the meaning of equal freedom. Wealthier bidders, according to Asirvatham, would invariably outbid poorer ones in competing for the best land. Hence, the old aristocracy would reacquire much of their former wealth (*Herbert Spencer's Theory of Social Justice*, pp. 237–8).[24] Plus, they would have the compensation paid to them by society for nationalizing their land to help them do it. Wealthier bidders will always enjoy bidding advantages and thus would have better than equal chances to exercise and develop their faculties. Being free to bid, in short, does not entail being equally free to use land.

Spencer's land reform theory in *Social Statics* is radical and sweeping. In Spencer's view, if the principle of equal freedom was to be more than a hollow profession of equity, more than an idle gesture, then everyone deserved equal access to land. But Spencer was unable to withstand the critical fury that his land reform proposals unleashed. Under the banner of the principle of general utility, he retreated. Precipitous land reform was cumbersome, destabilizing and thus inexpedient.

Spencer's liberal utilitarianism with respect to land ownership, then, proves to be nondeductive. As Sidgwick said of the principle of equal freedom, in light of Spencer's vacillation over land reform, "as we try to apply it, it changes."[25] And because the application of the principle of equal freedom to land ownership is so fluid, we again can't help but appreciate the fundamentally empirical nature of Spencer's liberal utilitarianism. Spencer abandoned land nationalization as a corollary of equal freedom not out of logical reassessment but because he concluded, on the basis of what he believed was credible empirical evidence, that land reform was not an effective utility-maximizing strategy after all.

Controversy over land reform haunted Spencer until 1895, when he published *Mr. Herbert Spencer on the Land Question*, a slim pamphlet of extracts about land nationalization from *Social Statics* and *The Principles of Ethics*.[26] With its publication, Spencer turned his back on

[24] For Maitland's fear that Spencer's land reform proposals would allow the land-owning aristocracy to reassert its control over land, see Maitland, "Mr. Herbert Spencer's Theory of Society," 515–16.

[25] Sidgwick, *Lectures on the Ethics of T. H. Green, Mr. Herbert Spencer and J. Martineau*, p. 284.

[26] Herbert Spencer, *Mr. Herbert Spencer on the Land Question* (New York: D. Appleton and Co., 1895).

land reform, vowing that "I must wash my hands entirely of the whole of the George business."[27]

PRIVATE PROPERTY AND EXCHANGE

The implications of Spencer's theory of land nationalization for his general theory of private property are not insignificant. These implications were not lost on Spencer giving him further reasons to reconsider the utility of land nationalization.

In *Social Statics*, Spencer defends the principle of private property by attacking Locke's labor theory of property:

> It might be argued that the real question is overlooked, when it is said that, by gathering any natural product, a man "hath mixed his labour with it, and joined to it something that is his own, and thereby made it his property"; for that the point to be debated is whether he had any right to gather, or mix his labor with that which by the hypothesis, previously belonged to mankind at large. The reasoning used in the last chapter to prove that no amount of labor, bestowed by an individual upon a part of the earth's surface, can nullify the title of society to that part might be similarly employed to show that no one can, by the mere act of appropriating to himself any wild unclaimed animal or fruit, supersede the joint claims of other men to it. It may be quite true that the labor a man expends in catching or gathering gives him a better right to the thing caught or gathered than any one other man; but the question at issue is whether by labor so expended he has made his right to the thing caught or gathered greater than the pre-existing rights of all other men put together. (pp. 114–15)[28]

[27] Spencer to James A. Skilton, February 22, 1895 in Duncan (ed.), *The Life and Letters of Herbert Spencer*, p. 342.

[28] In *A Perplexed Philosopher*, Henry George also accused Spencer of confusing equal use rights to land with joint-ownership rights when criticizing Locke's theory of property. According to George, Locke meant that humankind owns the earth's surface *only* in the former sense and that therefore permission from society to use the earth's surface becomes necessary only as good land becomes scarce. Equal use rights were not, for Locke, joint ownership rights and, consequently, the consent of society did not stem from our collectively owning all land but from scarcity. Scarcity of good land prevents all inhabitants from simultaneously utilizing their equal-use rights. Hence, society's consent becomes necessary simply from the lack of opportunity to use what nobody, including "mankind at large," owns. As George construes Locke: "For, where one man wants to use a natural opportunity that no one else wants to use, he has a *right* to do so, which springs from and is attested by the fact of his existence. This is an absolute, unlimited right, so long and in so far as no one else wants to use the same natural opportunity. Then, but not till then, it becomes limited by the similar rights of others . . . It is only then that any question of this right, any need for the action of society in the adjustment of equal rights to land, can come up" (pp. 48–9). If George is correct about Spencer, then Spencer joins those who interpret Locke as a "positive community" theorist as opposed to a "negative community" theorist. Interpreters who view

Spencer next suggests that private property can nevertheless be given a "legitimate foundation". By leasing a parcel of land from society, an individual obtains the consent of society to appropriate its produce as exclusively his own. Having "hired a tract of land from his fellow men," the lessee "has now, to use Locke's expression, 'mixed his labour with' certain products of the earth and his claim to them is in this case valid, because he obtained the *consent* of society before so expending his labor; and having fulfilled the condition which society imposed in giving that consent – the payment of rent – society, to fulfill its part of the agreement, must acknowledge his title to that surplus which remains after the rent has been paid." This surplus thereby becomes the lessee's private property "without any disobedience to the law of equal freedom" and the lessee "has therefore a *right* so to claim it" (*Social Statics*, pp. 116–17).

The "consent of society" as leaseholder provides a "legitimate foundation" for private property in *Social Statics*. And private property needs a "legitimate foundation" because it is so necessary to achieving happiness. According to Spencer, humans instinctively accumulate because the instinct to accumulate is a vital human faculty whose exercise generates considerable happiness. Hence, the instinct to accumulate "presupposes a right of private property" (p. 20). The right of private property is so basic because acquiring property is so hedonically rewarding.[29]

Spencer's treatment of private property after *Social Statics* changes little. In *The Principles of Ethics*, however, Spencer adds that different amounts of legitimately acquired property express different deserts. Deny the right to private property and desert is annulled. Annul desert and happiness is thwarted. Communism is odious precisely because it produces sub-optimal utility. Of course, in suggesting that legitimately acquired private property embodies desert, Spencer also implies that the former is necessarily compatible with the

Locke as a "negative community" theorist hold that, according to Locke, God did not give the world to humankind as a positive, joint possession. Hence, in using and appropriating a piece of unclaimed land, the consent of society is unnecessary. Mixing one's labor with a piece of land imparts ownership to it for the first time. For a discussion of Locke's theory of property in terms of "positive" versus "negative" community, see Istvan Hont and Michael Ignatieff, "Needs and Justice in the *Wealth of Nations*: An Introductory Essay" in Istvan Hont and Michael Ignatieff (eds.), *Wealth and Virtue* (Cambridge University Press, 1983), pp. 35–6. See also James Tully, *A Discourse of Property* (Cambridge University Press, 1980), Part II.

29 For an account of utilitarian justifications of property, including some found in *Social Statics*, see Lawrence C. Becker, *Property Rights* (Boston: Routledge and Kegan Paul, 1977), chapter 5.

principle of equal freedom. The principle of equal freedom and the principle of desert are, after all, different versions of the same principle for Spencer.[30]

Mill, likewise, argues in *The Principles of Political Economy* that private property, properly regulated, distributes desert fairly. Mill observes: "Private property, in every defense made of it, is supposed to mean, the guarantee to individuals of the fruits of their own labor and abstinence."[31] In Mill's view, however, no one deserves rewards associated with unimproved land. The value of unimproved land is not the result of anyone's labor. Mill therefore concludes, like Spencer, that land's unearned increment may not be legitimately owned. Summarizing Mill's view, Riley contends:

> The principle of desert prescribes property rights in the products of labor, that is, all man-made alterations to natural resources. But the natural resources themselves are not products of labor. Owners of labor and capital thus have desert-based rights to the long-run competitive rewards where possessors of natural resources have no such moral claims. Nonetheless, society may legally permit limited retention of natural resource rents to encourage selfish agents *efficiently* to develop the resources for public purposes.[32]

The right of private property was a fundamental moral right for Spencer as for Mill. The pursuit of happiness depended upon it. But insofar as Spencer held, like Mill, that legitimate acquisition of property rested upon fair access to land, the general distribution of wealth in Spencer's England was, by implication, inequitable in the extreme. Because land in England had been illegitimately appropriated, all wealth deriving from this illegitimate basis was necessarily illegitimate as well. As one of Spencer's detractors put it, "To attack the rights of private property in land is to attack property in its concrete form. If landed property is not secure, no property can be protected by law, and the transmission of wealth, be it large or

[30] In *The Principles of Ethics*, Spencer also claims that because manuscripts are mental products whose value is exclusively created by their authors, they are his or her property in a "fuller sense." Inventions, by contrast, should not be the exclusive property of their creators since other inventors would sooner or later invent them. Hence, patents on inventions should be limited in duration. See especially chapter 13, "The Right of Incorporeal Property," in Part IV.

[31] J. S. Mill, *The Principles of Political Economy* [1848] in Robson (ed.), *Collected Works* (1965), vol. II, p. 208.

[32] Jonathan Riley, "Justice Under Capitalism" in John W. Chapman and J. Roland Pennock (eds.), *Markets and Justice* (New York University Press, 1989), Nomos 24, pp. 141–2.

small, is extinguished."[33] Little wonder, then, that Spencer lost his appetite for land nationalization, eventually deciding to "wash [his] hands" of the whole "George business" as he came to appreciate the deeper egalitarian implications of the theoretical creature which he helped create and unleash. And too much egalitarianism, Spencer believed, was objectionable primarily because it produced sub-optimal utility.

When Spencer, furthermore, turns from the right to own private property to the right to exchange it, his reasoning is predictable. In *Social Statics*, he observes:

> Freedom to exchange his property for the property of others is manifestly included in a man's general freedom. In claiming this as his right, he in no way transgresses the proper limit put to his sphere of action by the like spheres of action of others. The two parties in a trade transaction, while doing all that they will to do, are not assuming more liberty than they leave to others. Indeed their act ends with themselves, does not affect the condition of the bystanders at all, leaves these as much power to pursue the objects of their desires as before. Hence, exchanges may be made in complete conformity with the law of equal freedom. (p. 131)

One might object to the claim, as many of Spencer's contemporary critics did, that market exchange leaves others unaffected. Market exchange can't but affect "bystanders" in innumerable significant and insignificant ways. Anticipating such criticism, Spencer adds that inasmuch as "everyone is entitled to offer, to accept, and to refuse . . . the closing of an agreement between two of the parties implies no infringement of the claims of the disappointed ones; seeing that each of them remains as free as ever, to offer, accept, and refuse" (*Social Statics*, p. 132). Naturally, whether the "closing of an agreement" proves merely disappointing, violating no one's rights depends upon the bargaining circumstances. The dividing line between driving a permissible hard bargain and making an impermissible coercive offer is arguably imprecise. As with competition for land leases, wealthy bargainers would often be able to manipulate their poorer counterparts especially with respect to the sale of scarce resources that they might happen to monopolize. What we need, then, is a criterion for distinguishing between bargaining circumstances which embody insignificant harms and those which embody significant ones. Now Spencer, as much as Mill,

[33] "The Nationalization of Land," *The Edinburgh Review* (January, 1883) and cited in George, *A Perplexed Philosopher*, p. 77. See also Lacy, *Liberty and Law*, p. 334.

appealed to general utility to settle such questions though Spencer held that a much less restricted form of permissible bargaining generated the best utilitarian results. Liberal utilitarian bargaining strategies can come in different empirically justified varieties.

Spencer's defense of market bargaining and exchange also stemmed from his belief that bargaining was simply mutual gift-giving. Insofar as unrestricted gift-giving unquestionably followed from the right of property as far as Spencer was concerned, minimally restricted bargaining and exchange followed as well. In *The Principles of Ethics*, Spencer claims that the right of gift followed from the right of property because completely owning something implies being able to transfer ownership to someone else. Moreover, for Spencer, the right of gift also implied the right of bequest or postponed gift. However, bequest understood as postponed giftgiving precluded testators from fixing what could be done with willed property because, in its "naked form, the proposition that a man can own a thing when he is dead, is absurd" and because property, being necessary to life, looses its justification when life ceases (vol. II, p. 138). Sidgwick responded, wondering why ownership implied the right to will to whom but not for what.[34]

Spencer nonetheless admitted that testators ought not to be entirely prevented from stipulating how their legacies should be used. When beneficiaries are immature children or when one's property has been acquired by "unusual industry" and "great skill" or by inventions "permanently valuable to mankind," testators may rightfully place conditions on their bequests. In these circumstances, Spencer concluded that "empirical compromise appears needful. We seem called upon to say that a testator should have some power of directing the application of property not bequeathed to children, but that his power should be limited; and that the limits must be settled by experience of results" (*The Principles of Ethics*, vol. II, pp. 141–2). Of course, settling limits by "empirical compromise" and the "experience of results" is the methodological stuff of empirical utilitarianism. As Sidgwick remarked in criticizing Spencer's approach to bequest, traditional "[u]tilitarianism comes in, clearly."[35]

For Spencer, the right of contract follows, in turn, from the right of exchange because contract is simply a "postponement, now

[34] Sidgwick, *Lectures on the Ethics of T. H. Green, Mr. Herbert Spencer, and J. Martineau*, p. 292.
[35] Ibid., p. 293.

understood, now specified, in the completion of an exchange."[36] Thus contracts are postponed exchanges of gifts. But the right of contract does not warrant selling oneself into slavery. According to *The Principles of Ethics*, "If we go back to the biological origin of justice, as being the maintenance of that relation between efforts and the products of efforts which is needful for the continuance of life, we see that this relation is suspended by bondage; . . . it becomes manifest that since a contract, as framed in conformity with the law of equal freedom, implies that the contracting parties shall severally give what are approximate equivalents, there can be no contract, properly so-called, in which the terms are incommensurable" (vol. II, p. 146).

Slavery is therefore incompatible with free contract because slavery violates the principle of desert. Contract, by contrast, respects the principle desert because parties to market contracts do no more than exchange equivalent deserts. In paying money for a service or a product, I purportedly exchange stored desert for something of equivalent value. Desert simply changes form and the integrity of principle of equal freedom is preserved.

Because he regarded market exchange and contract as affirming the principles of equal freedom and desert, Spencer labeled developed industrial societies where contract flourished, "contract" societies following Henry Maine. "Status" societies were pre-capitalist societies where contractual exchange had not yet become widespread. Recall in chapter 1 that, for Spencer, human social evolution was characterized by societies based on contract superseding those based on status.

By and large, Spencer viewed wage labor as a form of legitimate contract insofar as "free labour and contract are correlatives."[37] Hence, wage labor was compatible with the principles of equal freedom and desert. But the industrial realities of Victorian England were sobering. For instance, in *The Principles of Sociology*, he observes:

In their [factory workers'] social relations, too, there has been entailed retrogression rather than a progression. The wage-earning factory-hand does, indeed, exemplify entirely free labour, in so far that, making contracts at will and able to break them after short notice, he is free to engage with whom-soever he pleases and where he pleases. But this liberty amounts in practice to little more than the ability to exchange one slavery for another;

[36] Spencer, *The Principles of Ethics*, vol. II, p. 145.
[37] Spencer, *The Principles of Sociology*, vol. III, p. 509.

since, fit only for his particular occupation, he has rarely an opportunity of doing anything more than decide in what mill he will pass the greater part of his dreary days. The coercion of circumstances often bears more hardly on him than the coercion of a master does on one in bondage. (vol. III, p. 525)[38]

In "From Freedom to Bondage", a late essay, Spencer again laments the noxious yoke of working-class servitude. Modern "social organization is one which none who care for their kin can contemplate with satisfaction; and unquestionably men's activities accompanying this type [of organization] are far from being admirable." Capitalism has created "strong division[s] of rank" and "immense inequalities of means" wholly at "variance with that ideal of human relations on which the sympathetic imagination likes to dwell." Regrettably, "the distribution achieved by the system, gives to those who regulate and superintend, a share of the total produce which bears too large a ratio to the share it gives to the actual workers."[39]

Such conclusions must have been disappointing for Spencer especially coming when they did in Spencer's later years. If wage labor was a form of slavery, and if selling oneself into slavery is a fundamental violation of exchange as we saw earlier, then wage labor violates exchange. And if wage labor violates exchange, then it partially robs laborers of what they deserve. Hence, it contravenes the principle of equal freedom.[40]

[38] See also p. 492 where Spencer disparages the ostensible freedom of farm laborers: "Though nominally free, the laborer was coerced not only by restraints on his locomotion, and by the obligation to accept specified sums for his labor, but by the limitation of his liberty to labor, for he could not choose his occupation." See too Spencer, *The Principles of Ethics*, vol. II, p. 308, where he characterizes contracts between landlords and tenant farmers as coercive offers. Finally, see Spencer, *The Principles of Sociology*, vol. III, pp. 524–5, where he bemoans the debilitating alienation of rote factory routine: "Clearly, these self-adjustments, continually decreasing the sphere for human agency, make the actions of the workman himself relatively automatic . . . If we compare his life with that of the cottage artizan [*sic*] he has replaced, who, a century ago, having a varied muscular action in working his loom, with breaks caused by the incidents of the work, was able to alternate his indoor activities with outdoor activities in garden or field, we cannot but admit that this industrial development has proved extremely detrimental to the operative."

[39] Spencer, "From Freedom to Bondage," *Essays*, vol. III, pp. 448–9.

[40] Sidgwick's criticisms of Spencer are again germane. If society may prevent individuals from contracting themselves into full slavery, why cannot it prevent them from contracting themselves into the partial slavery of wage labor? In Sidgwick's words, "If a contract framed in accordance with the law of equal freedom implies that the contracting parties give what are approximately equivalents, and if the judgement of contracting parties as to equivalence is to be over-ruled here [slavery], why not interfere further [with wage contracts] to secure equivalence?" Sidgwick, *Lectures on the Ethics of T. H. Green, Mr. Herbert Spencer and J. Martineau*, pp. 294–5. Socialists also berated Spencer for undermining wage labor and

Spencer's deepening anxiety over the injustice of wage labor suggests that he was not always blind to what Mill saw more clearly. Even as he began recanting his theory of land nationalization, he nevertheless sensed what Mill came to understand more fully, namely that the unregulated exchange of wages for labor can often be coercive. Spencer's deepening anxiety over wage labor therefore belies Wiltshire's categorical claim that Spencer's "definition of freedom of contract in the context of industrial bargaining took no account of the inequalities in wealth, power, or influence between the parties (i.e. the industrial master and the individual employee)" (*The Social and Political Thought of Herbert Spencer*, p. 162). Spencer was, at least, not wholly inattentive to some of the more disturbing implications of his *definition* of freedom of contract. And the passages cited from "Freedom to Bondage" undermine Wiltshire's claim that the "class struggle did not exist" for Spencer as he saw "no essential conflict of interest between capital and labor" as well as Wiltshire's contention that Spencer regarded the appropriation of surplus value by capitalists as "perfectly equitable" (p. 160).

Spencer's misgivings about wage labor were also reflected in his position on trade unionism. While he sometimes decried unionism, at other times he defended it. Sometimes, that is, he regarded wage increases won through union agitation as distorting the exchange of equivalents that would otherwise prevail between workers and employers. Other times, however, he viewed union-negotiated increases as restoring the exchange of equivalents.

Spencer's most vigorous defense of unionism occurs in his chapter "Trade Unionism" in *The Principles of Sociology*, where he endorses unionism because it promotes "mutual aid" among union members,

capitalism on his own showing. H. Hyndman, using Spencer's definition of a slave as one forced to labor for another's benefit, complained that Spencer discredited capitalism by admitting that wage labor was moderated slavery. See H. Hyndman, *Socialism and Slavery: Being an Answer to Mr. Herbert Spencer's Attacks Upon the Democratic Federation* (London: Reeves, 1884), p. 10. Likewise the Belgian economist M. Emile de Laveleye complained to Spencer, "I maintain what you demonstrate in your *Social Statics* (chapt.ix) that when primary rights are violated, i.e. when the labourer or the tenant, deprived of all property, is forced to choose between the wages offered him by his employer or the owner of the land and starvation, he is no more free than the traveller when requested to deliver up his money or his life." See Emile de Laveleye to Herbert Spencer, April 2, 1885 in Duncan (ed.), *The Life and Letters of Herbert Spencer*, p. 246. Spencer's heightened sensitivity to the nominal freedom of wage labor may have been reinforced by his own experiences as an author. In *An Autobiography*, vol. II, p. 165, discussing the vulnerability of authors when negotiating with publishers, he grumbles that too often, the "penniless author . . . has to accept such terms as the capitalist offers; and they are usually hard terms."

because it forces employers to treat employees with "more respect" as well as forces employers to pay closer attention to workers' health and safety and because it disciplines union members for "living and working together" thereby making "men more available then they would else be, for such higher forms of social organization as will probably hereafter arise" (vol. III, pp. 551–2). Most importantly, unions help to keep wages fair (vol. III, p. 552).[41]

Spencer's rising doubts about the equity of wage labor mirrored his views about industrial cooperation. Spencer thought that workers' cooperatives represented the future of advanced industrial relations. Workers' cooperatives, by mitigating class distinctions between employers and employees, guaranteed that both groups earned what they deserved. But cooperative workers should be paid on a piecework basis:

> It [piecework cooperation] conforms to the general law of species-life, and the law implied in our conception of justice – the law that reward shall be proportionate to merit. Far more than by the primitive slave-system of coerced labour and assigned sustenance – far more than by the later system under which the serf received a certain share of produce – more even than by the wage-earning system under which payment, though partially proportioned to work, is but imperfectly proportioned, would the system above described bring merit and reward into adjustment. Excluding all arbitrariness, it would enable reward and merit to adjust themselves.[42]

In contrast to wage labor, then, piecework insured that cooperative members would be paid according to their abilities and initiative. They would be paid, that is, what they deserved.[43] Piecework

[41] For other discussions of trade unionism, see Spencer, *The Study of Sociology*, pp. 230–1; Spencer, "From Freedom to Bondage," *Essays*, vol. III, p. 469 and Spencer, "Regimentation," *Facts and Comments*, pp. 199–200. Note especially *The Study of Sociology*, p. 231, where Spencer defends union-led strikes as "not without justification." Spencer was favorably disposed towards unionism on balance. Hence, Wiltshire errs again in asserting that Spencer's "distaste for Trade Unionism verged on hysteria." Wiltshire, *The Social and Political Thought of Herbert Spencer*, p. 141.

[42] Spencer, *The Principles of Sociology*, vol. III, p. 573. See also pp. 571–2. And see Beatrice Webb, *My Apprenticeship*, [1926], 2 vols. (Harmondsworth, Middlesex: Penguin Books, 1938), vol. I, p. 54. Writing about her visits to the ailing Spencer just before he died, she says, "I saw him once or twice again, and both times he talked about the future society. Poor old man! Co-partnership and piecework seemed an adequate solution of all problems – inaugurating industrial peace and bringing about a decay of militarism!"

[43] Piecework cooperation, by fulfilling desert, also emancipates workers. Coerciveness diminishes "to the smallest degree consistent with combined action." The "system of contract becomes unqualified" as contracts become the very embodiment of equal freedom (pp. 572–3). Difficulties with piecework schemes, of course, abound. For instance, piecework payment may be ill-suited to the production of complex machinery. Anticipating this

cooperation is, of course, arguably a form of socialism as much as form of liberalism. Spencer acknowledged as much on at least one occasion, remarking that his view of capitalism did not "at all militate against joint-stock systems of production and living, which are in all probability what Socialism prophesies."[44]

Generally, though, Spencer denied that his vision of industrial cooperation was socialistic. He politely rejected Robert Buchanan's characterization of his political views as constituting a "higher Socialism" since, according to Spencer, liberal societies in the future would continue featuring modest competition and contract.[45] Yet, as Mill was well aware, it remains an open question whether or not societies dominated by worker cooperatives benignly competing with each other are more fundamentally socialist or capitalist.[46] George Lacy never accepted Spencer's disavowal of latent socialism with equanimity. Lacy was amused by the fact that both Henry George and Spencer denounced each other as socialists: "Each thus calls the other a socialist; and each sets up for a prophet of liberty!"[47]

Despite having misgivings about wage labor, Spencer never wavered in believing that contractual exchange, by and large, was compatible with justice. Government was thus obliged to enforce contractual obligations vigorously. Government had to be more than just "police-government." It should aggressively guarantee market equity and efficiency. In the words of "Specialized Administration," written in response to Huxley who accused Spencer of advocating the politics of "administrative nihilism":

While it [police-government] duly conveys the idea of an organization required for checking and punishing criminal aggression, it does not

difficulty, Spencer proposed that factory cooperatives be organized into teams which would bid against one another for the privilege of constructing, in effect, complex pieces. Accordingly, "pieces of work thus put up to auction, would be so arranged in number that towards the close, bidding would be stimulated by the thought of having no piece of work to undertake: the penalty being employment by one or other of the groups at day-wages." Spencer, *The Principles of Sociology*, vol. III, p. 572.

44 Spencer, *Social Statics*, p. 119.

45 Spencer to Robert Buchanan, February 5, 1890 in Duncan (ed.), *The Life and Letters of Herbert Spencer*, pp. 334–5.

46 For Mill, under nineteenth-century capitalism, workers have "little choice of occupation or freedom of locomotion, are practically as dependent on fixed rules and on the will of others, as they could be on any system short of actual slavery." See Mill, *The Principles of Political Economy*, p. 209. And for Mill a market system of worker cooperatives was part of the required antidote. See especially Riley, "Justice Under Capitalism," pp. 150–3, for Mill's cooperative version of capitalism.

47 Lacy, *Liberty and Law*, p. 333.

convey any idea of the no less important organization required for dealing with civil aggression – an organization quite essential for properly discharging the negatively-regulative function . . . Far from contending for a *laissez-faire* policy in the sense which the phrase commonly suggests, I have contended for a more active control of the kind distinguishable as negatively regulative . . . This doctrine, that while the negative-regulative control should be extended and made better, the positively-regulative control should be diminished, and that the one implies the other, may properly be called the doctrine of Specialized Administration – if it is to be named for its administrative aspect.[48]

Extending "negative-regulative" control entailed making civil litigation free. Like Bentham before him, Spencer proposed that justice be administered "without cost, in civil as well as in criminal cases," as every citizen ought to have equal access to the courts.[49] All citizens should have equal opportunities to seek legal redress when their basic rights had been violated.[50]

Concern for civil justice also led Spencer to decry the greed which often motivated railway companies to construct superfluous and ultimately unprofitable branch lines. In "Railway Morals and Railway Policy," he recommended that railway "proprietary" contracts be more narrowly interpreted and more vigorously enforced by compelling shareholders to honor the original purposes of incorporation. Hence, investment decisions were legitimate only insofar as they were consistent with the "specific" aims of incorporation and did not involve "unspecified" aims such as redundant

[48] Spencer, "Specialized Administration," *Essays*, vol. III, pp. 438–40. For Huxley, see T. H. Huxley, "Administrative Nihilism," *Fortnightly Review* (November, 1871). For other examples of Spencer's defense of the "negatively regulative" state, see Spencer, "M. De Laveleye's Error," *Various Fragments*, pp. 108–9 and Spencer, *The Principles of Ethics*, vol. II, pp. 60 and 227–8.

[49] See, too, Spencer, *Social Statics*, pp. 228–34, where Spencer insists that poverty ought not to penalize anyone from pursuing civil litigation. He deplored the inability of poor people to initiate civil proceedings as well as the risks that middle-class litigants faced of being financially ruined by being dragged from court to court, and from appeal to appeal, by wealthier litigants. See also Spencer, "Representative Government – What is it Good For?", p. 321 and Spencer, *The Principles of Sociology*, vol. II, pp. 660–1.

[50] In Spencer, *Social Statics*, pp. 232–3, Spencer denies that civil litigation would increase dramatically if it were made free, since open access to civil courts would deter dishonesty. Even if litigation multiplied, the evil must be tolerated, for otherwise we would be forced to admit that "an appeal to the law for protection is a greater evil than the trespass complained of!" Also note Spencer's recommendation that the state should not serve simply as an "umpire" but should become an "active investigator" in civil cases. For instance, in all civil suits, it should first appoint a court arbitrator to explain the law to plaintiff and defendant alike in hopes of precluding further court action. See Spencer to Wordsworth Donisthorpe, November 23, 1894 in Duncan (ed.), *The Life and Letters of Herbert Spencer*, p. 360.

branch lines and investments unrelated to railway construction and service. Such regulatory oversight would be "nothing but a better administration of justice."[51]

In one of his last essays, "The Reform of Company Law," Spencer proposed that *all* joint-stock companies be subject to such regulatory oversight. In order to insure that boards of directors kept to the original terms of incorporation, he proposed that "10 or more" state officials referee all stockholder meetings.[52]

Spencer's proposal that the fiduciary responsibilities of company managers be regulated by the state is probably rooted in his theory of political responsibility from *Social Statics*. There, Spencer insists that the "same principal holds" for both company management and politics. Both managers and political officials are bound "in all matters concerning the fulfillment of the objects for which they are incorporated; but no others" (p. 131). In the case of joint-stock companies, the "objects" of incorporation needing protection are the initial business objectives of incorporation. In the case of politics, the "objects" requiring protection are moral rights (including the right of contract of which joint-stock incorporation is an instance). In both cases, incorporation is legitimate insofar as these "objects" are respected.

[51] Spencer, "Railway Morals and Railway Policy," *Essays*, vol. III, p. 108.

[52] Spencer, "The Reform of Company Law," *Facts and Comments*, p. 328. This essay, as well as "Railway Morals and Railway Policy," betrays Spencer's appreciation of how managers have become divorced from stockholders allowing them to manipulate stockholders. See also Spencer, "The Morals of Trade," *Essays*, vol. III, p. 138, where Spencer laments the "demoralization" of business, thanks to increasingly widespread practices such as selling short and adulterating goods. He condemns the "commercial cannibalism" of everyday business life. As the law of animal life may be described as "Eat and be eaten" so the law of business may be described as "Cheat and be cheated." In Spencer, *The Principles of Ethics*, vol. II, pp. 301–2, he again bemoans contemporary business practices: "Competitive warfare carried on in this style, might not unfitly be called commercial murder; and were its flagitiousness to be measured by the pain inflicted, it might be held worse than murder originally so called." Hence, business must be conducted with more self-restraint: "Anyone who, by command of great capital or superior business capacity, is enabled to beat others who carry on the same business, is enjoined by the principle of negative beneficence to restrain his business activities, when his own wants and those of his belongings have been abundantly fulfilled; so that others, occupied as he is, may fulfill their wants also, though in smaller measure." And see Spencer, "A Business Principle," *Facts and Comments*, and Walter Troughton's comment that of "professional and business men generally he [Spencer] was always distrustful and his attitude towards them is sufficiently shown by the little essay entitled 'A Business Principle' in his last book." Troughton, "Reminiscences of HS," *The Herbert Spencer Papers*, MS. 791/355/3, p. 24. For Bentham's parallel reforms regarding the more effective oversight of companies, see L. J. Hume, *Bentham and Bureaucracy* (Cambridge University Press, 1981), chapter 5.

But, of course, the moral ends of politics are ultimately utilitarian for Spencer. So we shouldn't be surprised if the same holds for joint-stock companies as well. Railway enterprises, for instance, should be "confined within normal bounds" for the sake of "public" and shareholder welfare.[53] Business ventures must not ignore public utility:

> As trustee for the nation the government has to decide whether a proposed undertaking – road, canal, railway, dock, etc. – which will so change some track as to make it permanently useless for ordinary purposes, promises to be of such public utility as to warrant terms which, while they deal fairly with those who stake their capital in the enterprises, and while they protect the rights of the existing community, also keep in view the interests of future generations.[54]

"Public utility" never vanished from Spencer's thinking. Whether Spencer was contemplating land or business reforms, whether he was reflecting on land-use rights or commercial rights, utilitarian considerations were paramount. His liberalism never forsook the utilitarianism with which he began. And the utilitarianism with which he began, and with which he ended, was empirical utilitarianism.

Property rights, exchange rights and contract rights were "corollaries" of the principle of equal freedom for Spencer. Hence, they were basic moral rights. We have seen, however, that private land ownership was not a basic moral right, that it was not a corollary of the principle of equal freedom. Land possessed value that no one deserved because this unearned value was created by no one. This unearned increment belonged to the community hence justifying the community's nationalizing it.

But land nationalization, administered through a system of private tenancy under state ownership, was a radical proposal. No wonder Henry George seized upon Spencer's version of it from

[53] Spencer, "Railway Morals and Railway Policy," *Essays*, vol. III, p. 108.

[54] Spencer, *The Principles of Ethics*, vol. II, p. 231. Spencer continues: "In discharge of its duties as trustee, the ruling body [government] has to exercise a further control – allied but different. If not itself, then by its local deputies, it has to forbid or allow the breaking up of streets, roads, and other public spaces for the establishment or repair of water, gas, telegraph and kindred appliances" (pp. 231–2). "Public utility," however, proscribed public regulation of education, sanitation and poor relief. See the chapters in *Social Statics* and *The Principles of Ethics* specifically devoted to these questions. Spencer's antipathy to poor relief stemmed, no doubt, from his uncle Thomas Spencer's vigorous public opposition to the 1834 Poor Law Amendment Act. Spencer was close to his uncle.

Social Statics so enthusiastically. And little wonder that Spencer retreated from it as he began to appreciate its disruptive consequences if too quickly implemented. In the end, Spencer concluded that nationalizing land was a sub-optimal utilitarian strategy. At least, he concluded that it was a sub-optimal strategy for nineteenth-century England. If and when the average moral character of English citizens improved sufficiently, then land nationalization might prove worth the risk of the short-term turmoil that it would cause. When England was ready for it, Spencer thought, then land nationalization might be feasible, utilitarianly speaking. But we must bear in mind that Spencer's reassessment of the immediate viability of nationalizing land was grounded solely on *empirical* considerations. Even if we assume that "rational" utilitarianism is a credible alternative to "empirical" utilitarianism, in this case clearly the latter trumped the former hands down.

Conclusion

At the close of *Moral Thinking*, R. M. Hare insists with reassuring aplomb:

> in preferring what we prefer, morality compels us to accommodate ourselves to the preferences of others, and this has the effect that when we are thinking morally and doing it rationally we shall all prefer the same moral prescriptions about matters which affect other people (though in matters which do not, we remain free). Moral thinking is thus revealed as something that we do in concert, though each individual has to play his own part. What I am advocating, then, is less a form of descriptivism than, as I have called it, of rational universal prescriptivism. Reason leaves us with our freedom, but constrains us to respect the freedom of others, and to combine with them in exercising it.[1]

Hare's point, which is the major point of his book, is that we ought to adopt as our moral principles those principles that we would prefer were we others. The maxims that we propose to universalize as stringent moral principles, as sources of everyday obligation, must match those moral principles preferred by others so that each of us enjoys maximum freedom to satisfy his or her preferences compatible with the like freedom of all others to satisfy theirs. By each of us enjoying the most extensive equal freedom for satisfying our preferences, the happiness of each flourishes and thus the greatest happiness of all thrives.[2]

Now, Hare's two-tiered method of utilitarian moral reasoning

[1] R. M. Hare, *Moral Thinking* (Oxford University Press, 1981), p. 228.

[2] Jonathan Riley has suggested to me that Hare's two-tiered utilitarianism is less satisfactory than Mill's because it provides no criteria for distinguishing between actions which affect others and those which do not. Hence, according to Riley, how can we know when we ought to think morally by applying the principle of universalizability as opposed to when we are permitted to do as we please? In effect, Riley is faulting Hare's indirect utilitarianism for not being sufficiently liberal. Like Mill and Spencer's versions of indirect utilitarianism, Hare's version incorporates a liberty principle and thus seems liberal enough. However, unlike Mill and Spencer's versions according to Riley, Hare's version fails to specify the limits of liberty

comes from a distinguished liberal utilitarian pedigree that emerged in nineteenth-century England. Along with John Harsanyi's "critical rule utilitarianism," it is one of the most compelling and sophisticated modern versions of this venerated pedigree.[3] And, as we have seen, John Stuart Mill was not this pedigree's only energetic early advocate. Herbert Spencer was there at the beginning too. Together with Mill, Spencer fashioned the incipient contours of liberal utilitarianism, whereas Hare and others have modified it, sometimes with great skill and subtlety, by deploying the conceptual weaponry of modern analytic and metaethical theory.

Though Spencer's two-tiered liberal utilitarianism was not metaethically subtle like Hare's, still his liberal utilitarianism was, like Hare's, a liberal utilitarianism of equal freedom.[4] Spencer's liberal utilitarianism, to borrow from Hare, "leaves us with our freedom, but constrains us to respect the freedom of others" so that each of us enjoys an equal chance of cultivating our respective talents and of fulfilling our respective desires as best we can.

Hare aside, Spencer's liberal utilitarianism of equal freedom is also the practice of a *kind* of freedom, of a kind (albeit a moderated kind) of self-disciplining freedom requiring citizens to develop themselves morally as vigilant partisans in the cause of stringent moral rights. Only such partisanship advances the cause of equal freedom in turn, and ultimately advances the larger and far more important cause of utility. But zealotry in the cause of stringent moral rights is nevertheless, from our later perspective, a decidedly neo-Kantian enthusiasm. Taking rights seriously is the normative stuff of deontological moral theories preoccupied with ensuring that people are never served up in sacrifice, even marginally, to that great and allegedly tyrannical god of general utility. Taking rights seriously supposedly ensures that people treat each other as ends and never as means to something so impersonally dispiriting as the greatest

and thus fails to specify when we are compelled to think morally. It allows for "fanaticism" and thus may or may not generate genuine liberal utilitarianism.

[3] For Harsanyi's "critical rule utilitarianism," see especially John Harsanyi, "Rule Utilitarianism, Equality and Justice," *Social Philosophy and Policy*, 2 (1985).

[4] More recently, Hare has argued that Kant could have been a utilitarian thereby effectively devaluing the neo-Kantian features of his own (Hare's) moral theorizing. That is, for Hare, it's not so much that he should be considered some sort of neo-Kantian but rather that Kant must be considered some sort of utilitarian. Remember, in chapter 2, Spencer's claim that the categorical imperative was secretly utilitarian through and through. For Hare's recent account of Kant's disguised utilitarianism, see R. M. Hare, "Could Kant Have Been a Utilitarian?", *Utilitas*, 5 (1993).

happiness of the greatest number. As inviolable side constraints on what people may do to each other, stringent rights are every individual's precious armor.

Spencer also took rights seriously, and yet he was a utilitarian too. For Spencer, moral rights are stringent decision procedures of first importance. They stipulate how we should act. They are our most important sources of moral obligation. But their stringency is not the product of deontological obsessions because they are ultimately consequentialist in their justification. Moral rights, according to Spencer, best promote individual as well as general happiness. They do this on balance and over the long run, though not in all instances. Moreover, moral rights are historical practices, emergent in human history. Reason discovers them, though they are not reverentially inscribed in natural law. Their discovery is not a matter of deductively unearthing abiding maxims which have lain buried and hidden from the light of reason for so long. Their discovery, then, is not logical discovery. Rather, it is the discovery of consensus, of *empirical* reconciliation, on behalf of maximizing happiness. These discoveries are human artifacts even if it should turn out that only a sacrosanct array of them happens to maximize general happiness best.

Spencer, then, was a liberal utilitarian not only because he took the principle of equal freedom so seriously but because he specified the principle of equal freedom by strong moral rights. Strong moral rights constrain the pursuit of maximizing happiness for Spencer. Like Mill, Spencer struggled to make utilitarianism ethically attractive by investing it with a robust liberty principle constituted by sturdy moral rights. As in Mill, strong rights certified his indirect utilitarianism with its liberal credentials. And as in Mill, Spencer's moral and political theory aspired to retain its coherence insofar as it aspired to remain consistently utilitarian.

Because liberal utilitarianism has survived as an influential version of utilitarianism despite the relentless onslaught mounted against utilitarianism by its critics, past and present, Spencer's liberal utilitarianism remains as timely and as important as Mill's. Like modern liberal utilitarians after him, he labored to construct an ethically appealing yet, nevertheless, authentic utilitarianism that grounded the principle of equal freedom and derivative moral rights in the principle of utility itself.

As we have seen, Spencer's marriage of liberal decision procedures with a utilitarian theory of good was plagued by complex problems and disappointing vicissitudes. For instance, we have seen that Spencer's claim to have derived stringent moral rights from the principle of equal freedom by logical deduction is not persuasive. Contrary to what he maintains, moral rights are not logical derivations from the principle of equal freedom. Thus, his endeavor to replace "empirical" Benthamite utilitarianism with a more methodologically severe "rational" utilitarianism falls short. When all is said and done, Spencer's "rational" utilitarianism is just another variety of "empirical" utilitarianism, albeit a variety that tries to be more scientific. Spencer's later writings, especially *The Principles of Ethics*, plainly support such a conclusion.

Analysis of Spencer's efforts to apply his liberal utilitarian principles in practice leads to the same conclusion. The evolving permutations of Spencer's land nationalization proposal are particularly revealing. Spencer kept modifying his land nationalization strategy because he kept recalculating its likely empirical results and not because his skills in logical deduction improved.

In sum, Spencer's claim to have improved upon Benthamite empirical utilitarianism is overstated. Like Bentham and Mill, he was an empirical utilitarian. Spencer thought that he was something else because he seems to have understood terms like "empirical," "rational", "logic," and "deduction" so eccentrically. But such eccentricity of meanings, and the attendant confusions in his thinking that they generated regarding the kind of utilitarian methodology which he thought he was engaged in, does not alter the fact that Spencer was still a liberal utilitarian.

Another critical problem with Spencer's attempt to marry stringent liberal decision procedures with a utilitarian theory of good turns upon, of course, the very logic of such a conceptual marriage. As we have seen, trying to impose liberal constraints on the pursuit of utility may be logically incoherent inasmuch as such constraints introduce an alien criterion with separate "moral force." Thus, *insofar as* moral rights are indeed indefeasible for Spencer, they would appear to possess independent "moral force," implying that Spencer has abandoned utilitarianism. Either the right is prior to the good or the good is prior to the right. There is, many would argue, no third alternative. However, we have also seen, with Sumner's assistance, that indefeasible rights possessing their own "moral force" might conceivably prove to be the optimal decision procedure strategy after all. Though not probable, it is nonetheless possible, to recall Sumner, that "absolute rights are not an impossible output for a consequentialist methodology." Hence, Spencer's liberal utilitarianism may simply be improbable rather than logically impossible. But, of course, Griffin might caution us that such a version of liberal utilitarianism is barely recognizable as utilitarianism. He would probably say that, in this case, liberal utilitarianism has become, practically speaking, just liberalism. The impartial promotion of good would remain the sole, right-making criterion of morality in name only.

Now, matters may not be so trivial for Spencer. Perhaps, in the final analysis, Spencer does not end up championing indefeasible moral rights after all. Although he advocates absolute moral rights early on in *Social Statics*, he arguably forgoes indefeasibility by the time he wrote *The Principles of Ethics*. By *The Principles of Ethics*, moral rights only become indefeasible as societies achieve perfection. Hence, until then, moral rights are stringent though ultimately defeasible depending upon the circumstances. If enough added general utility is at stake, and one were certain that overriding basic rights would generate it, then overriding them may be justified. Hence, because Spencer became convinced that nationalizing land would considerably undermine general utility, he jettisoned the right to equal access to land *in practice* even though he continued to invoke it *in principle* as a "corollary" of the principle of equal freedom.

Considerable irony pervades Spencer's mature liberal utilitarianism with respect to moral rights indefeasibility. On the one hand, moral rights prove defeasible in practice. On the other hand, they remain indefeasible in principle. They become increasingly indefeasible in practice, however, as societies mature morally. Thus, moral rights finally become practically indefeasible once they become practically irrelevant. Because fully moral humans would invariably know with certainty which actions maximized utility, they would not need rights as decision procedures for guiding them in situations of uncertainty. Moral rights would lose their point as a second best strategy given uncertainty because uncertainty would no longer apply. They would lose their "moral force." What need would (empirical) utilitarian "archangels" have for decision procedures? What use could perfect act utilitarians plausibly have for rules of any kind? For such remarkable creatures, indefeasible moral rights would prove superfluous if not outright hindrances.

There is more than just irony to Spencer's mature theory of rights indefeasibility. Spencer's claim that rights can be both defeasible in practice yet indefeasible in principle is not coherent. If indefeasibility holds only for perfect humans, then indefeasible moral rights can't be said to exist at all given that we are anything but perfect. As Sidgwick, in effect, concluded regarding Spencer's theory of "absolute" ethics, "absolute" ethics are irrelevant and therefore are nonexistent. Or as Griffin has put it more recently:

> Moral norms must be tailored to fit the human torso. They are nothing but what such tailoring produces. There are no moral norms outside the boundary set by our capacities. There are not some second-best norms – norms made for everyday use by agents limited in intelligence and will – and then, behind them, true or ideal norms – norms without compromise to human frailty. Moral norms regulate human action; a norm that ignores the limited nature of human agents is not an "ideal" norm, but no norm at all.[5]

Spencer's liberal utilitarianism, then, has its shortcomings and they are several and important. But his liberal utilitarianism also has much to recommend it. Its principal virtue lies in the distribution-sensitive nature of its theory of maximization. Maximizing happiness *for* all individuals, as distribution-sensitive theories advocate, is no less credible a criterion of moral rightness than maximizing happiness *across* individuals. The former criterion operationalizes maximization *distributively* while the latter criterion operationalizes maximization *aggregatively*. The former, distribution-sensitive way of operationalizing maximization preserves everyone's personal integrity. No one may be sacrificed for the sake of aggregating utility.[6]

Spencer's liberal utilitarianism operationalizes maximization distributively. For him, right actions promote *everyone's* happiness. Moral rightness purportedly redounds to the flourishing of *each* person's individuality. Hence, as we noted in chapter 5, Spencer's liberal utilitarianism includes features of what Freeden calls "modified constrained consequentialism." It includes as a fundamental goal the protection and advancement of a value, namely personal integrity, extolled by rights-based theories.

[5] James Griffin, "Human Good and the Ambitions of Consequentialism," *Social Philosophy and Policy*, 9 (1992), 131.

[6] As we have seen, Mill was also a distribution-sensitive utilitarian, especially if we follow Riley. See also David O. Brink, "Mill's Deliberative Utilitarianism," *Philosophy and Public Affairs*, 21 (1992).

Spencer's utilitarianism is liberal, then, not only because it *externally* constrains the pursuit of utility by stringent moral rights but also because it builds *internal* constraints into the results it proposes to maximize. Maximizing happiness means maximizing everyone's happiness. It means, therefore, distributing happiness so that each person obtains a share of it. And because each obtains a share of happiness, nobody is reduced to being merely a vehicle of happiness conveyance. Each person's integrity remains reasonably intact.

Moreover, as we saw in chapter 2, Spencer also held that as each person becomes happier, each person becomes more moral as well. Thus, each person tends to become more adept at respecting everyone else's moral rights, enabling everyone else to become happier and more moral in turn. In effect, by operationalizing happiness maximization distributively, by building an *internal* constraint into the meaning of maximization, Spencer's liberal utilitarianism contains a mechanism that reinforces *external* constraints on happiness maximization. As a criterion of morality, maximizing each person's happiness leads each person to better respect moral rights. Our criterion of morality becomes the engine driving respect for utilitarian decision procedures.

Finally, even if we grant that Spencer's later liberal utilitarianism allows for the overriding of basic rights, the temptations to do so would, arguably, decline considerably. The temptations to override would emerge on only those rare occasions where we knew what to do with *certainty* and where considerable overall utility was *undoubtedly* at stake such as when people's lives (the very condition of personal integrity) were clearly at risk. The logical tension between liberalism and utilitarianism would thus presumably rear its irksome head only occasionally. And should everyone miraculously become utilitarian archangels making rights redundant, Spencer's utilitarianism might still be considered liberal insofar as maximizing *everyone's* happiness always remains the ultimate criterion of morality.

Liberal utilitarianism, to be sure, is a conceptually hazardous enterprise. It is a logical high wire, a theoretical flight of Icarus. Perhaps many of us find it so appealing precisely because of its perils, because it promises to reconcile the two horns of the rivalry between deontology and consequentialism. For those of us who find this enterprise appealing, Spencer's version of liberal utilitarianism demands our critical attention. Because Spencer's liberal utilitarianism combines such a robust theory of moral rights with an unswerving commitment to a distribution-sensitive utilitarian theory of good, it highlights, in an incomparable way, the logical tensions of liberal utilitarianism. Even if liberal utilitarianism is a misbegotten illogical endeavor, even if it bootlessly tries to reconcile the theoretically irreconcilable, Spencer's version at least helps to expose liberal utilitarianism's vanity in all its futility.

Liberal utilitarians and their critics may prefer to ignore their past aside from their obsessions with Mill. Proponents of liberal utilitarianism may prefer to return and luxuriate time and again in the lambent shadows of Mill. But there are other liberal utilitarians in our past who continue to remain timely and relevant for us. Other, earlier liberal utilitarians can help us avoid mirroring back distorted images of the history of utilitarianism. One of them is surely Herbert Spencer.

Bibliography

MANUSCRIPT SOURCES

The Huxley Collection, Imperial College of Science and Technology, London

The Herbert Spencer Papers, MS. 791, Senate House, University of London Library, London

Other relevant material at Senate House, University of London Library: A.L. 467, A.L. 217/3, A.L. 468, A.L. 112 and *Booth Collection*, MS. 797.

WORKS BY SPENCER

BOOKS

An Autobiography, 2 vols., London: Watts, 1904

[1861], *Education*, New York: D. Appleton and Co., 1924

[1868–74], *Essays: Moral, Political and Speculative*, 3 vols., London: Williams and Norgate, 1901

Facts and Comments, London: Williams and Norgate, 1902

[1862], *First Principles*, London: Williams and Norgate, 1915

[1884], *The Man Versus the State*, Indianapolis, Liberty Classics, 1981

Mr. Herbert Spencer on the Land Question, New York: D. Appleton and Co., 1895

The Principles of Biology, 2 vols., London: Williams and Norgate, 1864–7

[1879–93], *The Principles of Ethics*, 2 vols., Indianapolis: Liberty Classics, 1978

[1855], *The Principles of Psychology*, 2 vols., New York: D. Appleton and Co., 1897

[1876–96], *The Principles of Sociology*, 3 vols., New York: D. Appleton and Co., 1883

[1842], "The Proper Sphere of Government" in Herbert Spencer, *The Man Versus the State*, Indianapolis, Liberty Classics, 1981

[1851], *Social Statics*, New York: Robert Schalkenbach Foundation, 1970

[1873], *The Study of Sociology*, Ann Arbor: University of Michigan Press, 1969

[1897], *Various Fragments*, New York: D. Appleton and Co., 1898

ARTICLES

"Heredity Once More," *The Contemporary Review*, 68 (1895), 608
"The Inadequacy of 'Natural Selection'," *The Contemporary Review*, 63 (1893), 153–66
"The Inheritance of Acquired Characteristics," *Nature* (March 6, 1890), 414–15
"Professor Weismann's Theories," *The Contemporary Review*, 64 (1893), 743–60
"A Rejoinder to Professor Weismann," *The Contemporary Review*, 64 (1893), 893–912
"Replies to Criticisms," *Mind*, N.S. 6 (1881), 82–98
"The Survival of the Fittest," *Nature* (February 1, 1872), 263–4
[1852], "A Theory of Population Deduced From the General Law of Animal Fertility" in J. D. Y. Peel (ed.), *Herbert Spencer on Social Evolution*, University of Chicago Press, 1972, pp. 33–52
"Weismann Once More," *The Contemporary Review*, 66 (1894), 593–610

SECONDARY SOURCES

Asirvatham, E. *Herbert Spencer's Theory of Social Justice*, Lucknow: The Upper India Publishing House, 1936
Bagehot, Walter [1872], *Physics and Politics*, New York: A. A. Knopf, 1948
Bain, Alexander, "Critical Notices, The Data of Ethics," *Mind*, 4 (1879), 561–9
[1859], *The Emotions and the Will*, London: J. W. Parker, 1875
Moral Science, New York: D. Appleton and Co., 1880
The Senses and the Intellect, London: J. W. Parker, 1855
Becker, Lawrence C., *Property Rights*, Boston: Routledge and Kegan Paul, 1977
Bentham, Jeremy [1843], "Anarchical Fallacies" in Jeremy Waldron (ed.), *Nonsense Upon Stilts*, London: Methuen, 1987
[1817], "Plan of Parliamentary Reform" in John Bowring (ed.), *The Works of Jeremy Bentham* [1838–43], 11 vols., New York: Russell and Russell, 1962, vol. III
[1843], "Supply Without Burthen or Escheat Vice Taxation" in Jeremy Waldron (ed.), *Nonsense Upon Stilts*, London: Methuen, 1987, pp. 70–6
Berger, Fred, *Happiness, Justice and Freedom*, Berkeley: University of California Press, 1984
Berlin, Isaiah, *Four Essays on Liberty*, Oxford University Press, 1982
Bernard, Claude [1865], in H. C. Greene (trans.), *An Introduction to the Study of Experimental Medicine*, New York: Dover Publications, 1957
Bradley, F. H. [1876], *Ethical Studies*, New York: G. E. Stechert and Co., 1927
Brandt, R. B., "Utilitarianism and Moral Rights," *Canadian Journal of Philosophy*, 14 (1984), 1–19

Brink, David O., "Mill's Deliberative Utilitarianism," *Philosophy and Public Affairs*, 21 (1992), 67–103

Broad, C. D., *Five Types of Ethical Theory*, London: Routledge and Kegan Paul, 1930

Charvet, John, *A Critique of Freedom and Equality*, Cambridge University Press, 1981

Christiano, Thomas, "Sidgwick on Desire, Pleasure and the Good" in Bart Schultz (ed.), *Essays on Henry Sidgwick*, Cambridge University Press, 1992, pp. 261–78

Collini, Stefan, "The Ordinary Experience of Civilized Life: Sidgwick and the Method of Reflective Analysis" in S. Collini, D. Winch and J. W. Burrow (eds.), *That Noble Science of Politics*, Cambridge University Press, 1983, pp. 277–307

Combe, George, *Essay on the Constitution of Man and its Relations to External Objects*, Edinburgh: John Anderson, 1828

Cronin, Helena, *The Ant and the Peacock*, Cambridge University Press, 1991

Darwin, Charles [1892], *The Autobiography of Charles Darwin*, London: Collins, 1958

[1871], *The Descent of Man* in Charles Darwin, *The Origin of Species and the Descent of Man*, New York: The Modern Library, 1936

[1859] *The Origin of Species* in Charles Darwin, *The Origin of Species and the Descent of Man*, New York: The Modern Library, 1950

Darwin, F. (ed.) [1887], *The Life and Letters of Charles Darwin*, 2 vols., New York: Basic Books, 1959

Dan Otter, Sandra M., *British Idealism and Social Explanation*, Oxford University Press, 1996

Donner, Wendy, *The Liberal Self*, Ithaca: Cornell University Press, 1991

Dryer, D. P., "Mill's Utilitarianism" in John M. Robson (ed.), *The Collected Works of John Stuart Mill*, University of Toronto Press, 1969, vol. x, pp. lxiii–lxxxv

Duncan, David, *The Life and Letters of Herbert Spencer*, London: Methuen and Co., 1908

Farber, Paul, *The Temptations of Evolutionary Ethics*, Berkeley: University of California Press, 1994

Flathman, Richard, "Moderating Rights," *Social Philosophy and Policy*, 1 (1984), 149–71

Flew, A. G. N., *Evolutionary Ethics*, London: Macmillan and Co., 1967

Freeden, Michael, *The New Liberalism*, Oxford University Press, 1978

Rights, Minneapolis: University of Minnesota Press, 1991

Freeman, Derek, "The Evolutionary Theories of Charles Darwin and Herbert Spencer" in *Current Anthropology*, 15 (1974), 211–21

Gall, Franz Joseph, transl. Winslow Lewis Jr., *On the Functions of the Brain and of Each of Its Parts: With Observations on the Possibility of Determining the Instincts, Propensities, and Talents, or the Moral and Intellectual Dispositions of Men and Animals, by Configuration of the Brain and Head*, 6 vols., Boston: Marsh, Capen and Lyon, 1835

Gay, John [1731], *Concerning the Fundamental Principles of Virtue and Morality* in J. B. Schneewind (ed.), *Moral Philosophy From Montaigne to Kant*, 2 vols., Cambridge University Press, 1990, vol. II, pp. 400–13

George, Henry [1881], *The Land Question*, New York: Doubleday and Page, 1906

A Perplexed Philosopher, London: Kegan, Paul, Trench, Trubner and Co., 1893

Progress and Poverty, New York: D. Appleton and Co., 1880

Gewirth, Alan, "Can Utilitarianism Justify Any Moral Rights?" in John W. Chapman and J. Roland Pennock (eds.), *Ethics, Economics and the Law*, Nomos 24, New York University Press, 1982, pp. 158–93

"Political Justice" in Richard B. Brandt (ed.), *Social Justice*, Englewood Cliffs: Prentice-Hall, 1962, pp. 119–69

Gordon, Scott, "The London *Economist* and the High Tide of Laissez-Faire," *Journal of Political Economy*, 63 (1955), 461–88

Gray, John, *Hayek on Liberty*, Oxford University Press, 1984

"Indirect Utility and Fundamental Rights," *Social Philosophy and Policy*, 1 (1984), 73–91

"Liberalism and the Choice of Liberties" in John Gray, *Liberalisms: Essays in Political Philosophy*, London: Routledge and Kegan Paul, 1989, pp. 140–60

Mill on Liberty: A Defence, London: Routledge and Kegan Paul, 1983

"Mill's and Other Liberalisms" in John Gray, *Liberalisms: Essays in Political Philosophy*, London: Routledge and Kegan Paul, 1989, pp. 217–38

"On Negative and Positive Liberty" in John Gray and Z. A. Pelczynski (eds.), *Conceptions of Liberty in Political Philosophy*, New York: St. Martin's Press, 1984, pp. 321–48

"Spencer on the Ethics of Liberty and the Limits of State Interference," *History of Political Thought*, 3 (1982), 465–81

Gray, John and Smith, G. W., "Introduction" in John Gray and G. W. Smith (eds.), *J. S. Mill on Liberty in Focus*, London: Routledge and Kegan Paul, 1991, pp. 1–20

Gray, T. S., "Herbert Spencer on Women: A Study in Personal and Political Disillusionment," *International Journal of Women's Studies*, 7 (1984), 217–31

"Herbert Spencer's Theory of Social Justice – Desert or Entitlement?", *History of Political Thought*, 2 (1981), 161–86

"Is Herbert Spencer's Law of Equal Freedom a Utilitarian or a Rights-Based Theory of Justice?", *Journal of the History of Philosophy*, 26 (1988), 259–78

The Political Philosophy of Herbert Spencer, Aldershot: Avebury, 1996

Gray, Tim, *Freedom*, Atlantic Highlands: Humanities Press International, 1991

Greene, John C., "Comments on Freeman," *Current Anthropology*, 15 (1974), 224–5

Science, Ideology and World View, Berkeley: University of California Press, 1981

Griffin, James, "The Distinction Between Criterion and Decision Procedure: A Reply to Madison Powers," *Utilitas*, 6 (1994), 177–82

"Human Good and the Ambitions of Consequentialism," *Social Philosophy and Policy*, 9 (1992), 118–32

Guthrie, Malcolm, *Mr. Spencer's Data of Ethics*, London: The Modern Press, 1884

Halévy, Elie [1928], *The Growth of Philosophic Radicalism*, London: Faber and Faber, 1972

[1903], *Thomas Hodgskin*, London: Benn, 1956

Hare, R. M., "Could Kant Have Been a Utilitarian?," *Utilitas*, 5 (1993), 1–16

Moral Thinking, Oxford University Press, 1981

Harrison, Ross, *Bentham*, London: Routledge and Kegan Paul, 1983

Harsanyi, John, "Rule Utilitarianism, Equality and Justice," *Social Philosophy and Policy*, 2 (1985), 115–27

Hart, H. L. A., *Essays on Bentham*, Oxford University Press, 1982

Hattiangadi, Jagdish, "Philosophy of Biology in the Nineteenth Century" in C. L. Ten (ed.), *The Nineteenth Century, The Routledge History of Philosophy*, London: Routledge, 1994, vol. VII, pp. 272–96

Helfand, Michael S., "T. H. Huxley's 'Evolution and Ethics': The Politics of Evolution and the Evolution of Politics," *Victorian Studies*, 20 (1972), 159–77

Himmelfarb, Gertrude, "The Haunted House of Jeremy Bentham" in R. Herr and H. T. Parker (eds.), *Ideas in History*, Durham, N.C.: Duke University Press, 1965, pp. 199–238

Hobhouse, L. T. [1913], *Development and Purpose*, London: Macmillan, 1927

[1911], *Liberalism*, Oxford University Press, 1964

[1911], *Social Evolution and Political Theory*, New York: Kennikat Press, 1968

Hobson, J. A. [1909], *The Crisis of Liberalism*, New York: Barnes and Noble, 1974

Hodgskin, Thomas [1832], *The Natural and Artificial Right of Property Contrasted*, Clifton, N.J.: A. M. Kelley, 1973

Hofstadter, Richard, *Social Darwinism in American Thought*, Boston: Beacon Press, 1955

Hont, Istvan and Ignatieff, Michael, "Needs and Justice in *Wealth of Nations: An Introductory Essay*" in Istvan Hont and Michael Ignatieff (eds.), *Wealth and Virtue*, Cambridge University Press, 1983, p. 1–44

Hume, David [1734–40], *A Treatise on Human Nature*, Oxford University Press, 1978

Hume, L. J., *Bentham and Bureaucracy*, Cambridge University Press, 1981

Hutton, Richard, "Mr. Herbert Spencer on Moral Intuitions and Moral Sentiments," *The Contemporary Review*, 32 (1871), 263–74

"A Questionable Parentage of Morals," *Macmillan's Magazine*, 20 (1869), 266–73

Huxley, Leonard, *The Life and Letters of Thomas Huxley*, 2 vols., New York: D. Appleton and Co., 1901

Huxley, T. H., "Administrative Nihilism," *Fortnightly Review*, O.S., 1 (1871), 525–43

[1893], *Collected Essays*, 9 vols., London: Macmillan, 1894

[1893], "Evolution and Ethics" in T. H. Huxley, *Evolution and Ethics and Other Essays*, New York: D. Appleton and Co., 1929, pp. 46–116

Hyndman, H., *Socialism and Slavery Being an Answer to Mr. Herbert Spencer's Attacks Upon the Democratic Federation*, London: Reeves, 1884

Inge, W. R., "Liberty and Natural Rights," The Herbert Spencer Lecture, Oxford University Press, 1934

Kant, Immanuel [1797], Mary Gregor (trans.), "Metaphysical First Principles of the Doctrine of Right," *The Metaphysics of Morals*, Cambridge University Press, 1991

W. Hastie (trans.), *The Philosophy of Law*, Edinburgh: T. and T. Clark, 1887

Kelly, P. J., *Utilitarianism and Distributive Justice*, Oxford University Press, 1990

Kennedy, James G., *Herbert Spencer*, Boston: Twayne Publishers, 1978

Lacy, George, *Liberty and Law*, London: Swan Sonnenschein, Lowery and Co., 1888

Liddington, John, "Oakeshott: Freedom in a Modern State" in John Gray and Z. A. Pelczynski (eds.), *Conceptions of Liberty in Political Philosophy*, New York: St. Martin's Press, 1984, pp. 289–320.

Lyell, Charles [1830], *The Principles of Geology*, 2 vols., New York: D. Appleton and Co., 1960

Lyons, David, "Utility and Rights" in John W. Chapman and J. Roland Pennock (eds.), *Ethics, Economics and the Law*, Nomos 24, New York University Press, 1982, pp. 107–136

MacCallum, G. C., "Negative and Positive Freedom," *Philosophical Review*, 76 (1967), 312–34

Machan, Tibor, "Introduction" in Herbert Spencer, *The Principles of Ethics*, 2 vols., Indianapolis: Liberty Classics, 1978, vol. I, pp. 9–19

Mackie, J. L., "Can There Be a Right-Based Moral Theory?," *Midwest Studies in Philosophy*, 3 (1978), 350–9

Maine, Henry [1861], *Ancient Law*, New York: H. Holt, 1906

Maitland, F. W., "Herbert Spencer's Theory of Society," Part 2, *Mind*, 8 (1883), 506–24

Mill, J. S. [1863], "Austin on Jurisprudence" in John M. Robson (ed.), *The Collected Works of John Stuart Mill*, 33 vols., University of Toronto Press, 1984, vol. XXI, pp. 165–205

[1838], "Bentham" in John M. Robson (ed.), *The Collected Works of John Stuart Mill*, 33 vols., University of Toronto Press, 1969, vol. X, pp. 75–115

[1861], *Considerations on Representative Government* in John M. Robson (ed.), *The Collected Works of John Stuart Mill*, 33 vols., University of Toronto Press, 1977, vol. XIX, pp. 371–577

[1865], *An Examination of Sir William Hamilton's Philosophy* in John M. Robson (ed.), *The Collected Works of John Stuart Mill*, 33 vols., University of Toronto Press, 1979, vol. IX

[1849–73], *The Later Letters* in F. E. Mineka and D. N. Lindley (eds.), *The Collected Works of John Stuart Mill*, 33 vols., University of Toronto Press, 1972, vols. XVI–XVII

[1859], *On Liberty* in John M. Robson (ed.), *The Collected Works of John Stuart Mill*, 33 vols., University of Toronto Press, 1977, vol. XVIII, pp. 213–310

[1848], *The Principles of Political Economy* in John M. Robson (ed.), *The Collected Works of John Stuart Mill*, 33 vols., University of Toronto Press, 1965, vol. II

[1843], *A System of Logic* in John M. Robson (ed.), *The Collected Works of John Stuart Mill*, 33 vols., University of Toronto Press, 1973–74, vols. VII–VIII

[1861], *Utilitarianism* in John M. Robson (ed.), *The Collected Works of John Stuart Mill*, 33 vols., University of Toronto Press, 1969, vol. X, pp. 203–59

[1852], "Whewell on Moral Philosophy" in John M. Robson (ed.), *The Collected Works of John Stuart Mill*, 33 vols., University of Toronto Press, 1969, vol. X, pp. 165–201

Miller, David, *Social Justice*, Oxford University Press, 1976

Moore, G. E., Tom Regan (ed.), *The Elements of Ethics*, Philadelphia: Temple University Press, 1991

[1903] *Principia Ethica*, Cambridge University Press, 1984

Narveson, Jan, "Rights and Utilitarianism" in Wesley E. Cooper, Kai Nielsen and Steven C. Patten (eds.), *New Essays on John Stuart Mill and Utilitarianism*, Guelph: Canadian Association for Publishing in Philosophy, 1979, pp. 137–60

Nozick, Robert, *Anarchy, State and Utopia*, New York: Basic Books, 1974

Offer, John, "Introduction" in John Offer (ed.), *Herbert Spencer: Political Writings*, Cambridge University Press, 1994, pp. vii–xxix

Paradis, James, "*Evolution and Ethics* in Its Victorian Context" in James Paradis and George C. Williams (eds.), *Evolution and Ethics*, Princeton University Press, 1989, pp. 3–55

Paul, Jeffrey, "The Socialism of Herbert Spencer," *History of Political Thought*, 3 (1982), 499–514

Peel, J. D. Y., *Herbert Spencer: The Evolution of a Sociologist*, New York: Basic Books, 1971

Plamenatz, John, *English Utilitarians*, Oxford University Press, 1966

Priestly, Joseph, *Essay on the First Principles of Government*, London: J. Dodsley, 1768

Prior, A. N., *Logic and the Basis of Ethics*, Oxford University Press, 1965

Regan, Tom, *Bloomsbury's Prophet*, Philadelphia: Temple University Press, 1986

Riley, Jonathan, "Individuality, Custom and Progress," *Utilitas*, 3 (1991), 217–44

"Justice Under Capitalism" in John W. Chapman and J. Roland Pennock (eds.), *Markets and Justice*, Nomos 31, New York University Press, 1989, pp. 122–62

Liberal Utilitarianism: Social Choice Theory and J. S. Mill's Philosophy, Cambridge University Press, 1988
"One Very Simple Principle," *Utilitas*, 3 (1991), 1–35
Ritchie, D. G., *Darwin and Hegel*, London: Swan Sonnenschein, 1893
"Evolution and Democracy" in S. Coit (ed.), *Ethical Democracy: Essays in Dynamics*, London: G. Richards, 1900, pp. 1–29
"Has the Hereditability or Non-Hereditability of Acquired Characteristics Any Direct Bearing on Ethical Theory?," *Proceedings of the Aristotelian Society*, 3 (1895–6), 144–8
[1894], *Natural Rights*, London: George Allen and Unwin Ltd., 1952
[1891], *The Principles of State Interference*, London: Swan Sonnenschein and Co., 1896
Studies in Political and Social Ethics, London: Swan Sonnenschein and Co., 1902
Rosen, F., "Thinking About Liberty," Inaugural Lecture, University College London, 29 November 1990
Ryan, Alan, *The Philosophy of John Stuart Mill*, London: Macmillan Press, 1987
Scheffler, Samuel (ed.), *Consequentialism and Its Critics*, Oxford University Press, 1988
Schneewind, J. B., *Sidgwick's Ethics and Victorian Moral Philosophy*, Oxford University Press, 1977
Shelton, H. S., "Spencer's Formula of Evolution," *The Philosophical Review*, 19 (1910), 241–58
Sidgwick, Henry, *Lectures on the Ethics of T. H. Green, Mr. Herbert Spencer and J. Martineau*, London: Macmillan, 1902
[1907], *The Methods of Ethics*, 7th edition, Indianapolis: Hackett Publishing Co., 1981
"Mr. Spencer's Ethical System," *Mind*, 5 (1880), 216–226
Philosophy and Its Scope and Relations, London: Macmillan, 1902
"Philosophy and Physical Science," *The Academy*, 4 (1873), 131–4
"The Relation of Ethics to Sociology," *Miscellaneous Essays and Addresses*, London: Macmillan and Co., 1904, pp. 249–69
Review of Spencer's "Justice," *Mind*, N.S., 1 (1892), 107–8
"Symposium – Is the Distinction Between 'Is' and 'Ought' Ultimate and Irreducible?," *Proceedings of the Aristotelian Society*, 2 (1892–94), 88–92
"The Theory of Evolution in Its Application to Practice," *Mind*, 1 (1876), 52–67
Sidgwick, A. and Sidgwick, E., *Henry Sidgwick, A Memoir*, London: Macmillan, 1906
Smith, C. U. M., "Evolution and the Problem of Mind: Part I, Herbert Spencer," *Journal of the History of Biology*, 15 (1982), 55–88
Steiner, Hillel, "Land, Liberty and the Early Herbert Spencer," *History of Political Thought*, 3 (1983), 515–33
"Liberty and Equality," *Political Studies*, 29 (1981), 553–69

Stephen, James Fitzjames [1873], *Liberty, Equality and Fraternity*, University of Chicago Press, 1991

Stephen, Leslie [1900], *The English Utilitarians*, 3 vols., New York: P. Smith, 1950

"Ethics and the Struggle For Existence," *The Contemporary Review*, 64 (1883), 157–70

Sumner, L. W., *The Moral Foundations of Rights*, Oxford University Press, 1987

Taylor, Charles, "What's Wrong With Negative Liberty" in Charles Taylor, *Philosophy and the Human Sciences*, 2 vols., Cambridge University Press, 1985, vol. II, pp. 211–29

Taylor, M. W., *Men Versus the State: Herbert Spencer and Late Victorian Individualism*, Oxford University Press, 1992

Ten, C. L., *Mill on Liberty*, Oxford University Press, 1980

Thomson, David, *England in the Nineteenth Century*, Middlesex: Penguin Books, 1985

Tillett, Alfred W., *Militancy Versus Civilization*, London: P. S. King and Co., 1915

Tully, James, *A Discourse on Property*, Cambridge University Press, 1980

Vogel, Ursula, "When the Earth Belonged to All: the Land Question in Eighteenth-century Justifications of Private Property," *Political Studies*, 36 (1988), 102–22.

Wallace, A. R., "Herbert Spencer on the Land Question: A Criticism" in A. R. Wallace, *Studies Scientific and Social*, 2 vols., London: Macmillan and Co., 1900

My Life, 2 vols., New York: Dodd, Mead and Co., 1905

Webb, Beatrice [1926], *My Apprenticeship*, 2 vols., Middlesex: Penguin Books, 1938

Weinstein, D., "Between Kantianism and Consequentialism in T. H. Green's Moral Philosophy," *Political Studies*, 41 (1993), 619–35

"The Discourse of Freedom, Rights and Good in Nineteenth-Century English Liberalism," *Utilitas*, 3 (1991), 245–62

"Equal Freedom, Rights and Utility in Spencer's Moral Philosophy," *History of Political Thought*, 40 (1990), 119–42

"The New Liberalism of L. T. Hobhouse and the Reenvisioning of Nineteenth-Century Utilitarianism," *Journal of the History of Ideas*, 56 (1996), 487–507

Weinstein, W. L., "The Concept of Liberty in Nineteenth Century English Political Thought," *Political Studies*, 13 (1965), 145–62

Weismann, August, "The All-Sufficiency of Natural Selection: A Reply to Herbert Spencer," *The Contemporary Review*, 64 (1893), Part I, 309–38 and Part II, 596–610

"Heredity Once More," *The Contemporary Review*, 68 (1895), 420–56

Whewell, William [1852], *Lectures on the History of Moral Philosophy*, Cambridge: Deighton Bell, 1862

White, Alan R., *G. E. Moore*, Oxford: Basil Blackwell, 1958

Rights, Oxford University Press, 1984
Wilkinson, Martin, "Egoism, Obligation and Herbert Spencer," *Utilitas*, 5 (1993), 69–86
Williams, Bernard, "A Critique of Utilitarianism" in J. C. C. Smart and Bernard Williams (eds.), *Utilitarianism: For and Against*, Cambridge University Press, 1973, pp. 77–150
Wiltshire, David, *The Social and Political Thought of Herbert Spencer*, Oxford University Press, 1978
Youmans, E. L., "Spencer's Evolution Philosophy," *The North American Review*, 129 (1879), 389–403
Young, R. M., *Darwin's Metaphor*, Cambridge University Press., 1985
"Herbert Spencer and 'Inevitable' Progress," *History Today*, 37 (1987), 18–22
Mind, Brain and Adaptation in the Nineteenth Century, Oxford University Press, 1970

FURTHER READING

For a complete bibliography of Spencer's writings including selected translations of his books, as well as a complete bibliography of books and periodical literature about Spencer until 1930, see J. Rumney, *Herbert Spencer's Sociology*, London: Williams and Norgate, 1934, pp. 314–51.

Index

All entries in the index refer to Spencer's thought and writings unless otherwise stated. Titles of works by Spencer appear under the entry Spencer, Herbert.

IDEAS IN CONTEXT

Edited by Quentin Skinner (*General Editor*), Lorraine Daston, Wolf Lepenies, J. B. Schneewind and James Tully

1 RICHARD RORTY, J. B. SCHNEEWIND and QUENTIN SKINNER (eds.)
Philosophy in History
*Essays in the Historiography of Philosophy**

2 J. G. A. POCOCK
Virtue, Commerce and History
*Essays on Political Thought and History, Chiefly in the Eighteenth Century**

3 M. M. GOLDSMITH
Private Vices, Public Benefits
Bernard Mandeville's Social and Political Thought

4 ANTHONY PAGDEN (ed.)
The Languages of Political Theory in Early Modern Europe*

5 DAVID SUMMERS
The Judgment of Sense
*Renaissance Nationalism and the Rise of Aesthetics**

6 LAURENCE DICKEY
Hegel: Religion, Economics and the Politics of Sprint, 1770–1807*

7 MARGO TODD
Christian Humanism and the Puritan Social Order

8 LYNN SUMIDA JOY
Gassendi the Atomist
Advocate of History in an Age of Science

9 EDMUND LEITES (ed.)
Conscience and Casuistry in Early Modern Europe

10 WOLF LEPENIES
Between Literature and Science: The Rise of Sociology*

11 TERENCE BALL, JAMES FARR and RUSSELL L. HANSON (eds.)
Political Innovation and Conceptual Change*

12 GERD GIGERENZER *et al.*
The Empire of Chance
*How Probability Changed Science and Everyday Life**

13 PETER NOVICK
That Noble Dream
*The 'Objectivity Question' and the American Historical Profession**

14 DAVID LIEBERMAN
The Province of Legislation Determined
Legal Theory in Eighteenth-Century Britain

15 DANIEL PICK
Faces of Degeneration
*A European Disorder, c. 1848–c. 1918**

16 KEITH BAKER
Approaching the French Revolution
*Essays on French Political Culture in the Eighteenth Century**

17 IAN HACKING
The Taming of Chance*

18 GISELA BOCK, QUENTIN SKINNER and MAURIZIO VIROLI (eds.)
Machiavelli and Republicanism*

19 DOROTHY ROSS
The Origins of American Social Science*

20 KLAUS CHRISTIAN KOHNKE
The Rise of Neo-Kantianism
German Academic Philosophy between Idealism and Positivism

21 IAN MACLEAN
Interpretation and Meaning in the Renaissance
The Case of Law

22 MAURIZIO VIROLI
From Politics to Reason of State
The Acquisition and Transformation of the Language of Politics 1250–1600

23 MARTIN VAN GELDEREN
The Political Thought of the Dutch Revolt 1555–1590

24 NICHOLAS PHILLIPSON and QUENTIN SKINNER (eds.)
Political Discourse in Early Modern Britain

25 JAMES TULLY
An Approach to Political Philosophy: Locke in Contexts*

26 RICHARD TUCK
Philosophy and Government 1572–1651*

27 RICHARD R. YEO
Defining Science
William Whewell, Natural Knowledge and Public Debate in Early Victorian Britain

28 MARTIN WARNKE
The Court Artist
The Ancestry of the Modern Artist

29 PETER N. MILLER
Defining the Common Good
Empire, Religion and Philosophy in Eighteenth-Century Britain

30 CHRISTOPHER J. BERRY
The Idea of Luxury
*A Conceptual and Historical Investigation**

31 E. J. HUNDERT
The Enlightenment's 'Fable'
Bernard Mandeville and the Discovery of Society

32 JULIA STAPLETON
Englishness and the Study of Politics
The Social and Political Thought of Ernest Barker

33 KEITH TRIBE
Strategies of Economic Order
German Economic Discourse, 1750–1950

34 SACHIKO KUSUKAWA
The Transformation of Natural Philosophy
The Case of Philip Melancthon

35 Edited by DAVID ARMITAGE, ARMAND HIMY and QUENTIN SKINNER
Milton and Republicanism

36 MARKKU PELTONEN
Classical Humanism and Republicanism in English Political Thought 1570–1640

37 PHILIP IRONSIDE
The Social and Political Thought of Bertrand Russell
The Development of an Aristocratic Liberalism

38 NANCY CARTWRIGHT, JORDI CAT, LOLA FLECK and THOMAS E. UEBEL
Otto Neurath: Philosophy Between Science and Politics

39 DONALD WINCH
Riches and Poverty
*An Intellectual History of Political Economy in Britain, 1750–1834**

40 JENNIFER PLATT
A History of Sociological Research Methods in America

41 Edited by KNUD HAAKONSSEN
Enlightenment and Religion
Rational Dissent in Eighteenth-Century Britain

42 G. E. R. LLOYD
Adversaries and Authorities
Investigations in Ancient Greek and Chinese Science

43 ROLF LINDNER
The Reportage of Urban Culture
Robert Park and the Chicago School

44 ANNABEL BRETT
Liberty, Right and Nature
Individual Rights in Later Scholastic Thought

45 Edited by STEWART J. BROWN
William Robertson and the Expansion of Empire

46 HELENA ROSENBLATT
Rousseau in Geneva
From the *First Discourse* to *The Social Contract*, 1749–1762

47 DAVID RUNCIMAN
Pluralism and the Personality of the State

48 ANNABEL PATTERSON
Early Modern Liberalism

49 DAVID WEINSTEIN
Equal Freedom and Utility
Herbert Spencer's Liberal Utilitarianism

Titles marked with an asterisk are also available in paperback